TAX POLICY IN THE TWENTY-FIRST CENTURY

Edited by

HERBERT STEIN
Former Chairman of the President's Council of Economic Advisers

WILEY

JOHN WILEY & SONS

New York • Chichester • Brisbane • Toronto • Singapore

Published by John Wiley & Sons, Inc.

Based on a conference held in Washington, D.C., October of 1987, and sponsored by the University of Virginia and Erasmus University Rotterdam.

Library of Congress Cataloging in Publication Data

Tax policy in the twenty-first century.

Bibliography: p.
Includes index.
1. Taxation—Forecasting. 2. Twenty-first century—Forecasting. I. Stein, Herbert, 1916–

HJ2305.T18 1988 336.2 88–5443
ISBN 0-471-63618-5

Printed in the United States of America

10 9 8 7 6 5 4 3 2 1

Contents

Acknowledgments

Thanks for this book is due principally to the expertise of its distinguished authors, who were the main speakers at the "Tax Policy in the Twenty-First Century" conference on which this volume is based.

Erasmus University Rotterdam and the University of Virginia sponsored the conference. Special thanks to Alexander H. G. Rinnooy Kan, Rector Magnificus of Erasmus University and Marion B. Peavey, Vice President for Development and University Relations of the University of Virginia, who contributed their time and their resources to the development of this project.

I am also indebted to Sijbren Cnossen, Professor of the Economics Faculty, Erasmus University, and Charles O. Meiburg, Associate Dean of The Darden School, University of Virginia, who joined me in chairing the Advisory Board for this project.

Gratitude is due to all the members of this distinguished board who gave direction and substance to our exploration of a complex and demanding subject:

Andrew F. Brimmer, Ph.D., President, Brimmer & Co., Inc.
Don Fullerton, Ph.D., Associate Professor of Economics, University of Virginia
Harvey Galper, Ph.D., Associate National Director of Tax Analysis, Peat Marwick Main & Co.

Yuji Gomi, M.A., Chairman, Chuo Coopers & Lybrand Consulting Co., Ltd.
John A. Kay, M.A., Director, Centre for Business Strategy and Professor of Industrial Policy, London Business School
Charles E. McLure, Jr., Ph.D., Senior Fellow, Hoover Institution, Stanford University
Sylvia Ostry, Ph.D., Ambassador, Multilateral Trade Negotiations and Personal Representative of the Prime Minister of Canada, Economic Summit
Rudolph A. Oswald, Ph.D., Director, Department of Economic Research, AFL-CIO Headquarters
Stanford G. Ross, J.D., Senior Partner, Arnold & Porter
Vito Tanzi, Ph.D., Director, Fiscal Affairs Department, International Monetary Fund
Norman B. Ture, Ph.D., President, Institute for Research on the Economics of Taxation
Adalbert Krieger Vasena, Ph.D., Partner, Krieger Vasena & Asociados

The following individuals from the University of Virginia also offered their counsel:

Donald F. Kettl, Ph.D., Associate Professor of Government and Foreign Affairs
David M. Maloney, Ph.D., Associate Professor of Commerce, McIntire School of Commerce
John W. Rosenblum, D.B.A., Dean, The Darden Graduate School of Business Administration
Thomas R. White, 3rd, L.L.B., Professor of Law, School of Law

We are particularly indebted to Philip Morris Companies Inc. for the funding and follow-through that made the project possible.

To Charles McLaughlin, I am grateful for his tact as well as his editorial skills in working with our authors in fashioning this manuscript. I thank Glenn Follette, Research Assistant, American Enterprise Institute, who has added a glossary. Joan Mebane, the Twenty-First Century Project Consultant for Philip Morris, also deserves our thanks for her role in coordinating the conference and developing this book.

Washington, D.C.
April 1988

HERBERT STEIN

Contributors

Henry J. Aaron, Ph.D., Senior Fellow, The Brookings Institution, Washington, D.C.

James A. Baker, III, U.S. Secretary of the Treasury, Washington, D.C.

Jack F. Bennett, Ph.D., Senior Vice President and Director, Exxon Corporation, New York City

Richard M. Bird, Ph.D., Professor of Economics, University of Toronto, Ontario, Canada

Mario S. Brodersohn, Ph.D., Minister of Finance, Republic of Argentina, Buenos Aires

Sijbren Cnossen, Ph.D., Professor of the Economics Faculty, Erasmus University Rotterdam, The Netherlands

Yuji Gomi, M.A., Chairman, Chuo Coopers & Lybrand Consulting Co., Ltd., Tokyo, Japan

Bill Gradison, U.S. Representative (R.-Ohio), Washington, D.C.

Yolanda Kodrzycki Henderson, Ph.D., Economist, Federal Reserve Bank of Boston, Boston, Massachusetts

Hiroshi Kaneko, L.L.B., Professor of Law, University of Tokyo, Japan

John A. Kay, M.A., Director, Centre for Business Strategy, and Professor of Industrial Policy, London Business School, London, England

Donald F. Kettl, Ph.D., Associate Professor of Government and Foreign Affairs, University of Virginia, Charlottesville, Virginia

Charles E. McLure, Jr., Ph.D., Senior Fellow, Hoover Institution, Stanford University, Stanford, California

Ferenc E. Molnar, J.D., Associate (International Group), Arent, Fox, Kintner, Plotkin & Kahn, Washington, D.C.

Wallace E. Oates, Ph.D., Professor of Economics, University of Maryland, College Park, Maryland

Paul Craig Roberts, Ph.D., The William E. Simon Chair in Political Economy, Center for Strategic and International Studies, Washington, D.C.

Stanford G. Ross, J.D., Senior Partner, Arnold & Porter, Washington, D.C.

Dallas L. Salisbury, M.P.A., President, Employee Benefit Research Institute, Washington, D.C.

Joseph E. Stiglitz, Ph.D., Professor of Economics, Princeton University, Princeton, New Jersey

Lawrence H. Summers, Ph.D., Professor of Economics, Harvard University, Cambridge, Massachusetts

Vito Tanzi, Ph.D., Director, Fiscal Affairs Department, International Monetary Fund, Washington, D.C.

Klaus Vogel, Dr. iur., Professor of Public Law and Director of Research for Foreign and Tax Law, University of Munich, Federal Republic of Germany

Sir Alan A. Walters, M.A., Senior Fellow, American Enterprise Institute for Public Policy Research, Washington, D.C., and Professor of Economics, Johns Hopkins University, Baltimore, Maryland

Arnold H. Weiss, J.D., Senior Partner, Arent, Fox, Kintner, Plotkin & Kahn, Washington, D.C.

Introduction
The Urgent Need to Look Ahead

HERBERT STEIN

When the idea of thinking about tax policy for the 21st century was first raised, it seemed bizarre. We hardly seem capable of thinking about tax policy for next year. But taxation is one of the few things, according to an old maxim, that we can be certain will be with us in the 21st century. And we are used to making decisions in other fields that will have significant effects well into that century, even though those decisions rest on much uncertainty and speculation.

The Treasury issues, and people buy, bonds that are not due until 2018. The Pentagon plans ships and planes that are expected to be in service in the 21st century; some of them may not even enter service until after the year 2000. Private investors erect buildings that will be used in the 21st century. People have babies who will be alive well past the middle of the 21st century. So at least considering whether anything useful can be said about taxation in the 21st century seems worthwhile.

To consider this question an advisory committee of economists was assembled under the aegis of the University of Virginia and Erasmus University Rotterdam, with funding from Philip Morris Companies Inc. We singled out a number of factors we believed to be persistent and important. These issues were presented at an international conference of decision makers and thought leaders in Washington, D.C., in October 1987. This book is based on the proceedings and discoveries of that conference.

As with three earlier programs funded by Philip Morris—covering the future of working (1979), communications (1981), and agriculture (1983)—the hope is not to prescribe or predict but to open the minds of policymakers to some important facts. Our objective here is to recognize that tax systems will undergo major changes; that governments should try to influence the direction of these changes deliberately, rather than inching along shortsightedly; and that taxpayers should be aware of the main possibilities.

Looking as we always do to the difference between this year's taxes and last year's, we tend not to realize how far a tax system can go in 50 or 100 years. Some clue about how far that is can be obtained by comparing today's taxes in the United States with those of 1887 and 1937. In 1887, federal receipts were about 3 percent of gross national product (GNP). There was no federal income tax. More than 60 percent of the federal receipts came from customs. Almost all of the internal revenue came from excises on alcohol and tobacco. In 1937, federal receipts were about 5½ percent of GNP. Income taxes, corporate and individual, supplied 45 percent of the total, and employment taxes (for Social Security) about 5 percent. A family of four with an income of $10,000 paid about 3½ percent in federal income tax. "Progressive" income taxation was being carried to great lengths. A family with an income of $1 million paid almost 68 percent in federal income tax.

This year the federal government is collecting about 20 percent of GNP in revenue, of which 55 percent comes from income taxes and 35 percent from payroll taxes. The $10,000 income of 1937 would have to be about $80,000 now to have the same purchasing power. Using 1988 tax rates, a family with an income of $80,000 will pay about 14 percent in tax, compared with the 3½ percent paid by the $10,000 family in 1937. But the progression has low-income taxpayers—a contest intensified by the need to finance a rapidly growing government.

In the last decade, the tax struggle changed its nature again—to become the people versus the government itself. The legislative results of this shift in the public mood were remarkable. In 1980, Ronald Reagan was elected on a tax-cutting platform. In 1981, he signed the largest tax reduction in our history—approximately one-fourth of personal income taxes. In 1986, we cut tax rates further and broadened the base across business and personal incomes. It will be one of President Reagan's chief legacies that the top tax rate on the world's largest economy dropped from 70 percent to less than half that within a few short years.

Coinciding with these dramatic tax changes has been the longest peacetime expansion on record. Our economic growth, while not perfect, has nevertheless been much faster than most other countries, including Japan. Our employment growth of more than 13 million—has far exceeded that of other countries. And the fears that the tax cuts would cause inflation have not been realized: our inflation has averaged less than 4 percent during this expansion.

Finally, investment, a particular concern of those who opposed tax reform last year, is doing reasonably well this year and is expected to accelerate next year. Down the road, as tax reform takes full effect, we project that reform will increase the cumulative growth in gross national product (GNP) by 2 percent or so, and we will also have a more flexible and stronger economy overall.

These are the economic factors. The social changes are also significant. A new consensus among the American people has softened (although not erased) the old cultural and regional differences. There is a new understanding that both individuals and the economy had fared poorly under the old tax system. This was why we recently saw tax reform being supported by Democrats and Republicans, liberal and conservative economists, leaders ranging from Ralph Nader to the chairman of General Motors, and a majority of the American people.

Taxpayers blamed the economic difficulties in the 1970s on high taxes and other symptoms of a government grown too large. Millions of middle-class taxpayers were upset that inflation had forced them into higher tax brackets previously reserved for the wealthy. Special tax preferences were widely recognized as economically destructive, such as those causing widespread overbuilding in the real estate industry.

Certainly, much of the impetus behind tax reform was a desire to cut out loopholes for one undeserving soul or another. And indeed, fairness was an essential component of the President's reform proposal. But by and large—and this is my key point—this tax reform lacked the violent, often self-defeating passions of the past.

Perhaps most notable was the general acceptance, if not endorsement, of lower marginal rates. Not too many years ago, steeply progressive rates were widely popular in this country. This time, the desire to tax someone else was largely replaced by an agreement to lower tax rates for most people. All told, the tax changes of this decade were a triumph of the peaceful democratic process, somewhat untidy, of course—but landmark improvements in our economic system.

ECONOMIC INTEGRATION AND INTERNATIONAL COMPETITION

Of course, legislation that can change one way can be changed back in the future. But I believe these tax reforms are deeply rooted, not only because our economy and society have changed, but because the world economy has changed. An intensely competitive world will put pressure on policymakers of any political persuasion to keep taxes down.

This world integration is pervasive—in manufacturing, services, trade, and investment all over the globe. Rapid advances in technology are making it much cheaper and easier to move information, goods, money, people, and even factories across national borders. Moreover, the lifespans of products are shrinking dramatically, making it possible for companies to change corporate strategies (and locations) much faster. Telecommunications costs, to name one example, are expected in 20 years to be 1 percent of what they are today.

flattened out. This year's $8-million family will pay about 28 percent in taxes, compared with the 68 percent by the $1-million family in 1937.

There is always a tendency to think that history ends with us and that the future, in taxes as in other things, will not undergo changes as radical as occurred in the past. But a view of how far there may be to go, at least in one direction, can be obtained by comparing the United States with Sweden. In 1983, the marginal tax rate levied on the average production worker in the United States was 43 percent—when all taxes were combined. For Sweden the marginal tax rate was 73 percent (according to OECD studies). Who is to say that the inching-along process may not bring the United States to Sweden's present position in 50 years or less—or, indeed, that 50 years may not bring Sweden to the United States' present position?

The real question raised by the idea of studying tax policy for the 21st century is whether major developments that would influence the course of taxation so far ahead can be identified with some confidence.

One development that can be clearly foreseen is the increasing proportion of the population in most advanced countries that will be over retirement age. This has major implications for government expenditures and for revenue needs and raises important questions about the proper sources of that revenue.

A second factor that has become especially clear is the increasing ease with which business, capital, and labor will move across borders. This movement will intensify the efforts of business and individuals to find locations with tax advantages. It will force governments to try to find less mobile tax bases. International competition will tend to limit the tax rates that national governments can impose, which will also limit their expenditures. The conflict between the expenditures that governments consider necessary for their defense and social solidarity and the taxes they can afford to levy will become more acute.

This may generate a demand for international agreement on tax policy, to keep national revenues from being eroded by competition. But if there is to be international agreement on tax policy, there may have to be international agreement on other things as well. So the consequences of resource mobility through international tax competition could be profound.

Another example of possibly influential developments is the change in the technology of taxation. One thing I learned from reading a big book on the history of taxation is that the modern income tax would have been extremely difficult to administer if we still used the Roman numeral system. Perhaps a basic lesson is that tax systems adapt to the capacity of the administrative machinery.

What will the tax system be like when every economic transaction of every individual is instantly stored in a central data bank and instantly retrievable from it? Will the Internal Revenue Service (IRS) have a continuous up-to-the-minute file on each individual's lifetime income and lifetime tax payments and automatically credit or debit the individual's accounts with the amount required to keep the lifetime payments adjusted to the lifetime income? Will the IRS be able to attribute to each stockholder precisely that person's share of the retained earnings of a corporation and to tax the stockholder on it, making corporation profits taxation redundant? Certainly, ingenious people will find more ways to make use of the mass of additional data governments will have at their disposals.

Other factors that will influence the probable or desirable course of taxation during the next 50 years can be identified. Almost certainly, per capita incomes will be rising nearly everywhere. In the experience of the past century or more, rising per capita incomes have been associated with a rising demand for government services and rising willingness to pay taxes. The question is whether we are near a turning point in this process. Will there be a new attitude in which rising affluence is seen to reduce the need for government programs and thus for taxes? More generally, are the relative weights given to economic growth and efficiency, to "equity," meaning income redistribution, and to environmental concerns changing, with the necessary consequences for the level and character of taxation?

The essays contained in this volume are the thinking of experts from around the world on these and other foreseeable or imaginable developments in taxation. We believe that these essays fully confirm our initial judgment that useful and important things can be said.

1

The Momentum of Tax Reform

James A. Baker, III*

The checkered history of economic predictions serves as a caution to those of us who try to peer into the future. But at the same time, we can make some educated guesses that will likely come true—we have to, or else we'd be totally surprised by the future, and totally unprepared.

There are some basic trends today that point to an interesting, if not completely predictable future. The 1986 tax reform and the 1981 tax cut legislation in many ways reflected these powerful tides of change. Those who may wish to "revisit" reform must contend with these factors. They did not emerge overnight—they are deeply rooted in our past and will be influential in our future.

Several trends I see as particularly important:

*This chapter is based on the keynote address delivered by U.S. Secretary of the Treasury Baker at the "Tax Policy in the Twenty-First Century" conference on October 6, 1987.

- First, the rapid integration of the world economy is dramatically changing the effects of taxes—and creating vigorous tax policy competition among nations.
- Second, advances in technology will bring benefits for both tax collector and taxpayer, as well as some complications.
- Finally, changing demographic and social patterns will pose new challenges in tax policy.

INTEGRATION OF THE WORLD ECONOMY

The integration of the world economy has done many things, but in particular it has transformed the motives behind tax policy. It has changed the reasons why nations tax as they do.

Of course, taxation involves the power of one person to take property from another. Not surprisingly, it has from the earliest times inspired a wide range of human emotions—mostly negative feelings, from anger to fear to jealousy.

In fact, on the clay tablets of the Sumerian civilization—the first civilization in recorded history—reads this proverb: "You can have a lord, you can have a king, but the man to fear is the tax collector." And indeed, history has been punctuated with violent tax rebellions. These struggles have been tightly interwoven with—and often dominated by—regional disputes, class rivalries, cultural antagonisms, sectarian differences, and simple struggles for subsistence.

Our own United States came about largely through a tax revolt—combined with a desire for liberty, national independence, and other deeply held beliefs. The next great tax debate, over tariffs, pitted northeastern manufacturers against agrarians in the South and the West who imported factory goods. Tied in here were many familiar social conflicts—urban versus rural, rich versus poor, and farmer versus businessman.

The tariff issue was finally supplanted as a tax policy issue by the creation of the income tax in 1913. Tax debates lost much of their regional qualities as the U.S. economy integrated. In much of this century, tax policy was a contest between high-income and

Today, as much as one-third of world trade in goods is in intracompany trade, for example, shipments from a Sony parts plant in Japan to a Sony assembly plant in Mexico or San Diego. Commercial relationships that cross borders—such as joint venture, licensing, sourcing, and distribution arrangements—are growing by leaps and bounds. IBM is the second biggest computer company in Japan, and one of the biggest Japanese exporters of computer chips to America is Texas Instruments.

The point can be summed up in one simple question: Who will want to invest or work in a highly taxed country?

Of course, lower tax rates are not the only reason to invest in a country. But in this new world, when large quantities of capital are shifted because of tiny changes in interest rates, policies are often made on the margin—much more so than before. Political leaders are looking for something extra, a "competitive edge"—and let's face it, reducing taxes is often politically easier than cutting budgets or changing regulations.

The power of the 1986 U.S. Tax Reform Act has been recognized by our trading partners. The United States now has just about the lowest personal and corporate top rates in the industrial world and among the most favorable depreciation schedules for equipment.

If imitation is the sincerest form of flattery, then perhaps tax reform is one of the sincerest forms of competitiveness. Germany, France, Canada, Japan, and others have taken up tax reform campaigns, as foreign observers have indicated concern that the United States would become a tax haven and become the beneficiary of a so-called "brain drain." We would urge developing countries to follow suit, not only for their sakes, but because the rest of us need a healthy Third World economy. I might also add that many states in our own country are moving to lower rates and broaden their tax bases.

Let me note here that for competitive reasons, among others, the Reagan Administration has opposed the call for higher taxes in the United States. We don't want a tax bill to become a recession bill. Moreover, politicians always find it easier to raise taxes than to cut spending. And even talk of raising taxes tends to dissipate any spending discipline in the Congress. (And excessive spending is the primary cause of the deficit in the first place).

What is overlooked by those favoring new taxes is the tremendous progress already made in lowering the deficit. The President has been willing to take the political heat on budget reductions. (In fiscal 1987, the U.S. budget deficit was reduced by almost $73 billion, a decline of 1.9 percent of GNP. Moreover, in late 1987, the Administration and the Congress implemented a $79 billion deficit reduction agreement covering the next two years.)

Over the past four years the United States has reduced its deficit by 2.9 percent of GNP—the largest deficit reduction of any of the major industrial countries over a comparable period. At 3.4 percent of GNP, our deficit will not be substantially greater than that of most other industrial countries.

INTERNATIONAL TAX COOPERATION

The world community can prosper by making tax systems more consistent with each other. Incompatible tax rules can be as dangerous and self-defeating to the flow of commerce as the more obvious trade barriers. In the past, the United States has sometimes acted unilaterally in setting tax regulations and given little thought as to how the world would follow along. But now I think we recognize that an incompatible American tax policy may harm not only our own businesses in the international arena but also may allow other countries to take unfair advantage of our tax system.

With our 1986 tax reform enacted, the United States hopes soon to sign at least eight or ten bilateral tax treaties. These agreements should help to free up the flow of capital, reduce double taxation, and improve the exchange of tax information. In addition, we should explore ways to improve our multilateral efforts at tax cooperation.

Of course, political pressures may continue to impose excessive taxes on investment in many places—in the United States as well as abroad. But balanced against these pressures will be the growing numbers of voters who depend directly on international capital flows, such as the employees of subsidiaries of foreign companies.

Other factors determine the course of taxation and tax policy. In fact, some events could transform the landscape entirely. We shall do well to remember the forecaster in the last century who predicted that traffic in the streets of New York would ultimately be impossible because of horse manure. He evidently made some laborious mathematical calculations, but he had no way of measuring something that had not happened yet—the advent of the automobile.

TECHNOLOGICAL CHANGES

Likewise, we can make cautious observations about technology and taxation but give no guarantees. Besides speeding up economic integration, technology will greatly change tax collection itself. Collection is one tax policy that will probably affect Americans more dramatically than any other—and if we play our cards right, it can be for the better.

Tax collection has the potential to be cheaper for the government and less painful for the taxpayer. Our system is moving rapidly from paper to electricity. In five to ten years electronic filing could be used by as many as 40 million Americans. Computer records will also replace many of the paper-filled warehouses that burden the Internal Revenue Service. Computers will enable officials to answer the public's questions almost instantly, and lap-top computers will enable agents in the field to complete audits much faster and with much less discomfort to the taxpayer.

Of course, technology, the unlimited phenomenon that it is, will also cause difficulties in tax policy. The proliferation of new financial instruments and business structures could mean more complicated taxes. For example, the legal dividing line between partnerships and corporations is becoming hazier. Computers now make it possible for a large partnership to distribute profits to its partners much like a corporation dispenses its profits to stockholders. On the other hand, computers will enable small businesses—many of whom use only rudimentary accounting techniques—to keep more comprehensive and accurate records. This will make filing less of a chore for both the IRS and the taxpayer.

We will have to wait and see. If I may dare a guess about the next few years of technology: businesses invariably will be faced by a larger array of choices—which in turn imply a wider array of tax consequences. As for the large majority of taxpayers, filing should be quicker and easier.

As the capacities of computers expand, our protections of privacy must expand accordingly. Those who administer taxes must always treat the taxpayer with respect, courtesy, and professionalism. And all Americans must preserve the very strong tradition of freedom in this country and the very strong laws that safeguard our freedoms.

It is heartening to note that technology, so often depicted as the ally of Big Brother, is probably aiding the cause of freedom these days. We need only observe how radio, television, satellites, and copying machines have opened up totalitarian regimes. And here at home, we who administer taxes can rest assured that our conduct will continue to be under close public scrutiny—and occasionally will be widely publicized—in the years ahead.

DEMOGRAPHIC CHANGES

Demographics may not have the drama of technological changes, but its effects can be powerful. The growing numbers of dual-earner families, remarriages, and retirees who work part-time all mean new challenges for makers of tax policy. These changes have involved us in such issues as withholding schedules and the treatment of dependents and alimony payments. I would expect future adjustments as social patterns evolve. Such a changing environment is another reason why a nation needs a flexible tax system with low rates and broad base.

And there is something else important. The average age of populations here and in other industrial countries will continue to rise, and so will social security and health care expenses.

In 1982 and 1983, this Administration and Congress forged a compromise to strengthen Social Security—and guaranteed the integrity of its retirement benefits into the 21st century.

In the years ahead, policymakers must maintain a watchful eye on the Social Security system and keep its resources adequate. But we should also know that young people cannot bear ever-increasing payroll taxes, any more than retirees can be expected to take cuts in benefits earned over a lifetime of hard work.

Our efforts to encourage long-term economic growth are all the more crucial as a way to generate revenues to support the system. Our nation should also tap the great reservoir of talent and experience in our elderly, who are far more vigorous and healthy than ever before. As a matter of public and private policy, we should not coerce these older Americans into premature retirement.

CONCLUSION

I think our preparations for the century ahead should be based on sound economic and social principles. I don't think our economy is ever served very well by a lot of political tinkering, either in taxes or other areas of policy. Revisiting tax reform, to name one example, could open a Pandora's box of all kinds of problems.

Instead, let us fully recognize the competitive nature of this changing world, and therefore the need to keep taxes reasonable and the economy resilient. Let us reaffirm our commitment to restraining the growth of government, because such growth is a fundamental cause of higher taxes. Finally, and not least, let us think carefully about how to balance the benefits of technology against the needs of privacy.

With these things in mind, we can make progress toward a world where each citizen is treated with dignity and each nation is allowed to reach its potential.

2

A View from the Legislative Front

Bill Gradison

I think that if Rip Van Winkle fell asleep in 1988 and woke up in the year 2000, he would recognize the tax system and many of its forms—and could fill out the returns needed to calculate the taxes, penalties, and interest that accumulated during his 13-year slumber.

I am comfortable with this forecast because in 1974 such a projection would have proven correct. In that year, federal government receipts were 18.6 percent of output, about the same as today, and state and local government tax receipts were 10.3 percent, also about the same. Even the most recent changes in the tax code—in 1981, 1982, 1984, and 1986—did not dramatically change the level of federal taxation.

Looking into the more distant future, we must recognize that taxes are not an independent variable. They are related in some way, however, to the level of spending, the size of the surplus or deficit, which unit of government raises the money, and, perhaps, to international considerations as well.

SPENDING

With regard to the level of spending as well as spending priorities, there was an impasse in Washington when the same public that elected Ronald Reagan elected a Congress as strongly committed to domestic spending as the President was to defense and foreign aid. This impasse resulted in compromises only a politician could love—increased spending for both defense and domestic programs.

The new strategy embodied in the revised Gramm-Rudman balanced budget law gave a choice between a rather mindless process called "sequestration," which seeks deficit reduction solely through spending cuts, and so-called "reconciliation," which seeks the same goal but through a mix of revenue increases and spending restraint. How this choice is resolved helps to determine both the level of spending and the level of taxation. Of course, to the extent that cuts in federal domestic spending merely shift responsibilities to the state and local levels the tax burden is not reduced, although the mix of taxes is altered with heavier weight on consumption taxes.

I do not subscribe to the thesis that spending is a function of taxation; in fact, I consider that notion entirely backwards.

BUDGET SURPLUS OR DEFICIT

What, then, is the proper level of budget surplus or deficit? While so-called "automatic stabilizers" remain in place, countercyclical fiscal policy, including countercyclical tax policy, seems to be dead or at least dormant. But as the deficit is reduced over time, the implication is that the tax burden will not be reduced. That is to say, net tax cuts do not appear in the picture as long as deficit reduction is our highest fiscal priority.

I think our goal should be a substantial federal surplus, achieved, perhaps, by balancing the overall budget but running a large Social Security surplus.

I would argue that the objective of fiscal policy ought to be to maximize social welfare and that an appropriate indicator is society's preference over a long period of time for consumption. After all, we live to consume, not to save. Analytically, this means we can learn how far we have to go, and in which direction, by studying saving patterns.

Not long ago I did some rough calculations, starting with the assumption that government policies distort private savings behavior. This is not to say that government policies are undesirable or even unnecessary—only that such policies as government capital formation justify some public dissaving, while our unfunded Social Security system and taxation of capital income discourage private saving and should be balanced by public saving. I tried to estimate the fiscal deficit or surplus necessary to correct for these distortions—to determine the optimum budget margin. Without any distortive government policies, I asked, what would people save? My model suggests that government planners can do no better than the sum of private individual choices in determining aggregate savings over time.

Not surprisingly, and despite the considerable imprecision in the numbers, I found that U.S. fiscal policy should be adding to, not reducing, aggregate national savings; that is, we should run large federal surpluses.

Tax policy is important in this context to the extent it pushes saving in the right or wrong direction. For example, a country like the United States, which needs to increase aggregate saving, ought to consider carefully tax proposals that hold promise for nudging us in the direction of more saving. To be sure, it is far from clear—based on the experience since 1981—that we know how to use the tax system to increase saving. But this should not discourage us from trying.

INTERNATIONAL COMPETITIVENESS

The United States in recent years has been an exporter of tax policy—specifically, the idea of lower marginal rates—but has resisted importing foreign ideas, such as the value-added tax (V.A.T.). This could be characterized as a mercantilist tax policy. One can speculate that during the balance of the 20th century domestic fiscal policy will have to be set with much more attention to international considerations than in the past. Much the same, of course, can be said of monetary policy. Perhaps the criticism most frequently heard of the Tax Reform Act of 1986 was its perceived effect on the "competitiveness" of the United States, and I suspect that this criterion will be used for future tax bills. Just as the investment tax credit has risen from the dead twice before, there is no reason to doubt its possible revival again in the future.

However, using the vague standard of competitiveness to evaluate our tax system, and especially to focus on the cost of capital in doing so, is the wrong approach. Investment demand is not very sensitive to the cost of capital, and the amount of savings available for investment is not closely tied to the return on capital. It would seem, therefore, that capital formation is more dependent on the amount of savings available for investment than on a return-driven demand for investment.

Moreover, the "competitiveness" perspective on taxation has a more fundamental flaw. Changes in the tax code do affect the ability of individual firms or industries to compete internationally, but this is not true of the nation as a whole. The mechanisms of international trade, particularly the exchange rate, adjust so that the overall level of trade will not be affected, though its composition will. In a world of floating exchange rates, the notion of a country's competitiveness is nonsense.

Nonetheless, a possible outgrowth of the maturing international economy could be increased pressure for countries to engage in tax competition in order to attract or keep business, and this is a danger that concerns me. As the availability of international capital, educated workforces, and levels of productivity become more equalized, the importance of tax considerations in the investment equation increases. Just as the states of the United States have been bidding for commercial enterprises, countries could be forced into similar competition. Such a bidding war would not only harm the efficient allocation of world resources, but it could also strengthen the protectionism that is flourishing in today's world.

Avoiding such a situation could prove difficult. While protectionist policies could derail tax competition, I doubt that many analysts would encourage this solution. And the prospects for international cooperation have considerable barriers. While economic forces may push countries toward similar, more efficient tax codes, I doubt that nations will, by working together, reach such a harmony.

A good example of the difficulty of cooperation is international monetary reform, an idea to which many pay lip service, but which so far has produced few tangible results. That international monetary cooperation has proved so difficult raises greater questions about the ability of nations to agree on even basic tax policy questions. The operation of monetary policy, in the United States at least, is largely shielded from political pressures. To get our unwieldy legislature to agree with those of other nations on divisive economic issues such as taxation is a daunting task. Perhaps this is a topic for the future of the General Agreement on Tariffs and Trade (GATT), following what we hope will be a successful treatment of intellectual property rights and trade in services. But a GATT solution might not be reached even in the long run.

TAX POLICY

Central to any discussion about future tax trends is the role of broad-based federal consumption taxes. My prejudice is for such levies in order to reduce the pressure on income taxes. However, we receive a mixed signal from abroad.

Western Europe adopted the V.A.T. as a reform measure to replace existing, selective excise taxes. But Japan, which like the United States has few such levies to build upon, gets cold feet every time the V.A.T. is seriously considered, and my guess is so will we.

This is largely political, but not entirely. A V.A.T. offers no immediate relief to our hard-pressed fiscus, since it takes time to gear up and put into effect. And the V.A.T. would add complexity to an already arcane tax system, opening up compliance problems every bit as serious as those we have with income taxes.

For some years, the United States has been shifting away from income taxes based on ability to pay toward payroll taxes, user fees, and a flatter individual income tax. These trends are likely to continue. Our recent means of financing the environment Superfund, the highways and airways trust funds, the pension benefit guarantee fund, and the means being discussed for financing catastrophic health benefits suggest that we have hit upon a politically acceptable means of raising more revenue. Even President Reagan, who opposes tax increases, agrees.

I played a major role in developing the idea of financing a portion of Medicare benefits by taxing the actuarial value of the subsidy to the beneficiaries. To describe this, I have hit upon the term "income-related mandatory users fee." Whatever one may think of the terminology, this appears to be an idea whose time has come, and the notion could be applied well beyond Medicare financing. Indeed, such a concept could be applied to the next major step in health care for the elderly—long-term care, which could well be on the books by the year 2037.

No discussion of tax policy would be complete without mention of nontax taxes, that is, expenses mandated by government but paid for largely by business and not run through the Treasury.

This is not a new development. Workers compensation and minimum wage laws have been on the books for years. The subsidy costs of government credit programs have, up to now, been missing or misstated in the budget accounts. Costly regulations of all sorts, such as farm marketing orders, do not show up in the budget either, yet they impose costs as surely as increased taxes.

Today, perhaps because of fiscal stringency, more off-the-books proposals are under consideration, and some, like mandatory employer health insurance coverage, are quite expensive. To the extent these devices are used widely, our analysis of tax burdens cannot be limited to examining the books of government.

Two major steps already taken, however, will stabilize our tax code. The 1986 Tax Reform Act is a giant step toward a tax system based on economic income. Combined with our high budget deficits, this development will make it more difficult to provide benefits to special pleaders.

The other step, which I consider my most significant legislative accomplishment, was the indexation of the tax code that went on the books in 1981. Indexing makes raising taxes harder, which was my intent. The Treasury no longer can count on revenue windfalls generated by inflation. Results of that historic decision are being played out in the news almost daily.

When Rip Van Winkle wakes up in the year 2000 or 2037, he will recognize the tax world of 1988. Whether this is good news or bad news, we leave to Mr. Van Winkle to decide.

3

Experience from a Century of Change

RICHARD M. BIRD

What does a look in the rearview mirror tell us about what lies ahead? People who are 50 and older have in their lifetimes experienced a global war, political upheavals in much of the world, major economic crises, rapid technological change, and substantial economic progress. These momentous changes have been accompanied by equally significant changes in the scale and structure of the public sector. In most Western countries, government spending taken as a share of national income is now double or more than what it was 50 years ago. The structure of government spending has also changed drastically. More emphasis is put on social expenditures than ever before. This greatly expanded public sector has been financed to a large extent by increasing taxes on income and consumption to levels never before considered sustainable. Even so, in recent years the tax yields of many countries have proven insufficient to eliminate deficits or banish the specter of increasing public debt.

What is most interesting about this characterization of the last 50 years, perhaps, is that exactly the same words could have been written in 1937. Fifty years ago, someone looking back on the development of the public sector would have seen a huge increase in government spending and taxation. In the United States, for example, government spending—federal, state, and local— was probably only about 6 percent of gross national product (GNP) in 1887; by 1937, this ratio had more than doubled, to 14 percent. In Britain, the comparable increase was from about 15 percent to 30 percent; in Germany, from 9 percent to 31 percent; and in Canada, from 8 percent to 20 percent.[1] Taxes, too, particularly those on income, were much higher in 1937 than anyone in 1887 would have conceived to be possible.

It seems equally unlikely that anyone in 1937 would have predicted that the next 50 years would be much like the past 50 years, at least with respect to the growth of the public sector. Yet the size of governments in most Western countries has again more than doubled from 1937 to 1987. Government spending as a proportion of GNP is now close to 40 percent in the United States, close to 50 percent in Britain, Canada, and Germany, and well over 50 percent in a number of other European countries.[2] Even in Japan and Switzerland, always the laggards where government expansion is concerned, the public sector share of GNP is now more than one-third. In all countries, the major growth in spending has been on social welfare and social security.

The picture on the tax side is similar, with taxes now taking more than one-quarter of GNP in every country comprising the Organization for Economic Cooperation and Development (OECD) except Turkey, and close to 50 percent of GNP in a number of European countries. Income taxes claim a much bigger part of this impressive total than they did 50 years ago, while consumption taxes and wealth taxes are correspondingly less important. Another less noticed but striking change in tax structure in many countries has been the rise in prominence of payroll taxes earmarked to finance that part of the welfare state called "social security."

Since 1937, not to mention 1887, many other important changes have taken place in tax policy as well as in the political and economic environment. However, the great growth of the public sector throughout the industrialized world during the past 100 years—

despite, or perhaps because of, the traumatic effects of two world wars and the Great Depression—is surely one of the most striking phenomena of the 20th century. The question of whether this prolonged period of growth has now come to an end, as many seem to assume, is critically important to all those concerned with social and economic matters, including tax policy.

The surprisingly close historical parallels between today and 50 years ago do not, of course, suggest that the future will necessarily be like the past. I am not predicting that the tax level in, say, Sweden will continue to double every 50 years, so that by 2037 it will exceed 100 percent of GNP, or that even in such "moderate" countries as the United States tax ratios will climb inexorably upward to 60 percent or higher. However, the history of taxation so far in this century does suggest at least three important lessons for those who wish to consider how tax policy will or should respond to the economic, political, and social changes ahead.

FISCAL INERTIA

In many ways, the future is most unlikely to be like the past. Who would have predicted 30 years ago the return to intellectual respectability of consumption taxation? But 30 years before that, who would have predicted that the income tax would have become the chief pillar of the fiscal system in many countries? Nevertheless, although old taxes may not always be good (or even popular), they are likely to be long lasting. The first lesson of fiscal history is that "the first law of finance is inertia" (in the words of a leading book on the subject: *A History of Taxation and Expenditure in the Western World,* by Carolyn Webber and Aaron Wildavsky).[3]

The taxes now in place in any country are likely to be around for years to come. The relative weights of different taxes in the tax mix may alter: Consumption taxes may increase relative to income taxes, or payroll taxes may grow relative to both consumption and income taxes. The precise characteristics of different taxes may also change, sometimes in important ways. Savings exemptions may turn an income tax into something close to a consumption tax, or exemptions and rate differentiation may turn a general sales tax into something akin to a collection of excises. Still, the tax policy debate 50 years from now, like that of 50 years ago, will center on the same old questions such as the effects of various features of tax design on growth and equity—objectives that, then as now, are held with varying degrees of fervor by different groups in society. Moreover, the basic tax institutions around which the debate takes place are likely to be similar to those we have come to know—if not always to love.

It is surprising that the many governments in the world, most of which are trying to raise more revenues, have not come up with more ingenious ways of doing so. The lure of the familiar and the apparent desire of most governments—like most people—not to be the first to do anything new doubtlessly account for the relative lack of fiscal innovation in the last 50 years. Moreover, it is likely that a careful search through the jumbled warehouse of tax history would reveal that almost every conceivable tax has already been tried somewhere over the years, as sovereigns, dictators, and more or less democratic governments have grappled with the perennial problem of collecting sufficient revenue to carry out their various beneficent or nefarious purposes.

Every once in a while, a government seems to rummage through this warehouse, haul out some antique tax, dust it off, and present it to the world as a brilliant new solution to a currently pressing problem. A striking recent instance of this is the new "community charge" method of financing local services in Britain, which suspiciously resembles the ancient poll tax. For the most part, however, a first lesson suggested by history is that the fiscal problems of the next 50 years will probably have to be dealt with using taxes very much like those on hand today. As with most social and political institutions, there seems to be little or no chance of a "quick technological fix."

ON SIMILARITIES AND DIFFERENCES

In the future as in the past, the way in which each country sets about the task of securing adequate revenue in an acceptable way will continue to be both similar to and different from every other country's course of action. As Rudyard Kipling wrote, "There are nine and sixty ways of constructing tribal lays, and every single one of them is right."

Within the Organization for Economic and Cooperative Development (OECD), for example, the tax system of every country is both similar to that of every other country in terms of the basic problems faced and the major taxes used and different from all others in terms of the relative importance of the different taxes and their precise natures. Detailed examination of the personal income tax in the OECD countries reveals numerous and often important differences in structure and operation.[4] Some countries index rate brackets and exemptions for inflation; others do not. Some tax income on an individual basis; others tax on a family basis. Some tax some or all capital gains; some do not tax such gains at all. Some have highly progressive rate structures; others levy virtually flat-rate taxes.

Differences also may be found in corporation income taxes, wealth taxes, and even sales and payroll taxes. Not only are most taxes different in many respects in individual countries, but they also change in each country at a different pace, in different ways, and—so it usually seems—for quite different and locally specific reasons.

Viewed from a broader perspective, however, many of these differences tend to vanish, and all countries behave in a surprisingly similar fashion. From 1955 to 1984, for example, the yield of income taxes as a proportion of Gross Domestic Product (GDP) increased, on average, from 9 percent to 15 percent in the 19 OECD countries for which the information was available. This ratio increased by somewhat more in those countries in which such taxes were less important at the beginning of the period and by somewhat less in those in which they were more important, but nonetheless, the ratio increased substantially in virtually every country, no matter how much the countries differed in other respects. In Turkey as in Switzerland, in Japan as in Sweden, income taxes went up. Interestingly, the sole exception was that frequent outlier in international comparisons, the United States, where in this period income taxes actually declined slightly in relation to national income.

With respect to other aspects of tax systems, similarly uniform movements are evident when viewed over a period of time for a number of countries—including the very heterogeneous group of developing countries. Two examples in recent years are the spread of the value-added tax (V.A.T.) and the considerable interest shown by many countries in integrating corporate and personal income taxes through such devices as dividend tax credits.

These patterns traced by fiscal developments in various countries have stimulated a number of scholars to postulate grand theories that attempt to explain the development of a country's tax structure. Some emphasize the way in which changing economic structures alter the technological possibilities for raising revenue by giving access to new "tax handles."[5] Illustrations of this thesis are the growth of foreign trade taxes in developing countries and the importance of large business organizations as tax collectors in industrial countries. Other analysts have developed more explicitly political models, ranging from relatively simple scenarios of revenue maximizing governments to more complex and elaborate political-economic models that attempt to track the influence of changing political, economic, and administrative conditions on fiscal structures.[6]

Despite such worthy efforts, however, it is too soon to claim that anyone understands the multitude of forces determining the level and choice of taxes used in a particular country or by industrial or developing countries as a group. About all that can be said is this: While the precise details of what happens and when in any particular country depend upon its particular circumstances—including (as emphasized earlier) its prior fiscal history—the same sorts of things often tend to happen in a number of countries more or less simultaneously.

The most important factor behind this apparent internationalization of something as inherently domestic as tax policy is, of course, world economic development. The rapid pace of economic expansion in the decades up to the early 1970s, and the halting progress thereafter, undoubtedly explain much of what has gone on in many countries both in tax policy discussions and in tax practice. Another factor may be the increased speed and ease of global communications, coupled with the desire to copy apparent fiscal successes achieved elsewhere, whether as a defensive measure (as in the case of cuts in the rates of corporate income taxes) or out of simple emulation (as in the case of the V.A.T.).

Whatever the reason, a second lesson from fiscal history is that (to paraphrase John Donne) no country today is an island, sufficient unto itself. Rather, each is a part of the whole and consequently is influenced, directly and indirectly, by what happens elsewhere. At the same time, the precise manner in which such influences are reflected in fiscal change will doubtlessly continue to depend upon a wide range of social, political, historical, and institutional factors peculiar to each country.

THE HAZARDS OF FISCAL PROPHECY

A third general lesson suggested by fiscal history is (with apologies to Alexander Pope) that fools rush in, where experts fear to tread. Any attempt to forecast what will happen to tax policy in the next 50 years is likely to be as futile in 1987 as it would have been in 1937 or 1887.

The fiscal equivalent of the fictional hunt for the Great White Whale is the search for a single, all-encompassing explanation of fiscal developments. In the end, most such explanations turn out to be some variant of constrained revenue maximization. The constraints considered in the various approaches range from maintenance of the tax base (whether in such modern versions as the Laffer curve or, as the 17th century Japanese ruler Tokugawa Ieyasu put it when asked how heavily peasants should be taxed: "So that they may neither live, nor die") to the existence of tax handles, the possibility of electoral defeat, and the simple desire of governors to lead a quiet life undisturbed by vocal protests from their flocks. Exhilarating as the chase for a single, simple answer may be, most such explanations, like Moby Dick, eventually turn on their hunters and destroy them.

To avoid such a fate, I shall simply comment on five key features of postwar tax policy:

1. the rise (and perhaps impending decline) of the personal income tax
2. the decline (and perhaps rise) of corporate taxes
3. the apparent rejuvenation of consumption taxes
4. the fading away of wealth taxes
5. the inexorable growth of payroll taxes.

PERSONAL INCOME TAXES: PARADISE LOST?

Unquestionably, the outstanding feature of tax policy in the 20th century has been the rise of the personal income tax to a predominant position in the revenue structures of most industrial countries. In many of them, the income tax was introduced during the First World War, remained in place after the war primarily as a relatively modest tax on higher incomes, became a mass tax during or soon after the Second World War, and rose to prominence during the next three decades of unparalleled increases in real and, especially, nominal incomes.

During the past decade, however, both popular and intellectual opinion seem to have turned away from the personal income tax to the point where its future as a major source of public revenues seems open to question. Increasingly, the direction of tax reform in countries such as the United States and Canada has been to remove as many taxpayers as possible from the income tax rolls and to reduce the tax rates levied on those still within the net. A particularly striking sign of the times is the sharp contrast between the 1966 Report of the Canadian Royal Commission on Taxation—which marked the high point of postwar enthusiasm for the personal income tax—and the 1987 tax reform proposals in Canada, which express only muted approval of the tax while simultaneously trying to reduce its visible impact on as many voters as possible.

This tendency has been spurred by widely expressed dissatisfaction with taxation in general and the personal income tax in particular. It has also been reinforced by the growing literature, both scholarly and popular, on the pernicious effects of income taxes on effort, savings, and economic growth. Some critics want to reduce income tax rates to the point of making them flat; others want to simplify the tax system in some drastic manner that usually involves reducing the role of the progressive personal income tax; still others simply want to reduce taxes—and government activity—as much as possible.

What the future holds for the personal income tax is far from clear. Will Western countries gradually replace it by some form of personal expenditure tax or V.A.T.? Or will the income tax, modified somewhat, remain in place for decades to come? Although only time will tell, and the subject is vast, three additional points are worth noting.

First, income tax revenues, relative to national income, have increased only slightly in Western countries in recent years. Indeed, in Britain and Germany the relative importance of the personal income tax has been declining steadily for a decade or more. The extent to which recent fiscal discussions have centered on this tax is thus somewhat surprising. Most likely, the high public profile of the tax makes it a lightning rod for fiscal discontent, whatever the real cause.

Second, and more importantly, the apparent turn away from the income tax may have substantial symbolic meaning. The extent to which a nation's finances rely on taxation of income has recently been characterized as "a mirror of democracy," in the sense that the tax has come to symbolize the strength of egalitarianism and commitment to social justice.[7] The power of this symbol has obviously been weakened, at least in some countries, by the perceived failure of redistributive taxation, by well-publicized defects in most income taxes, and, not least, by the renewed importance attached to economic growth as a result of the less-than-satisfactory performance of the world economy since the early 1970s.

Nevertheless, it seems unlikely that the character of modern democracies will soon alter so much that they will no longer need to finance their activities from what is perceived to be the only real progressive element of the tax system, albeit one that is at best only modestly progressive and far from comprehensive in scope. In his influential prewar treatise, *Personal Income Taxation,* Henry Simons disparagingly referred to such taxes as "dipping deeply with a sieve."[8] It may well be, however, that both the dip (progressivity) and the sieve (tax loopholes) are essential ingredients of fiscal balance in a capitalist democracy.

The third point about the personal income tax is that it is highly visible. Indeed, the tax's visibility lies at the root of my preceding comments. The extent to which most Western countries were able to finance the huge growth of government in the postwar period in this highly visible fashion—albeit aided by the partial shield of wage withholding and the invisible boost of inflation—is a great testimony to the strength of democracy. It is easy to understand why the current disenchantment with the efficacy and efficiency of government spending and resentment of declining real private incomes take the form of a reaction against the obvious target of the income tax. The interesting question, however, is whether less use of the personal income tax will result in smaller (and perhaps more efficient) governments or simply in governments that hide even more of the real cost of their activities from the public than they already do. For those who care about the economic efficiency of government or the future of democracy, not all the omens in this regard are good.

TAXING BUSINESS INCOME: THE TAXMAN ALWAYS KNOCKS TWICE?

One such omen is the shift in emphasis on personal taxes to business taxes in the 1986 U.S. tax reform—a shift subsequently emulated in Canada. Another is the curious invention of a minimum alternative corporate tax. Some experts have rationalized such moves to increase taxes on business as satisfying the need for "perceived fairness" in the tax system. The people, it is said, dislike seeing large businesses pay few taxes or none at all, and, of course, the people are also especially happy to learn that their own taxes can be reduced at the expense of these "fat cats."

As economists quite properly never cease to remind us, however, in the end, business taxes, too, are inevitably paid by people. The main difference between business taxes and the personal income tax is that with business taxes, nobody is sure exactly who pays what. Given the political usefulness of such ambiguity, it is in a way surprising that in most countries so little use has been made of corporate taxes.

This strange reluctance is probably based less on the persuasive words of economists worried about the pernicious effects of taxing capital income than on the desire of governments to respond to the wishes of powerful producer groups, and especially to direct economic activity into politically useful channels. The first law of politics throughout the postwar period in many countries has been that the government can and should "do something" to help this industry, that region, or the other interest group. Tax incentives have been used so often, so widely, and for such purposes that one feels if the corporate income tax had not existed, it would have had to be invented simply so that it could be reduced to order.

Tax incentives, like all policy instruments, are subject to cyclical fashions, and currently they are out of favor. However, the temptation to use fiscal instruments to achieve nonfiscal purposes is unlikely to be held down for long. The new broader corporate tax bases now being put in place in the United States, Britain, Canada, and elsewhere may again be eroded as governments continue to respond both to the perceived needs of their constituents and to their own need to be active.

The growing internationalization of business will also continue to exert downward pressure on the level of business taxes in many countries. Whether or not the structure of business taxes will in time tend to converge is substantially less clear. At one point, for example, it seemed that those who believed in the integration, at least in part, of corporate and personal income taxes would win the day. Indeed, two recent converts to this cause are Australia and New Zealand.

The former has adopted, and the latter proposes to adopt, imputation schemes that are more complete than those that exist elsewhere.

Despite these recent successes, however, there are countertrends. The resolute refusal of the United States to move in the integrationist direction, the recent reduction in the dividend credit by such a longtime partisan of this approach as Canada, and the failure of the European Economic Community (EEC) to make any progress toward a uniform policy with respect to corporate-personal tax integration—all cast doubt on once confident forecasts of a few years ago that integration would be the wave of the future.

CONSUMPTION TAXES: PARADISE REGAINED?

The future is clearer with respect to the third member of the traditional "big three," the general sales tax. After years of second class citizenship, consumption taxes have been readmitted to fiscal respectability. Furthermore, the coming of the V.A.T. has provided governments with a form of sales taxation that is free of the economic distortions of such predecessors as the turnover tax and the manufacturer's sales tax, while still providing a copious flow of revenue. Renewed interest in fostering economic growth, disillusionment with the redistributive role of the tax system, and public dissatisfaction with income taxes all suggest that indirect taxes, especially the V.A.T., are likely to continue to play a large role in many countries.

Such taxes are already very important in several countries. In the EEC, consumption taxes are more important than personal income taxes, with the larger part of consumption tax revenues coming from V.A.T.s. The increase in the relative importance of the V.A.T. in recent years, however, has come largely at the expense of other taxes on goods and services, such as the traditional excises on "vices" (smoking, drinking, and driving). There is as yet little evidence that consumption taxes are likely to recapture the position they held some 50 years ago, when they were the most important source of tax revenue in most countries.

THE TAXATION OF WEALTH: R.I.P.?

In contrast, there is all too much evidence that the future of wealth taxation in most countries is likely to be as bleak as its past. In this century, taxes on wealth—in the form of impersonal taxes on real property, net wealth taxes, or taxes on bequests and gifts—have never been major revenue producers in any industrial country. Moreover, their importance has declined steadily over time. Wealth taxes are now significant only in a few countries in which local governments are important and real property taxes are the main tax they levy.

Except in primitive agricultural countries, however, the role of such taxes has never been simply to produce revenue. Even more than with the progressive personal income tax, their primary role has been to symbolize the commitment of the state to redress some of the more egregious inequalities generated by the market economy. Viewed in this light, the recent complete abandonment by such countries as Canada and Australia of any attempt to tax bequests, and the very feeble efforts elsewhere to do so, such as in the United States, offer still more support to the thesis of declining public support for egalitarian tax policies. Death, alas, is still certain everywhere; taxes on death certainly are not.

SOCIAL SECURITY TAXES: LEVIATHAN BY THE BACK DOOR?

Finally, the most rapidly growing component of tax revenues in many industrial countries in recent decades has been the least discussed, perhaps because it is frequently not even thought of as a tax. This magnificent deception has been achieved, of course, by the payroll taxes ("contributions") levied to finance social insurance schemes.

Personal income taxes increased in importance in the postwar period when inflation and growth moved large numbers of people up the progressive rate schedule, and thus there was no need for politically painful discretionary increases in rates. Although sales taxes increased mainly as a result of expansions in base and increases in rates, as a rule such changes caused no great fuss. In Canada, for instance, the rate of the federal sales tax went up by 25 percent in the early 1980s, with no noticeable public discussion or reaction. The probable fate of any government that had attempted to increase income tax rates by a similar proportion in those years may be readily imagined. In contrast, payroll taxes, which in principle are as visible to most taxpayers as is the income tax withheld from their wages, in most countries have increased steadily and substantially through explicit rate changes with almost no public discussion or dissent.

One explanation for the very different reception given income and payroll taxes by the ordinary workers who pay most of both may be that there continues to be wide public support for at least the social insurance segment of the welfare state. It seems people remain willing to pay at least some explicit tax price for programs they consider to be of direct benefit to themselves. Such earmarking of revenues to particular expenditure programs is one of the most ancient of fiscal practices. The considerable success achieved in financing modern social insurance programs in the face of widespread public dissatisfaction with taxes in general suggests that there is still a good deal of life in this old idea, at least in political terms. Whether public placidity with payroll taxes will continue in the face of the further substantial increases demography seems to require remains to be seen.

CONCLUSION

"To tax and to please, no more than to love and be wise, is not given to men," Edmund Burke once said. Viewed in one light, taxation is a dull, unpleasant business, at best accepted as a painful necessity ("the price we pay for civilization," according to Justice Oliver Wendell Holmes), at worst seen as a threat to economic progress, political regimes, and even whole civilizations—as some have argued. From this perspective the proper task of those who study and design tax policy, then, is primarily to reduce its inevitable economic and political damage. If by luck and skill they achieve some marginal improvements in distribution or allocation, these are at best minor bonuses. In this view, tax policy is little more than an exercise in damage control.

From another perspective, however, the design and implementation of tax policy are among the most fascinating activities. In their formulation is revealed not only the naked play of vested interests, but also deep-seated cultural attitudes and the impress of economic exigencies. Taxation, in this scenario, is less the villain than the victim. It does not so much determine the nature of social, economic, and political changes as it reflects the resolution of such changes in the fiscal arena. The political and economic turbulence of the past decade, for example, has called into question propositions once viewed as graven in stone, such as the superiority of personal income taxes over taxes on consumption.

Tax theory may follow tax practice or precede it, but it is clear that both theory and practice generally reflect developments in the real world, in which ideas are formulated and taxes collected. Lord Keynes wrote that those in authority often do little more than mouth the words of long-dead philosophers. His point was, of course, that the power of ideas is often underestimated. Undoubtedly, he was correct, but one may equally well say that the extent to which ideas are accepted often depends more upon the context in which they are expounded than upon their inherent merits.

In particular, the greater the degree of perceived crisis, the more acceptable it is to make changes in long-established institutions, such as tax systems. For most of the past 100 years, equity has been a central concern of tax policy in much of the Western world. It remains to be seen whether the crisis of confidence that has precipitated the revival of economic liberalism in the post-OPEC (Organization of Petroleum Exporting Countries) years has penetrated deeply enough to reverse this emphasis.

Periods that historians view from the calm of their studies as having been interesting were probably, as a rule, very uncomfortable for those who had to live through them. "May you live in interesting times" is said to have been an ancient Chinese curse. I would not wish such a fate on anyone, but I suggest that the pace and nature of future tax policy changes in various countries will, in the end, be governed primarily by how "interesting" their future turns out to be. Such, at least, is the major lesson I derive from a brief review of tax policy in the 20th century.

4

Demographic Shark in the Fiscal Water

CHARLES E. MCLURE, JR.

Anyone asked to speculate about the likely and desirable contours of the world economy 50 years from now faces a problem similar to that of a man sitting in a dugout canoe in the middle of a coral reef surrounded by sharks. He may have little idea what lies beyond the next threatening piece of jagged coral. He is too close to the water to know whether it is an even more dangerous reef or a quiet lagoon. Furthermore, his attention is likely to be focused on the circling sharks and the narrow passage in the reef he has just navigated.

We economists are "too close to the water" to see clearly what lies over the economic horizon in the 21st century. Moreover, our perceptions of the future are likely to be conditioned, consciously or unconsciously, by such factors as the international debt crisis and the federal budget deficit, current sharks of no mean consequence. In looking forward, our thinking may also be unduly affected by what we see when looking backward, for example, to the energy crisis of the last decade or to the recent experience with federal tax reform.

It is useful to try to see beyond the economic horizon; after all, there is reason to think that our present causes for concern will eventually pass away, presumably to be replaced by others. However, we must recognize that the economic world of the 21st century, in particular, the tax system of the United States, will be significantly affected by how we deal with current crises and those that will occur in the foreseeable future.

The single most important variable in predicting tax policy in the 21st century is the size of government. That will be determined by a number of factors. Lasting peace would allow substantial reductions in expenditures on national defense and in federal taxation. On the other hand, the spread of an AIDS epidemic throughout the population could significantly increase requirements for medical care, while decimating the supply of workers. A strong ideological shift toward either the left or the right could also make it either more or less difficult to raise enough revenues to finance the public sector.

There is, however, one important determinant of the likely size of government in the 21st century that is not imponderable and cannot be neglected. Demographic factors will affect dramatically the size and composition of public expenditures and the need for tax revenues. The first important manifestation of such demographic influences will begin to be felt early in the 21st century when the baby-boom generation retires. How that temporary fiscal crisis is handled is likely to cast a long shadow through the remainder of the century. Even before that, the means chosen to deal with the current budget deficit of the federal government will significantly affect the tax policy we carry forward. The comments that follow begin with consideration of these two "sharks."

CUTTING THE FEDERAL DEFICIT

There appears to be a growing consensus that the United States cannot much longer tolerate federal budget deficits of the magnitude it has experienced during the first six years of the Reagan Administration. While there appears to be little chance that a meaningful tax increase will be enacted before 1989, a tacit agreement seems to be developing that taxes should be increased as quickly as possible after that. This development reflects a realization, reached reluctantly by some and joyously by others, that the prospects of making substantial inroads into the budget deficit by reducing spending are not bright. While supporters of a balanced budget amendment to the Constitution see it as a means of curtailing the growth of expenditures and avoiding the necessity for a tax increase, this view is apparently not widely shared. My opinion is that while the intent behind these proposals—a mandate for fiscal responsibility—is laudable, such an amendment might do more harm than good by stimulating the greater use of "off budget" programs to circumvent that intent.

There are three obvious candidates for a major attack on the federal deficit (not counting the various types of tinkering that are unlikely to be adequate to the job, for example, asset sales and increases in federal excise taxes and user charges). Perhaps the easiest and most obvious would be simply to raise the tax rates applied to the newly expanded income tax base resulting from the Tax Reform Act of 1986. This would have the substantial disadvantage of reversing the reduction of disincentives and economic distortions provided by high rates. In addition, it would accentuate pressures for the reintroduction of the type of loopholes closed by the 1986 act and stymie efforts for further reform. The likely result would be a downward spiral of higher rates, greater inequities and economic distortions, deterioration of the newly improved perception that the tax system is fair, greater evasion, loss of revenue, and a further round of higher rates, with all that this entails. This is not an attractive alternative.

A substantially better alternative would be to rely on further base broadening. The report on tax reform submitted to President Reagan by the U.S. Treasury Department in 1984 ("Tax Reform for Fairness, Simplicity, and Economic Growth," hereafter Treasury I) provides much of the unfinished agenda in this area. Without attempting to be exhaustive, one can note simply that employer-provided fringe benefits should be taxed; deductions for all state and local taxes should be ended; interest on debt of state and local governments should be subject to tax; and the benefits of home ownership should be reduced, perhaps by gradually phasing out the deduction for interest on home mortgages.

In addition, remaining sources of divergence between taxable income and real economic income, such as immediate deduction on intangible drilling costs and accelerated depreciation, should be reduced. If this were done, it should be possible to dismantle most of the complex antishelter provisions of the 1986 Tax Reform Act, notably the limitations on the ability to use losses in one activity to offset income in another, the limitations on interest deductions, and the alternative minimum tax. It should be recognized, however, that not all reforms required to bring rationality to the federal income tax would increase revenues. In particular, both inflation adjustment (to be discussed at greater length later) and the elimination of the double taxation of dividends would result in the loss of revenue.

There is much to be said for this second alternative, since it would raise revenue while eliminating existing distortions and inequities. Yet it would be difficult to achieve, precisely because it would adversely affect potentially powerful interest groups which are able to make politically persuasive, if not well-founded, arguments. (Consider, for example, the national defense arguments for preferential treatment of the oil and gas industry which result in benefits to the rich and regional inequities, while inducing overallocation of resources to this industry and premature depletion of the nation's resources.) Whether the miracle of 1986 can be repeated is not clear.

It is possible that Congress will look to an alternative source of revenue rather than reopen the tax reform debate. In that case, the most likely candidate is a general sales tax, in particular, a value-added tax (V.A.T.) of the type imposed in some 40 other countries, including those of the European Common Market and much of the rest of Western Europe.[1] A retail sales tax would be a reasonable alternative, considering American experience with state retail sales taxes and the greater ease of dovetailing state and federal sales taxes. A distinctly inferior alternative, but one that has received much favorable mention, is a "business transfer tax" of the type recently proposed for Canada under the name "goods and services tax."

A federal sales tax has both considerable advantages and important disadvantages. Unless filled with preferential treatment for various items of consumption, the V.A.T. would be relatively neutral in its impact on the economy—certainly much more neutral than the present income tax. Thus it would interfere less with economic decisions than the present tax system.

One of the primary disadvantages of the V.A.T. (or any form of general sales tax) is its regressivity. Being imposed on consumption, it would impose a substantial burden on low-income families, one that would be larger in relation to income than that on those with higher incomes. If, as seems likely, the United States eventually adopts a general system of low-income relief patterned after proposals for a negative income tax, this would be a matter of less concern. By comparison, techniques of reducing regressivity, such as exemptions for food, are very blunt and inefficient; substantial amounts of revenue are lost through exemption of food consumed by families that are not poor in order to gain relatively small benefits for the poor.

One characteristic of such a tax, with a foot in both the "advantages" and "disadvantages" columns, is that it would raise a substantial amount of revenue relatively easily. Liberals see this as a great attraction of the V.A.T., while conservatives see in it the specter of increased government spending. While I share the latter viewpoint, I have come to fear even more than increased spending the continuation of large federal deficits.

Perhaps the most widely heralded feature of the V.A.T. is irrelevant to the discussion of tax policy for the 21st century: the supposed competitive advantage that would result from the fact that the V.A.T. is collected on imports and rebated on exports. (Much the same can be said of retail sales taxes; they are also imposed on imports but not exports. Yet hardly anyone makes the same claim about them.) Any short-run competitive advantage that might be gained from use of the V.A.T. would be absorbed by movements in exchange rates over periods beginning as long as a decade from now.

It appears unlikely, then, that the world will tolerate continuation of federal budget deficits anywhere near the size of those experienced during the 1980s. Experience since the stock market crash in October 1987 supports this view. The most likely means of dealing with the deficit problem appear to be these: the raising of rates on the still highly defective base resulting from the 1986 Tax Reform Act; the broadening of the income tax base in ways that should have been followed in the 1986 act; or the introduction of a federal sales tax. Either of the last two alternatives would be substantially better than the first or resorting to "nickel and dime" tinkering.

THE DEMOGRAPHIC TIME BOMB

The need to reduce the federal budget deficit seems like a friendly dolphin compared to the demographic shark lurking in the waters of the 21st century. As the baby-boom generation retires, the fiscal system of the United States will experience a "double whammy." Expenditures for retirement benefits and medical care will increase tremendously just as the labor force shrinks in relation to the retired population. Even a cursory examination of the fiscal implications of demographic trends indicates how important it is to make responsible choices now.

The percentage of the population over the age of 65 is expected to grow from less than 10 percent as recently as 1970 to almost 14 percent in 2010, to 17 percent only a decade later, and to 21 percent by 2030. Whereas between now and 2010 the number of pensioners will be only about a fourth as large as the labor force, by 2030 this ratio will exceed 40 percent. The elderly dependency ratio (the ratio of population aged 65 and over to that aged 15 to 64) will rise from about one-sixth to perhaps twice that.

In the long run, the retirement and disability part of the Social Security system, Old Age, Survivors and Disability Insurance (OASDI), is likely to run an actuarial deficit, except under quite optimistic scenarios. This problem will be accentuated by large deficits expected for hospital insurance (HI) beginning in the 1990s.

Professor Michael Boskin of Stanford University has estimated that the deficit in the Old Age and Survivors Insurance (OASI) portion of Social Security could be handled with a modest rate increase of only about one-half of one percent, provided it were enacted now and surplus funds were allowed to accumulate for the next 25 years, rather than permitted to dissipate.[2] The question is whether we have the political will to do this.

During the next 25 to 30 years, while the baby-boom generation is at the peak of its earning power, a substantial surplus will accumulate in OASI if currently legislated real benefits and tax rates are not changed. This accumulated surplus is projected to peak at nearly 30 percent of gross national product (GNP). This is approximately equivalent to the current ratio of the national debt to GNP. It is this short-term surplus that must be allowed to accumulate if we are to accommodate the retirement of the baby-boom generation without cutting benefits or raising taxes substantially.

There will be tremendous pressures to divert this surplus to other uses, notably to reduce tax rates, to increase benefits, to bail out HI, or to finance other programs. The disastrous result of such a diversion can be seen by supposing that the tax rates for OASI during this period of potential surplus were to be sufficiently lower than under current law to eliminate the surplus. (For this purpose we use the intermediate scenario of the Social Security Administration.) Under this "pay-as-you-go" scenario, by 2001 or so combined employee-employer tax rates for OASI could be reduced from their current level in excess of 10 percent of payroll to well below 9 percent. However, by about 2020, rates would return to their currently scheduled level, and by the middle of the 21st century they would be approaching 14 percent.

Of course, cutting tax rates during the next two decades may not be the most likely scenario; an increase in benefits is probably more likely. During the period of potential surplus, benefits could be raised substantially, reaching a peak of roughly 30 percent above levels provided in current legislation by about 2010. However, by 2020, they would fall to currently projected levels and to only 80 percent of current law levels by the middle of the 21st century.

Cuts of this magnitude—from 130 percent of currently legislated benefits to only 80 percent—are, of course, not likely to be politically feasible. This raises the possibility of an even scarier scenario, that is, a rise in benefits to their peak level just before the retirement of the baby-boom generation and maintenance of that level of benefits thereafter. Under this "benefits ratchet" scenario, tax rates would stay at currently projected levels until about 2010 and then rise dramatically to finance the payment of increased benefits to a rapidly growing retired population. By the middle of the 21st century, a combined tax of almost 18 percent would be required just to finance OASI. Under any of these scenarios, higher taxes would also be required to finance HI.

It may appear at first glance that the increases in tax rates hypothesized here are not very large; after all, an increase of three to four percentage points seems relatively small. However, it is worthwhile to place it in context. If we allow the potential surplus to be dissipated and thus are obliged to raise taxes above current levels after 2020, we could be talking about a tax increase of at least 30 percent to finance OASI. If we allow benefits to be "ratcheted" upward, the increase may be on the order of 70 percent. These are not small changes.

In combination with income tax rates (and perhaps a federal sales tax) as well as state and local taxes, tax increases of this magnitude will create tremendous disincentives for work effort. These disincentives would be softened somewhat by a belief that increases in Social Security contributions actually purchase increases in future retirement benefits and medical care. But given existing estimates of the real rates of return that are to be expected on investments in Social Security wealth, especially by those in the middle class who will be subject to relatively high income tax rates, there is a hollow ring to this argument.

There may be some impetus to shift partial financing of Social Security to general revenues. This has pros and cons that cannot be discussed fully here. Such a policy would not, of course, reduce the basic demographic fact that substantially higher taxes on the working population are likely to be required in order to provide benefits for the elderly. Indeed, such a shift would likely worsen the disincentive effects by further weakening the "insurance myth" that has traditionally supported the Social Security system.

CHOOSING A TAX BASE

A substantially less frightening topic is the need for the United States to choose between two competing models for direct taxation. Historically, the federal government has relied on taxation of income as compared to taxation of personal consumption expenditures, or what can be called consumed income. (This discussion pertains to a personalized tax on consumption collected in much the same way as the present income tax rather than to an impersonal tax on transactions, such as the V.A.T. or a retail sales tax.) However, many features of the current income tax are really more appropriate for a tax on consumption, and many provisions essential for a fair and neutral income tax are missing. The results are quite predictable: inequities, economic distortions, and complexities.

One hopes that sometime during the next few decades the United States will choose to replace the existing hybrid system containing both income and consumption tax features with either a more comprehensive and sensible income tax or a tax based explicitly and consistently on consumption.

INFLATION ADJUSTMENT

Many well-known shortcomings plague the U.S. income tax: A few of the most important gaps in the tax base have already been mentioned. One defect demands further consideration, however, both because its adverse consequences are not adequately recognized and because it is likely to become more important over the coming decades. This is the need for inflation adjustment in the measurement of income from business and capital. This is an entirely different topic from the need for inflation adjustment in monetary magnitudes fixed in nominal terms, such as personal exemptions, the standard deduction, and rate brackets. That is handled more or less satisfactorily under current law.

The measurement of taxable income under current law is based on historical values. That is, the bases for calculating depreciation allowances and capital gains are not adjusted for inflation, and the full amount of interest expense is recognized as income and allowed as a deduction. As long as there is little or no inflation, this poses little or no problem; there may be some mismeasurement of income, but not enough to justify instituting an inflation-adjusted system.

If, however, the rate of inflation is high and variable, the situation is quite different. Unexpected inflation creates windfall gains and losses. Tax is paid on the full amount of interest income even though the value of principle is being eroded by inflation; similarly, deductions are allowed for interest expense that is not real. Tax is paid on capital gains that are not real, and perhaps even when real losses occur. Depreciation allowances based on historical costs do not allow tax-free recovery of capital invested in depreciable assets.

When inflation is perfectly forecast by both borrowers and lenders, the problem is not so much a lack of fairness as the distortion of economic choices. Taxpayers are encouraged to borrow too much and to save too little. They are also discouraged from investing in depreciable assets and those that yield their return as capital gains.

A common response to this type of potential inequity and distortion is to provide ad hoc adjustments for inflation. For example, depreciation allowances may be accelerated; last-in, first-out (LIFO) inventory accounting may be allowed; and preferential treatment may be accorded to capital gains. This ad hoc approach to dealing with inflation has several undesirable consequences. First, the various adjustments are likely to be correct only for a particular rate of inflation (and perhaps other economic parameters); at any other rate of inflation, tax treatment will be either too generous or not generous enough. When the rate of inflation is varying, it is especially unlikely that any particular ad hoc tax regime is appropriate. As a result, inequities and distortions are not eliminated and may even be exaggerated. Beyond this, ad hoc adjustment is seldom extended to interest income and expense. As long as these items are treated incorrectly, equity and neutrality are not possible, and opportunities for tax arbitrage and tax shelters are likely to abound. Particularly important in this respect is the stimulus for overinvestment in owner-occupied housing.

A comprehensive system of inflation adjustment was proposed in Treasury I. This proposal was not favorably received for a number of reasons. These included its complexity, its revenue cost, the inadequacy of transition rules, and the apparent lack of need for such a system now that inflation rates have subsided from the double-digit range experienced only a few years earlier. Still, I believe it was a major mistake to reject this proposal. Inflation will almost certainly accelerate before the end of this century, if only because of the effects of the weakening of the dollar. When this occurs, we shall go through another episode of inequities and distortions resulting from the interaction of inflation and an unindexed tax system. We shall learn that a period of low inflation is precisely the best time to introduce a system of inflation adjustment.

If the inflation is rapid enough and lasts long enough, however, we may see the introduction of inflation adjustment. Such a system undoubtedly will be complicated, but I view this as a reasonable price to pay for insurance against the undesirable effects described earlier.

INCOME VERSUS CONSUMPTION

Economists generally emphasize the following key economic difference between a tax on income and a tax on consumption: The consumption tax, because it effectively excludes the return to saving from the tax base, is neutral with respect to the choice between present and future consumption and is therefore likely to be more favorable to saving than the income tax. In a world with too little saving, this difference is seen as a major advantage of a consumption-based tax.

My view is that neutrality toward the choice between saving and consumption and the potential positive effects on saving are not the important advantages of a consumption-based direct tax. Frankly, it seems rather quixotic to be advocating such a fundamental shift in tax policy based on hypothesized changes in saving behavior at a time when the federal government is borrowing $200 billion a year and we face the demographically driven budgetary problems described earlier. If we are really worried about national saving, we should reduce the budget deficit and prevent dissipation of the temporary surplus expected in OASI. I believe, rather, that the important advantage of a consumption-based direct tax is its relative simplicity. Both the need for inflation adjustment and the complex timing issues so prominent in the 1986 Tax Reform Act simply vanish under a consumption-based tax.

However, important concerns and stumbling blocks exist along the route to a consumption-based direct tax. These include transition from the present income-based system, the equity implications of exempting capital income from taxation, the proper treatment of gifts and bequests, and the taxation of flows of income and expense moving among nations. These must be fully studied as we assess whether movement to a consumption-based system is appropriate.

Two alternative ways of treating individuals under a consumption-based tax system have received considerable attention from tax experts. Under the cash flow alternative, individuals would include the proceeds of borrowing and interest income in their tax base but would be allowed a deduction for repayment of debt and interest expense. It can be shown that under certain circumstances this is equivalent to exempting the marginal return to capital from tax.[3]

The second alternative, sometimes called the tax-prepayment approach, achieves this result directly by explicitly exempting capital income received by individuals (for example, as interest and dividends) and allowing no deduction for interest. (Capital transactions such as borrowing and lending have no tax implications.) I believe that the cash flow approach is substantially more complicated than the tax-prepayment approach, so much so that it is not a viable alternative for consideration. These crucial differences have received such minimal attention that the nation really is not adequately prepared to make a choice between these alternatives, much less to choose between one of them and a reformed income tax.

LOOSE ENDS

A few other steps may—and perhaps should—be taken in the fiscal area during the next half century. The first concerns technology. Improvements in information processing should make it possible for the Internal Revenue Service to calculate the tax liabilities of many taxpayers without the necessity of their filing an income tax return. Such a "return-free" system, proposed in Treasury I, would be facilitated by the adoption of comprehensive income tax reform. It would be even simpler under a prepayment-based tax on consumption (but not under the cash flow alternative). Some experts are concerned about the infringement on privacy such a system would entail. It seems, however, that this concern is misplaced since under such a system little information that is not already required would flow to the IRS. The concern that taxpayers would fail to realize the magnitude of their liabilities under a return-free system also seems to have little force unless we are willing to dismantle withholding—a concession to taxpayer awareness that is unlikely to be made.

A few obvious improvements in state and local taxation would also be desirable. A greater conformity of federal and state income taxes would facilitate both taxpayer compliance and administration. State sales taxes would be more equitable and neutral if taxation extended to services as well as goods. Of course, if the federal government enacts a sales tax, there will also be important issues of conformity between the sales taxes of the various levels of government. One possible (if unlikely) outcome would be the replacement of existing state and local sales taxes with shared revenues from a federal V.A.T. Finally, it is to be hoped and expected that the indefensible distinction between nondeductible sales taxes and fully deductible income and property taxes contained in the 1986 Tax

Reform Act will soon be eliminated, preferably by disallowing deduction for all state and local taxes.

For many years, economists have been arguing that economic decision making would be improved if "effluent charges" were imposed on goods, services, and activities generating costs to society not paid for by those responsible for them. Long and bitter experience suggests that this is not an idea whose good sense immediately recommends itself to the public or to lawmakers. Thus one must be slightly wary about suggesting that within the next 50 years the use of effluent charges will be widespread. And yet, the combination of an increasing degradation of the environment and the increased difficulty of raising public revenues in acceptable ways suggests that effluent charges may eventually come into their own.

CONCLUSION

The federal deficit and the sobering fiscal implications of demographic trends seem to leave little room for optimism. I believe, however, that by the year 2000 we will have a federal sales tax, an improved income tax, or substantially higher income tax rates. Though the need for increased federal revenues seems to be inevitable, it is not a development I particularly welcome.

I am relatively complacent, however, about that prospect compared with what I foresee in the financing of Social Security. I am concerned that the near-term potential surplus will not be allowed to develop and that Social Security taxes will need to be raised dramatically toward the end of the first 25 years of the 21st century. Alternatively, general revenue financing may be utilized for Social Security; but, of course, such a rearrangement of the deck chairs on the fiscal ship of state would not much affect the dismal prognosis.

5

We're Not Getting Any Younger

DALLAS L. SALISBURY

Demographics determine how many taxpayers there are, how many people those taxpayers must support, what is possible in terms of redistribution and reallocation of the tax dollars, and thus what programs the government and employers can provide.

In recent decades, the United States has been experiencing dramatic demographic change, and for many decades to come it will continue. Women's participation in the labor force is up dramatically and continuing to climb. With it have risen the numbers of two-income households and "latch key" children. So, too, there has been a rise in the numbers and proportion in the population of unmarried people and single parents. Most important for future tax and spending policies, family size has dropped below the point of zero population growth, and people are living longer. This changing age mix of the U.S. population—more old, less young—(as described in the middle-series assumptions of the U.S. Bureau of the Census) is our focus here, along with certain trends related to this change.

The age mix of the population determines the monetary flow in programs funded in advance, such as private sector pensions, and whether one can expect contributions to such programs to exceed the eventual benefit payments. When benefit payments exceed contributions plus investment earnings, assets must be sold to meet those payments. If these assets are government bonds, the government may have to raise taxes to redeem them. Indeed, in the 21st century, Social Security will be paying benefits in excess of contributions, a situation that will require debt redemption of its four-year reserve and thus additional revenue.

Demographics also determine the cash flow requirements of such programs as Medicaid, Medicare, and private health insurance. The average cost per individual rises with age, guaranteeing that for a given level of benefit promised, the shares of gross national product (GNP), government expenditures, and (in the case of the private programs) individual compensation or assets going to health care will increase. The Employee Benefit Research Institute has projected that if health care expenditures continue to grow at the pace of the last 15 years, 100 percent of GNP will be spent on health care by the year 2035—an obvious absurdity. So action will eventually have to be taken. No small part of this cost growth is brought about by the aging of the population. The United States has been talking about the "pig in the python" for years but has done little to change policies to reflect the future implications of today's demographics.

DEMOGRAPHIC TRENDS

Our population is moving along a trend line identifiable since the turn of the century: that of an aging population. The Census Bureau points out that in 1982 the median age of the U.S. population was at an all time high of 30.6 years, with the trend line moving us to 36.3 years at the turn of the century, 40.8 years in 2030, and 42.8 years in 2080. The population pyramids of Chart 1 show the tremendous change brought about by the passage of the baby boom and continued moderate fertility. Chart 2 provides a picture of the

Chart 1 Population Pyramids

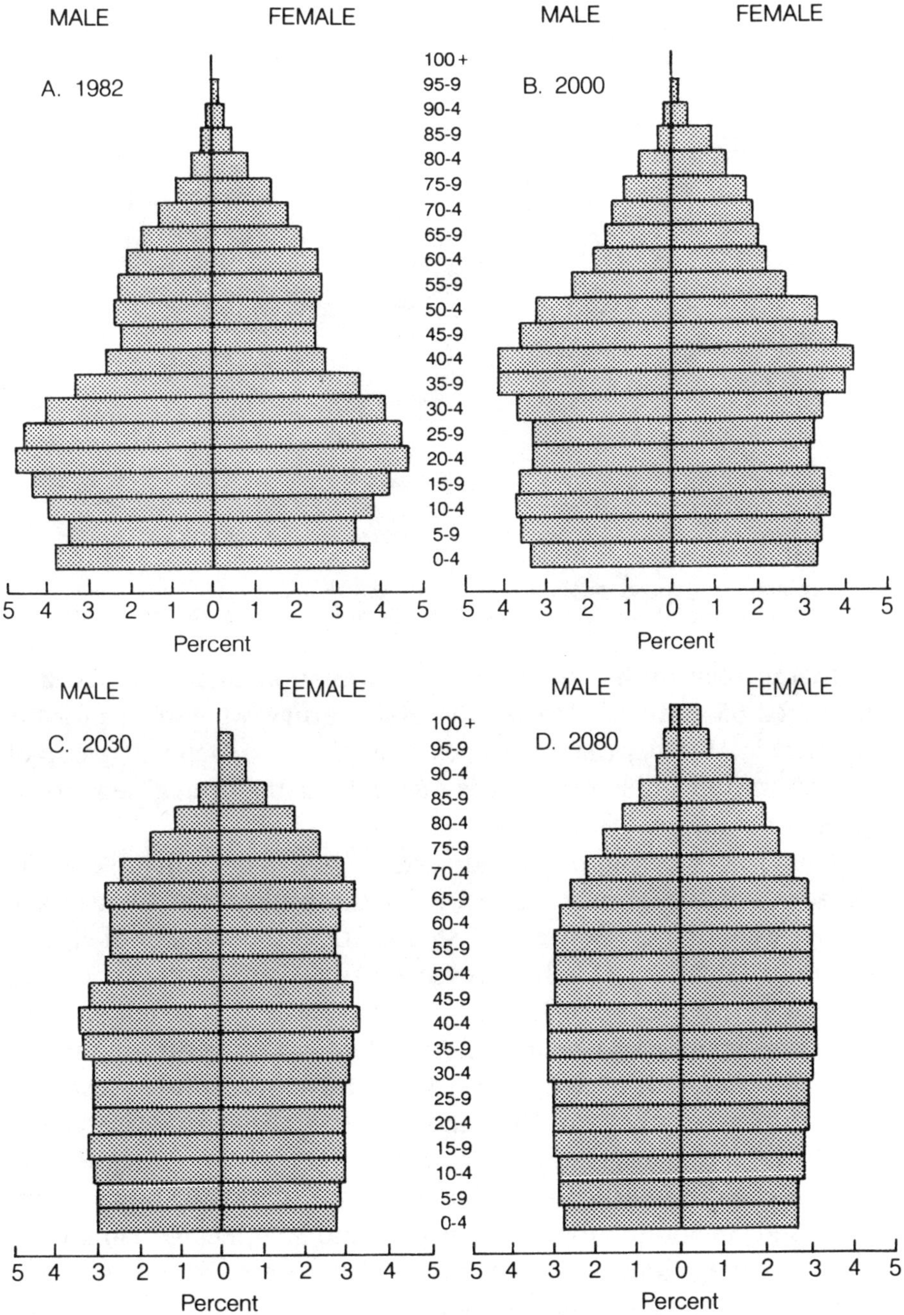

Source: U.S. Bureau of the Census, *Projections of the Population of the United States by Age, Sex, and Race: 1983–2080.* Series P-25, N. 952.

Chart 2 Cumulative Ratio of the Under 20 and Over 65 Populations to the Working Age Population, 1900–2080

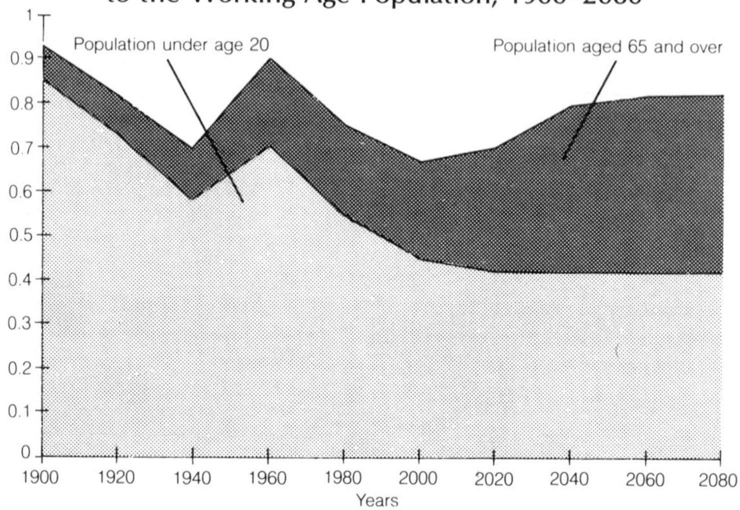

Source: U.S. Bureau of the Census, *Statistical Abstract of the United States, 1986,* and *Projections of the United States, by Age, Sex, and Race: 1983–2080.*

changing relationship between the population under age 20 and that aged 65 and over. During the 21st century, we will face for the first time in history the challenges of an elderly dependent group of the retired and disabled that is larger than the young dependent group of children.

The growth of the population age 65 and older during coming decades will be unprecedented in both absolute and percentage terms (see Chart 2). Between 1985 and 2080, the number of elderly persons (65 and over) will increase 2.5 times, and their percentage in the total population will nearly double. By 2050, one out of every five Americans could be age 65 or older, and by 2080 it could be nearly one in four. Chart 3 shows the relative percentage growth of different age groups from 1900 and projected through 2080; Chart 4 shows the actual age distributions and projections for the same time span. Since the elderly population is far more dependent on government and corporate support for income and health care than are the young, this age shift translates directly into an effect on spending and thus on taxes and the cost of goods.

Chart 3 Percent Age Distribution of the United States Population, 1900–2080

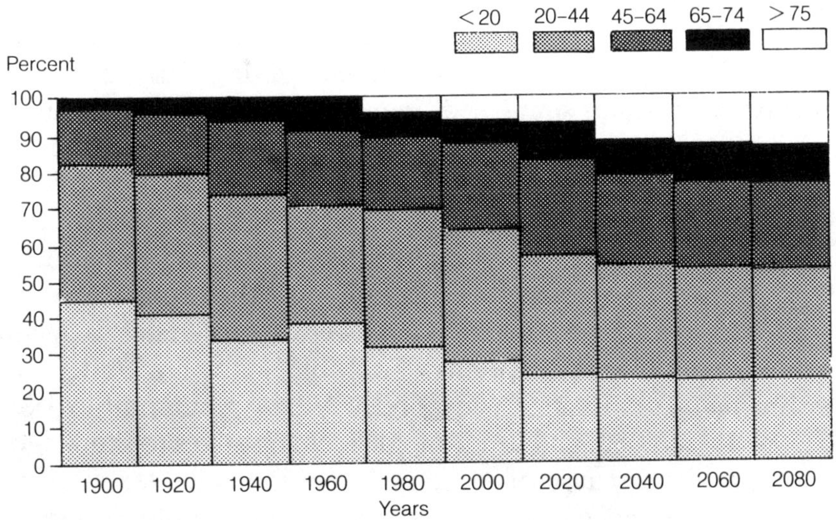

Note: For 1900–1960, age greater than 75 is included with persons 65–74.

Source: U.S. Bureau of the Census, *Statistical Abstract of the United States, 1986, and Projections of the United States, by Age, Sex, and Race: 1983–2080.*

Chart 4 Age Distribution of the United States, Actual and Projected, 1900–2080

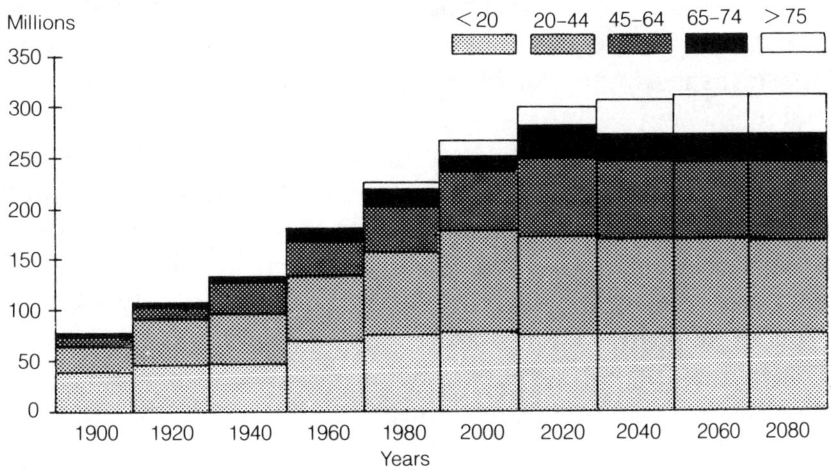

Note: For 1900–1960, age greater than 75 is included with persons 65–74.

Source: U.S. Bureau of the Census, *Statistical Abstract of the United States, 1986, and Projections of the United States, by Age, Sex, and Race: 1983–2080.*

The change in population mix changes the relative balance of workers to program beneficiaries, that is, those paying the highest taxes and having their take-home pay reduced and those paying lower taxes because of lower income but getting much of that income from programs supported financially by the workers who pay the highest taxes (see Table 1). This comparison is defined as the dependency ratio. Based upon intermediate assumptions, the dependency ratio is predicted to decrease by about 50 percent, from 3.3 percent in 1985 to 1.9 percent in 2040 (having been at 5.1 in 1960). Were life expectancy to increase more than is now expected (as a result of medical advances), and were fertility rates to decline further, pessimistic assumptions would come into play. Under these pessimistic assumptions, the dependency ratio would fall to 1.8 in 2025, to 1.4 in 2040, and to 1.2 in 2065. No one likes to think about this possibility because of its stark implications for tax rates and employer spending levels that would be required to support present benefit promises.

Health and long-term care expenditures are particularly sensitive to an aging population, as usage of these services increases with age. The larger the old-old population (age 85 and older) grows, the greater will be the expense—and that population is growing. Even under the intermediate assumptions, growth of the population aged 85 and over is expected to be dramatic. Today, one out of every 88 Americans is 85 years or older, and by 2080, one in 17 will be 80 or older.

In sum, the United States is locked in to a greatly expanding population of older Americans in absolute terms. Regardless of fertility levels, this trend makes it certain that the cost of services for older Americans will climb. Should present fertility assumptions prove accurate, the older population will also greatly expand in terms of its proportional share of the total population. Tax policy and policies regarding economic security programs are already changing in response to these shifts, but the future will bring even more change.

Table 1
Ratio of Covered Workers to Beneficiaries, Actual 1960–1986, and Projected 1986–2065

Actual:		
1960	5.1	
1965	4.0	
1970	3.7	
1975	3.2	
1980	3.2	
1985	3.3	
1986	3.3	
Projected:	**Assumption II B**	**Assumption III**
1987	3.3	3.3
1990	3.3	3.1
1995	3.2	3.1
2000	3.3	3.1
2005	3.1	2.9
2010	2.9	2.7
2015	2.6	2.4
2020	2.3	2.0
2025	2.1	1.8
2030	1.9	1.6
2035	1.9	1.5
2040	1.9	1.4
2045	1.9	1.3
2050	1.9	1.3
2055	1.9	1.2
2060	1.9	1.2
2065	1.9	1.2

Source: 1987 Annual Report of the Board of Trustees of the Federal Old-Age and Survivors Insurance and Disability Insurance Trust Fund, pp. 72–73.

DEMOGRAPHICS AND HEALTH CARE SPENDING

While people age 65 and over represent less than 12 percent of the population today, they receive more than 35 cents of every dollar spent on health care in the United States. In 1984, the per capita amount spent on these older Americans was more than four times that spent on the remainder of the population, and the discrepancy has become greater in recent years. As the proportion of the population age 65 and over, and particularly that of 85 and older, continues to grow, this trend can be expected to persist.

RETIREMENT PATTERNS

For many years, Social Security, Medicare, employer-provided pensions, and employer-provided health insurance programs have been designed to allow older Americans to stop working at the "age of maturity." Public and private employers have used these programs in recent years to adjust workforces and make room for the aging baby-boom generation. Employees have retired at earlier and earlier ages. Government employers and large private employers now provide sufficient pension and health benefits to allow more than half of their workers to retire before age 60. Labor force participation continues to decline, and so does the age at which individuals first claim Social Security benefits.

Among the cost implications of early retirement is a sizable reduction in tax revenue, both in income taxes and Social Security taxes. One way to measure this reduction is to estimate what those workers would have contributed to the tax rolls if they had gone back to work. In 1983, the General Accounting Office (GAO) did just that, estimating the aggregate amount of tax revenues generated if early retirees (defined as those under 65 who did not work and gave retirement as the reason for not working) resumed work (see Table 2). The GAO estimates that in 1983, if 10 percent of early retirees (those between 50 and 64) had returned to the workforce,

Table 2
Estimates of Average Additional Tax Revenues per Person, If Retired Pension Recipients Had Returned to Work in 1983, by Sex and Age (Recipients in thousands).

Sex and Age	Income Tax	Social Security Tax	Total	Number of Retired Pension Recipients[a]
Men:				
50–54	$4,600	$2,600	$7,200	46
55–61	3,200	2,200	5,400	368
62–64	2,800	1,700	4,500	482
Women:				
50–54	2,000	1,600	3,600	16
55–61	1,400	1,200	2,600	166
62–64	1,400	1,100	2,500	209
Both sexes:				
50–61	2,800[b]	1,900[b]	4,700[b]	596
62–64	2,300[b]	1,500[b]	3,800[b]	691

Source: United States General Accounting Office. *Retirement Before Age 65: Trends, Costs and National Issues* (July 1986), p. 47.

[a]Pension recipients who gave retirement as reason not worked. Excludes recipients who gave health or disability, unemployment, or home responsibilities as reason not worked.

[b]Average additional tax weighted by number of retired persons receiving pensions in each sex-age group.

$550 million in additional taxes would have been generated. If 75 percent had returned, $4.1 billion would have been generated. Application of this same analysis to later decades would produce much larger numbers because the size of the group would be far larger. Further, this analysis does not include an estimation of the benefit savings that would accrue were these individuals to defer retirement.

Although demographics cannot be unilaterally altered, benefits payable at retirement can. The 1983 amendments to Social Security require that the age for full benefits be gradually extended from 65 to 67. Eventually, workers retiring at age 62 will be subject to a 30 percent reduction in benefits (the reduction today is 20 percent), and for those retiring at age 65, the reduction will be 13 percent, whereas there is no such reduction today. The amendments also provide that, beginning in 1990, the delayed retirement credit—for workers who postpone retirement beyond the normal retirement age—will be gradually increased, and the reduction in benefits for each dollar earned above the maximum will fall from one half to one third. In other words, the penalty for continuing to work and earn will be decreased.

Today the average individual files for initial Social Security benefits before the age of 63. Surveys find 20 percent retiring before age 55, 34 percent before age 60, 55 percent before age 63, and 86 percent by age 65. The level of income for households headed by individuals age 65 and over continues to climb. It is likely that only a policy change reducing benefit levels and increasing the cost of retirement will cause retirement and work patterns to change.

U.S. President Carter's Commission on Pension Policy, which was in operation from 1979 to 1982, proposed the creation of a "fourth pillar" of economic security for older Americans to help make policy change possible. This fourth pillar (after Social Security, employer pensions, and individual savings) would be represented by generating part-time work opportunities for the retired, thus extending the point at which they end all attachment to the workforce. A recent U.S. Department of Labor report entitled "Workforce 2000" states that the workforce will change so dramatically in the decades ahead that individuals will move in and out of it during their life spans, so that retirees will want to work part-time. Were the fourth pillar to develop, it would increase tax revenues from the growing population of older Americans and might ease the pain of benefit adjustments.

CHANGING PENSIONS

Employer-sponsored pensions are expected to become an increasingly important part of total retirement income for baby-boom retirees, especially for the single individual (see Table 3). Changes in federal law since 1974 have made the receipt of pensions certain for millions, and the spread of defined contribution pensions in the public and private sectors will make it increasingly difficult for employers to change retirement behavior. Why? Because the employer cannot change the value of the pension significantly at a moment's notice, as the traditional defined benefit pension—like Social Security—allows.

In a defined contribution plan employers contribute a fixed percentage of pay to the plan, which then grows with investment earnings. The individual can carry the money from job to job, and if it is invested well, the employee will have a large account available for

Table 3
Percent of Total Retirement Income at Age 67 from Various Sources Among Retiree Families of Different Generations

Income Source	Workers Currently Retiring[a]	Baby Boom Retirees[b]
All Retiree Families		
Social Security	46.1	39.7
Employer-Sponsored Pensions	22.7	37.8
Earnings	28.8	22.2
Supplemental Security Income	2.1	0.3
Married Couples		
Social Security	47.1	37.7
Employer-Sponsored Pensions	22.7	36.6
Earnings	29.8	25.7
Supplemental Security Income	0.3	—
Single Individuals		
Social Security	43.8	43.8
Employer-Sponsored Pensions	22.7	40.2
Earnings	26.0	15.3
Supplemental Security Income	7.4	0.7

Source: Employee Benefit Research Institute tabulations of the Pension and Retirement Income Simulation Model (PRISM) as presented in *Future Sources of Retirement Income: Whither the Baby Boom* (EBRI, 1986).

[a]Age 55 to 64 in 1979.

[b]Age 25 to 34 in 1979.

income during retirement. On the other hand, the defined benefit pension provides a benefit that is a percentage of earnings, and the employer can quickly change the formula, the age for retirement, and other factors that affect cost and benefits. The growth of defined contribution plans means that employers may spend more on pension programs during the workers' careers and have less control over the retirement decision. After the workers retire, the employer may save funds since there is no defined benefit to be increased for inflation.

How employer-provided pension plans are structured and how beneficiaries will fare has become an issue of growing concern to policy makers studying these demographic trends. As a result, Congress has been active in this area, making three major changes in pension tax policy. First, it has repeatedly reduced the maximum amount that can be contributed to pensions or paid in benefits tax free. Second, it has expanded the rules that seek to assure that the greatest possible number of workers receive a pension. Third, it has changed the tax law so that pensions reaching the maximum allowable ceilings (ranging from $35,000 to $90,000 a year) and taken before age 65 are reduced fully to reflect the additional years of payment. Taken together, these changes have served to reduce the amount spent by employers on pensions, reduced the amount that individuals can place in defined contribution pensions or individual retirement accounts, and thus increased current government revenue by keeping more money currently taxable.

PAYING FOR BENEFITS WITH TAXES

As a means of adjusting to the growing population of older Americans, Congress has been moving to restrict benefits and increase revenue of Social Security and Medicare as well. The rise in the age for Social Security eligibility has been mentioned previously. The percentage of final preretirement income replaced by Social Security has also been adjusted so that it decreases over time, and taxation of Social Security benefits has been enacted. If adjusted gross income exceeds $25,000 for single persons or $32,000 for a married couple, the benefit may be taxed. The more inflation there is, the larger is the proportion of retirees who face some tax payment.

There has also been discussion in Congress of taxing all Social Security benefits, and as the aging trend continues, this discussion can be expected to intensify. If all Social Security benefits were taxed beginning in 1987, it is projected that federal revenues would increase by $104.8 billion for the period 1987 to 1991. While this is not a small figure, full benefit taxation would raise a far greater amount in the years beyond 1991 as the retiree population grows. The taxation of Social Security benefits at current levels will reduce necessary payroll taxes by .59 percent in 2060, compared to 0.17 percent in 1987. While the percentages seem small, they represent billions of dollars in tax revenue. Full taxation of Social Security benefits would significantly increase this value.

Social Security and Medicare will increase total tax burdens in the 21st century if major program changes are not made. Under intermediate assumptions, the Social Security rate will move from 10.1 percent in 1987, to 14.25 percent in 2035, and to 13.83 percent in 2060. Under pessimistic assumptions, the rates would be 19.63 percent in 2035 and 23.61 percent in 2060. While most observers do not use the pessimistic assumptions, these assumptions do not appear all that extreme, considering a projected maximum inflation rate of 5 percent, long-term unemployment of 7 percent, and a long-term fertility rate of 1.6 percent versus the present 1.8 percent. The intermediate assumptions of inflation, unemployment, and fertility are 4 percent, 6 percent, and 2 percent respectively.

Medicare also promises to force reconsideration of present tax policy as present demographic trends play out. Under intermediate assumptions, payroll tax rates to support Medicare move from the present 2.66 percent, to 7.36 percent in 2035, and to 7.58 percent in 2060. Under the pessimistic assumptions, the rate would rise to 15.4 percent in 2035. Since for years the actual inflation in medical costs has far exceeded the pessimistic assumptions that were made, a future rate between the intermediate and the pessimistic is most likely. Furthermore, the introduction of catastrophic protection today and coverage of prescription drugs and long-term care tomorrow would only make the tax rates higher. If the nation were willing to allow the total tax burden to increase to the levels entitlement programs require, then no change in spending or tax policies would be necessary. It is unlikely, however, that this course of action will be viewed as acceptable.

Evidence of the changing view of how to distribute the tax burden of entitlement programs can be found in the proposals for catastrophic protection in the Medicare program. Members of both houses of Congress proposed that the cost of the program be paid by present beneficiaries, not through the intergenerational mechanism of the payroll tax. The new program would move the total premium to levels that begin to represent real money, with some proposals requiring beneficiaries to pay as much as $1,079 per year in premiums, compared to $312 per year under the program in effect in 1987. Repeated changes in the Medicare program have increased premiums to the point where out-of-pocket health care expenditures for retirees now exceed the level of 1965, when Medicare was enacted.

As with Social Security taxation, so in the medical area, the tax policy of the 21st century can be expected to increase dramatically the taxes of older Americans.

DEMOGRAPHICS, TAXES, AND INDIVIDUAL CHOICE

There was a time when people retired after the age of 70 and lived for only a few golden years. What savings they had could be spent relatively quickly without adverse consequences. Average retirement age today is closer to 61, and retirees have an increasing prospect of living into their 80s or beyond. Yet surveys indicate that many people do not believe they will live as long as the mortality tables indicate.

When people were retiring late and living a few golden years, few had an employer pension. If they did, it was likely to be a defined benefit pension plan from which they received a monthly check. Well over half of new retirees today have a pension, but many take advantage of the legal option of receiving one check in a lump sum from either a defined benefit or a defined contribution pension plan or one from each.

Many workers who change jobs now receive a lump-sum payment from the pension plan(s) rather than the promise of a benefit to be paid at retirement. Surveys indicate that 87 percent of those who received lump-sum payments before 1983 spent the distribution rather than saving it or rolling it over into an individual retirement account (IRA). As a result, they reduced their ultimate retirement income.

The U.S. Tax Reform Act of 1986 eliminated tax rules that served to encourage individuals to take lump-sum distributions prior to retirement and introduced a penalty tax to encourage the funds to be rolled over into an IRA. The act also significantly increased taxes for a retiree taking a lump-sum distribution at retirement if the retiree was younger than 50 in 1986.

Proposals now pending in Congress under the title of pension portability would either make the penalties more severe for taking a lump sum into current income or would disallow it. Some of the proposals would require that a lump sum be rolled over into another pension plan or IRA and that it be withdrawn as a stream of payments over the retiree's life expectancy. These proposals are being driven by demographics at a time when the aging of the population has only begun to show. As the trends previously discussed take hold, the movement to change tax-pension rules significantly can be expected to take hold as well.

Tax policy in the 21st century can be expected to end retirement plan lump-sum distribution. Dollars accumulated in tax-deferred pension plans would have to be paid out over the projected period of retirement. This would target dollars first to the supplementation of entitlement programs and second to the enjoyment of the golden years. This partial sacrifice of individual freedom would bring with it the prospect of lower government spending.

CONCLUSION

Were the United States a demographic "closed group," with the population structure in perfect symmetry year after year, then policy could remain constant. Behavioral and preference changes would be the primary reasons for changes in tax policy. Social Security, Medicare, employer pensions, and health care could all be relatively constant, as could other spending programs.

Obviously this is not the case, since demographics of the United States and the world are changing dramatically. Given the programs we have structured for retirement income and retiree medical insurance and the payment methods we have devised for them, the most profound effects of the changing demographics stem from the aging of the population. When the number of older Americans was small relative to the working population and the taxes it paid, public and employer policies could provide benefits without putting a significant burden on the workers paying most of the cost. This is no longer the case. The population of those age 65 and over, and those 85 and older within that group, is growing so quickly that tax policies, as well as social and employer policies, must change. Benefit levels must be severely reduced, taxes and employee payments for benefits (direct and through cash compensation reductions) must be increased, or both of these actions must be taken.

The nation is slow to act and to react to demographic changes that are already with us. The growth of the older end of the population is predictable for years to come, and the areas of potential change in the population as a whole are limited to the relative rates of fertility and mortality. Will families suddenly go back to having four children? Will diseases like AIDS reduce some age groups far beyond predictions? Will a major medical advance suddenly add ten years to the average life expectancy?

The most likely change from present assumptions is a further extension of life expectancy. This is also the change that would produce the greatest challenges. Tax and social policy decisions of the past indicate that we would not handle such a change well, yet the tax and spending consequences of not handling it quickly could be devastating to the nation. The demographics now in place could also be devastating if economics takes us down the path of the pessimistic assumptions of the trustees of the Social Security and Medicare programs. We need not be pessimistic, however, for who can imagine inflation staying above 5 percent or unemployment at 7 percent?

6

Taxation in a Small World

LAWRENCE H. SUMMERS

Until recently, international taxation has been an arcane subspecialty among American tax lawyers, and international considerations have rarely influenced the thrust of tax reform. Instead, tax rules have been crafted in consultation with domestic interests; tax incentives have been instituted to spur American individuals and companies to work toward perceived national goals; and the overall level of tax collections has been determined on the basis of American business conditions. Such a provincial approach to tax policy may have been appropriate in an earlier era, but the increasing economic integration of the world requires a more global approach to tax policy. The emphasis in recent American tax reform debates on competitiveness is only a precursor to a time in which international considerations will play a pervasive role in shaping tax policies.

Almost every indicator demonstrates the rapid internationalization of economic life. Since 1965, the volume of international trade in goods and services has risen more than 15-fold. American multinational corporations have almost $1 trillion in foreign assets and now account for more than three-quarters of all American exports—and the proportion continues to increase. Last year net capital inflows into the United States exceeded $150 billion. Around the world, foreign currency-denominated bank liabilities now total more than $2 trillion, compared with only $7 billion in 1963. And some $200 billion in foreign exchange is traded every day!

Growing economic interdependence is a consequence of continuing improvements in transportation and communication technology. A single 747 is able to transport more passengers across the Atlantic in a year than the largest ocean liner ever could. A call from New York to London today costs (after adjusting for inflation) less than half of what a call from New York to Chicago cost in 1965. Technology is easily transferred across international borders, as demonstrated remarkably first by transformations of the Japanese economy and now by other Asian economies. It took decades for improved steel production techniques to diffuse throughout Europe and the United States in the 19th century. Already Brazil and Korea are producing sophisticated personal computers on a substantial scale.

Barring a major upsurge in economic nationalism, there is every reason to expect this increase in economic interdependence to continue. What it may mean can be glimpsed in the history of the American states as their economies have grown more and more integrated. This integration has developed to the point where large corporations choose their "home state" as a legal and financial convenience, and almost any form of economic regulation can be justified by the federal government as bearing on interstate commerce.

Similar developments are transforming the global economy. Indeed, many national economies are as open to international trade as comparably sized regions of the United States are open to interregional trade. It has been estimated that the Philadelphia metropolitan area, with a population of 4.8 million, exports about 40 percent of its output outside the region. In comparison, Austria, with a population of 7 million, exports 36 percent of its output, and Canada, with a population of 24 million, exports 28 percent of its output.

Increasing international economic integration has important implications for domestic tax policies and creates an increased need for international harmonization of tax policies. As the volume of international transactions expands, two broad issues become more and more pressing:

- realistically defining capital income and enforcing tax rules without ruinous tax competition between jurisdictions.
- curbing disruptive short-term flows of capital that create exchange rate misalignments and trade frictions.

Neither of these problems will be easy to resolve within the current nationalistic approach to international taxation.

THE PROBLEM OF INTERNATIONAL TAXATION

Because the flow of international capital dwarfs the volume of international labor migration, the principal issues and problems in international taxation involve the taxing by nations of capital income. Before taking up these problems, it is helpful to describe the ways in which international considerations complicate the choice of domestic tax policies.

In a closed economy, one that does not interact with the rest of the world, there is no fundamental distinction between taxes on saving and on investment. Any tax on capital income, whether placed on the corporations that invest or on individual savers, drives a wedge between the total return to capital and the amount received by its owners. At least in the short run, before changes in saving and investment can have a large impact on the capital stock, taxes on capital are borne by the owners of capital.

In an open economy, on the other hand, there is a fundamental distinction between taxes on saving and investment. Taxes on saving burden domestic residents who receive capital income regardless of its source. Such taxes affect savers' decisions about how much to save but not the allocation of capital between domestic and foreign uses. Taxes on investment, however, burden capital located in the home country, whether or not it is domestically owned. These taxes will have their primary impact on the location of capital rather than on the saving decision.

In crafting their tax rules, nations must decide how to tax saving and investment income. Both provide attractive targets for taxation. Since profits earned, for example, by an American in Great Britain represent saving income to the American tax authorities and investment income to the British tax authorities, the possibility of double taxation arises. One conceivable solution for treating transnational transactions would involve each country taxing only investment income generated within its borders and allowing foreign governments to tax any foreign income generated by its citizens. This is the practice followed by some countries but not by the United States, which asserts a tax claim on the worldwide income of its citizens, both individual and corporate. The American approach of asserting a tax claim against worldwide income is perhaps natural, given the large volume of American direct foreign investment.

Taxing worldwide income resolves the problem of citizens escaping taxation by investing abroad but creates problems of its own: most obviously, the difficulty of enforcing a tax claim on profits earned and reinvested abroad. Because of this problem, the United States generally defers the taxation of business income earned abroad until it is repatriated (numerous exceptions are spelled out in subpart F of the current tax code).

Double taxation is also possible if an American company earning profits in foreign countries must pay taxes to both the foreign and American governments. Thus American firms might be at a disadvantage in competing abroad. This problem is addressed by the American policy of allowing firms and individuals credit for foreign taxes paid up to the American rate. Double taxation is thus eliminated: American firms pay taxes at a rate above the American rate only when they invest in high-tax countries, and on these investments they pay no American taxes.

Permitting firms to defer their tax liabilities until profits are repatriated and to receive credits for foreign taxes paid is necessary to offset the bias against foreign investment created by national efforts to tax both domestic income earned by foreigners and foreign income earned by domestic firms and individuals. However, the deferral and credit provisions create problems of their own. Deferral substantially reduces effective tax rates on income earned abroad. The foreign tax credit may give foreign governments a free ride in taxing U.S. companies up to the American rate. Firms investing abroad will not be concerned with minimizing tax liabilities as long as any taxes they pay are credited against their U.S. tax liabilities. Foreign countries can then costlessly raid the U.S. Treasury by raising their tax rates on American multinational corporations.

A further problem arises in connection with the foreign tax credit. Companies that invest in high-tax jurisdictions will find themselves with excess foreign tax credits. If they are permitted to use these credits to offset income earned in low-tax jurisdictions, the possibilities for countries to freeload on the U.S. Treasury are enhanced. The 1986 U.S. tax reform addressed this concern and related concerns about the use of tax havens by setting up an elaborate system of "baskets" designed to limit somewhat the transferability of excess foreign tax credits.

EFFECTIVELY TAXING MULTINATIONALS

The difficulties that the current approach to taxing multinational corporations will increasingly encounter may be illustrated by imagining what would happen if the separate American states levied taxes in a similar fashion. Suppose each American corporation had a home state that attempted to tax its nationwide income but allowed credits on taxes paid to other states and deferred the recognition of profits earned and reinvested out of state. How would firms respond?

First, firms would seek to locate their tax home in low-tax states and would try to bargain with state legislatures over their tax rates.

Second, having located their tax home in a low-tax state, firms would likely find themselves in excess foreign tax credit positions and so would seek to locate profits in low-tax rather than high-tax jurisdictions. Further, firms deferring taxes by not repatriating profits would also have an incentive to minimize tax liabilities by using accounting devices to take losses in high-tax jurisdictions and gains in low-tax jurisdictions. Finally, firms would locate physical investments in low-tax jurisdictions to the greatest extent possible.

States that recognized the likely responses of firms would have a very strong incentive to lower tax rates in order to induce firms to report higher profits. Even for jurisdictions not concerned with attracting businesses, maintaining a higher-than-average tax rate would have a substantial cost by causing firms to relocate their profits. States with high tax rates would have very strong incentives to impose and enforce rules governing the allocation of income across states. Given the arbitrariness involved in transfer pricing and the allocation of fixed costs, such rules would inevitably be exceedingly complex. Some income would fall between the cracks, and other income would be taxed twice.

These possibilities are not just hypothetical. In the early part of this century, American states' tax policies relied on specific apportionment schemes in which corporations were taxed on the basis of profits earned within each state. This system proved unworkable for the increasing number of large, integrated businesses which had no clear-cut way of allocating profits across jurisdictions. As a consequence, all state corporate income taxes now rely on some type of formula apportionment in which the nationwide profits of a company are allocated among the states on the basis of more easily measured variables, such as sales, payroll, and assets in place. This system eliminates incentives to use accounting devices to move profits between states. Since companies do not have the option of using accounting devices to reallocate profits, the elasticity of state tax bases with respect to their tax rate is reduced, making it easier for states to maintain high tax rates. Of course, there is still an incentive to cut tax rates because reduced tax rates give firms an incentive to relocate capital and employment.

In many respects, the evolution of the world economy parallels—with a lag—that of the American economy. The rise of international economic integration presents national tax authorities with problems very similar to those that American state tax authorities confronted in the 1920s. International trade among affiliates of multinational corporations has increased much faster than overall trade, to the point where trade among the affiliates of multinationals now accounts for about one-third of all U.S. exports. The volume of international trade within multinational corporations dwarfs their foreign profits, so the even relatively small changes in transfer prices can have large tax consequences.

International tax authorities face an additional problem not faced by state tax authorities. Multinational firms can move profits across borders not only by manipulating transfer prices but also by altering their means of financing. They can, for example, relocate profits by issuing debt and taking interest deductions in high-tax jurisdictions.

The incentive to use accounting devices to move income across international boundaries creates pressures on countries to change their tax laws. It may help to explain the trend in many countries toward reforms, like the U.S. Tax Reform Act of 1986, that reduced corporate tax rates and scaled back investment incentives. These reforms have been popular despite an important economic argument against them: that they reduce the tax burden on old capital while raising the tax burden on marginal new investments. Because of accounting changes, reductions in tax rates may enlarge the tax base even though they do not affect the amount of capital in place. Something of this kind may lie behind suggestions that the United States, despite increases in the effective rate of taxation on new investments, has become a tax haven.

The need to avoid a large spread in tax rates relative to the United States is an important element in recent Canadian tax reform proposals. Tax experts in a number of other countries also see a possible need for rate reductions in light of the reduction in U.S. rates. In addition to the possibility of moving income, this reflects the fact that the reduction in the U.S. tax rate will reduce the amount of foreign taxes that are creditable.

Pressures to maintain nearly equal tax rates are an inevitable element in any system in which tax payments can be altered by accounting changes that move income across jurisdictions. The problem is accentuated when some countries make gifts to other countries through their foreign tax credit provisions. These pressures will grow with the increasing international integration of the economy. One defect in aligning tax rates is that countries may have valid economic reasons for wanting to maintain different tax rates. An alternative approach is to rely on formula apportionment, which obviates the need to locate a multinational's home country and eliminates the incentive to use transfer prices to manipulate tax liabilities.

Radical reform in the tax law governing international transactions is certainly not on the current policy agenda. But I believe that the pressures described here make it inevitable that by the time the 21st century arrives major new cooperative steps will have been taken to tax multinational corporations. Just as specific apportionment became obsolete as a basis for state taxation, many of the concepts underlying current tax rules are becoming archaic. It would be premature to conclude that the system used by America's 50 states is the right one for the world economy, but it is time to begin thinking of ways to address the technical problems created by world economic integration.

TAXATION AND INTERNATIONAL COMPETITION

While tax competition among jurisdictions to attract investment has long been practiced, a different possible interaction between taxation and international competition has come to the fore in recent years. Tax policy has been singled out by some observers as a lever that can be used to spur the competitiveness of American industry. The President's Commission on International Competitiveness devoted a significant share of its report to structural tax policies directed at enhancing competitiveness. Many other observers have stressed the connection between federal deficits and trade deficits in the United States. Federal deficits in turn are the direct result of legislated tax cuts.

Discussions of linkages between tax policy and competitiveness have not been confined to the United States. Some observers have attributed part of Japan's economic success to tax measures that kept the cost of capital low. Others have blamed Japan's chronic current account surpluses on a high national saving rate caused by tax incentives directed at saving. Because trade frictions are a pressing international economic problem and because they are likely to continue in the future, it is worthwhile to consider the impact of tax policy on national trade patterns and on the competitiveness of industry.

The key to understanding the relationship between tax policy and trade performance lies in recognizing a basic national income accounting identity. The difference between a nation's saving rate and its investment rate determines its current account balance, which is essentially the difference between its exports and imports. This point is illustrated in Table 1, which presents information on the saving rate, investment rate, and current account balance for Japan and the United States in recent years. When a nation saves more than it invests—as Japan has in recent years—and so accumulates foreign assets, it must finance them by exporting more than it imports. Similarly, when a nation spends more than it earns and so saves less than it invests—as the United States has done in recent years—it must inevitably export less than it imports.

This basic economic arithmetic has important consequences for tax policy. It implies that there is no way economic policy can affect competitiveness without altering national saving or investment. Consider, for example, a tariff on a particular type of imported goods. It is tempting but wrong to conclude that reducing one type of imports will improve the trade balance. Since a tariff on a single good will not alter national saving or investment, it cannot affect the overall trade balance. Instead, the reduction in the demand for foreign currency that is caused by the tariff will

Table 1
National Saving, Investment, and the Trade Balance
(as a Percent of GNP)

	Japan			United States		
Year	Net National Saving %	Net National Investment %	Current Account Balance %	Net National Saving %	Net National Investment %	Current Account Balance %
1975	19.4	19.9	−0.5	2.8	2.1	0.7
1980	18.3	19.5	−1.2	4.4	4.2	0.2
1981	18.5	18.6	−0.1	5.3	5.2	0.1
1982	17.9	17.5	0.4	2.0	2.0	0.0
1983	17.0	15.5	1.5	2.0	3.2	−1.2
1984	18.2	15.7	2.5	4.5	7.1	−2.6
1985	16.7	13.0	3.7	3.2	6.2	−3.0
1986	***	***	***	2.0	5.5	−3.5

Source: Quarterly Income Accounts, OECD, various issues. Japanese data for 1985 are annualized first-quarter estimates. Japanese data for 1986 are unavailable. (Differences between saving minus investment and the current account balance are due to net capital transfers and statistical discrepancies in the OECD accounts.)

cause an exchange rate appreciation, which will lead to increased imports and reduced exports of other products. Tariffs or tax policies that do not affect national saving or investment can influence the composition but not the overall volume of a nation's trade balance.

Tax policies that influence saving and investment can exert a decisive influence on overall trade patterns. It is instructive to consider the American and Japanese experiences of recent years. In 1981, the United States embarked on a program of major tax cuts and investment incentives. The revenue lost dramatically increased federal budget deficits and substantially reduced national saving to 2 percent of GNP in 1986. Reduced national saving has led to a current account deficit that is now equal to 3 percent of GNP. Conversely, in Japan, extremely high saving rates have led to large capital outflows and a substantial current account surplus. It is tax and budget policies, not specific industrial policies, that account for the substantial trade imbalances between the United States and Japan.

This analysis has one important implication that is often overlooked in discussions of tax policy and trade. Investment incentives are likely to make a nation's producers of trade goods less competitive in the short run. By drawing funds into the country, they lead to a real exchange rate appreciation, which reduces the price of imports and raises the price of exports. As long as investment is increased, the adverse effect of altered exchange rates on competitiveness must outweigh the beneficial effects of a reduced cost of capital.

Elimination of current trade imbalances will require some combination of increased American saving, reduced American investment, increased Japanese investment, and reduced Japanese saving. Tax and budget policies are the natural way of bringing about these outcomes. It is ironic from this viewpoint that the Japanese government and not the American government has recently debated the introduction of a broad-based tax on consumption. The curtailment of Japanese saving incentives and limitations on the deductibility of consumer interest contained in the most recent American tax reform are more welcome developments from this perspective.

Current economic strains between the United States and Japan presage problems that are likely to become pervasive in the future if action to coordinate tax and budget policies is not undertaken. The magnitude of the capital flows into the United States (or out of Japan) is still quite small when contrasted with the enormous difference in the two countries' national saving rates. Historically, there has been a very strong association between national saving and investment rates, which implies that net international capital flows have been relatively small (see Table 1). In part, this has been a consequence of capital controls and various institutional restrictions on international investment. As controls and restrictions are lifted and the international economy grows more integrated, capital flows are likely to increase unless countries make more extensive efforts to balance incentives for saving and investment. International cooperation will be required either to insure that national saving-investment targets are mutually consistent or to prevent large trade imbalances, which are an inevitable concomitant of large capital flows, from interfering with policy commitments to free trade.

THE KEY CHOICE AHEAD

There is every reason to think that the world economy in 2037 will be as different from the world economy of today as today's world economy is different from the world economy of 1937. No one in 1937 could have anticipated the problems and challenges we face today, and no one today can accurately anticipate the economic problems that lie ahead. The only judgment confirmed by historical trends is that as long as the world remains at peace, economic integration will continue. As the example of the American states and the European Common Market demonstrate, increased economic integration can promote growth and prosperity. At the same time, these examples suggest that economic integration must inevitably limit national sovereignty.

Tax policy is one area in which international coordination will be increasingly important. If nations pursue tax policies without regard to international objectives, the result will inevitably be economic conflict. Competition among nations will make it difficult to effectively tax multinational companies, and inconsistent policies toward saving and investment will give rise to disruptive trade imbalances. On the other hand, if used cooperatively, tax incentives for saving and investment can insure that capital is efficiently allocated and that levels of investment sufficient for rapid economic growth are maintained.

7

The Search for Compatible Tax Systems

KLAUS VOGEL

Toward the end of the 20th century, coordination among tax systems is still insignificant, almost nonexistent. Save for trifling exceptions, each state enacts its own tax legislation. Among the states, there are similarities of tax structures. There is also some imitation, and with regard to direct taxation, there is a network of double taxation treaties; but on the whole, diversity prevails. Even in common markets, harmonization has been accomplished only in customs duties and, to some extent, the value-added tax (V.A.T.). This lack of coordination inevitably affects resource allocation. The disparities among tax burdens tend to direct investment away from the countries or sites where it would be employed most efficiently.

Such distortions, while they are detrimental to rich countries, are disastrous to poor countries, who have the least advantages and are particularly in need of investment capital and know-how. They cannot, as rich countries can, make up for forfeitures incurred as a consequence of unreasonable tax policy (which is sometimes their own policy and sometimes that of other states). To the less advanced countries, therefore, it is even more important than to the advanced ones that unintentional tax barriers as well as other obstacles to the international flow of goods, services, investment capital, and know-how are eliminated to the greatest extent possible.

The most radical way to remove these tax barriers (apart from removing taxation altogether) would be to harmonize tax systems and rates on a universal basis. But it would not be realistic to expect a worldwide agreement to this effect in the time for which a forecast may be ventured, let us say for the next 100 years. Lack of flexibility, the desire to show a nation's independence, and sometimes sheer self-interest induce governments to cling to their own ways and even to introduce new particularities.

Moreover, it is doubtful that a sweeping harmonization would be desirable. Considering the strong tendency of politicians to expand rather than to restrict expenditures, a universal agreement on harmonization—with some governments insisting on high taxes and others not firmly resisting—in all likelihood would result in the highest possible level of taxation. Thus harmonization might frustrate and, for the future, prevent all national efforts toward a limitation of tax burdens and expenditures.

If, therefore, an all-embracing harmonization is not to be expected and is not even desirable, it is important to search for instruments by which the different tax systems may be adapted so that they are compatible with the goal of investment efficiency and, at the same time, in accordance with equity.[1] With respect to indirect taxes, these questions have been discussed extensively, and solutions are relatively obvious (e.g., assigning taxation to the country of destination).[2] Therefore, this discussion focuses on direct taxes. First, it briefly describes and evaluates the instruments used at present to adapt systems of direct taxation to each other. Then it asks which method, whether applied at present or not, is most advantageous to efficient resource allocation. Finally, it discusses whether the instruments suggested by considerations of efficiency are consistent with or adverse to equity standards.

ADAPTATION OF TAX SYSTEMS IN CURRENT PRACTICE

Until very recently, the interaction of tax systems was viewed predominantly from the angle of double taxation, its causes, and its avoidance. Double taxation arises primarily as a consequence of worldwide taxation in one country and source or situs taxation in another country. Most countries, in particular most industrial countries, levy income taxes on their residents' worldwide income, regardless of whether the income has been earned in the country of residence or abroad. The United States goes even further and taxes the worldwide income of its citizens, nonresidents as well as residents (and so do Mexico and the Philippines). On the other hand, all states that levy an income tax impose it on all income raised in their territory. Consequently, if the residence state or the state of citizenship levies income tax on a worldwide basis, foreign income is taxed twice: first, by the state of residence (or the state of citizenship), and second, by the state of source. Even without worldwide taxation, occasional overlapping of tax claims occurs because legislation may "source" income in different ways; that is, two (or more) states may consider the same item of income as having been produced in their territories. Finally, in regard to wealth taxes and estate taxes, identical problems arise, the criterion of source in these cases being replaced by situs.

To avoid such conflicts, two methods are applied today: credit and exemption. These methods derive from two different philosophies. The credit method assumes that the problem is exclusively to eliminate the double burden on the taxpayer, that is, not to tax the individual more than if the state of residence (citizenship) and the source of income or the situs of asset were the same. This result is achieved by the residence state granting a credit for taxes paid in the state of source or situs, though not for a higher amount than the amount of tax of the residence state which falls on the foreign income or the assets.

The exemption method, in contrast, presumes that, though worldwide taxation may be acceptable, the source or situs state in principle has a more legitimate right to tax than the state of residence or of citizenship. Therefore, if a conflict arises, the state of residence or of citizenship gives way to the source or situs state by exempting the foreign income or assets.

The credit method originally was developed in U.S. and British domestic tax law (specifically in the Revenue Act of 1918, Statute 40, 1057, sections 222 and 238). More recently, it has been adopted increasingly by European and Third World states. The exemption method is provided in some countries under their domestic law. Switzerland exempts income from permanent establishments and real property located abroad; the Netherlands and Australia exempt foreign income in general if it is subject to any taxation in the country of source. Very few states, among them Argentina and Uruguay, and also Hong Kong, go beyond such individual exemptions and impose no tax on foreign income at all (the so-called "territoriality" rule). The same is true in France and Brazil with regard to corporate income tax.[3]

Even more than domestic legislation, however, international treaties have widely accepted the credit and exemption methods as instruments for the avoidance of double taxation.[4] This is due in particular to treaty models elaborated first by the League of Nations, then by the Organization for Economic Cooperation and Development (OECD), and recently by the United Nations. Both the OECD and UN treaty models suggest use of exemption and tax credit methods as alternatives, but in each case as modified by elements of the other method.

The United States has adhered to the tax credit method more rigidly than other states have. It has insisted on inserting in all its double taxation treaties a "saving clause," according to which the United States reserves the right to tax its residents and citizens as if no treaty had come into effect. In other words, the United States concedes treaty benefits mainly to nonresident aliens (with respect to their U.S. source income), but not, as a rule, to its own residents and citizens. In this regard, the treaty practice of the United States is paralleled only by that of the Soviet Union.

Similarly, the United States includes no treaty provision on so-called "tax sparing," which refers to tax incentives granted by the foreign source state. Generally, as a consequence of the tax credit mechanism, a reduction of tax in the state of source only means less credit and, therefore, higher tax in the state of residence. In other words, the incentive is absorbed by the tax law of the residence state, an outcome that is particularly annoying to developing countries. Tax sparing upholds the incentive by awarding a credit equivalent to the amount of tax that would have been levied by the source state had the incentive not been granted. The U.S. Senate has consistently refused to accept tax sparing provisions; nearly all treaties concluded by European countries with developing countries, in contrast, include such rules.

Application of the exemption method may result in certain income or assets being taxed by neither contracting state. This is not, however, in contradiction to the philosophy underlying this method, according to which the source state is entitled to decide whether a particular item of income or wealth shall or shall not be taxed. In certain cases, on the other hand, both methods may fail to eliminate double taxation. This situation may occur, for example, under the credit method when, on account of losses incurred by the taxpayer in his country of residence, there is not enough domestic tax due against which the foreign tax can be credited (and when a carry-forward or carry-back is not admitted by domestic law or is not successful).

However, these deficiencies are merely technical. It is more important in the present context that double taxation be recognized as only part of the problem. Even if double taxation has been totally eliminated in a certain type of situation, it does not follow that distortions of resource allocation have been eliminated. We must ask more generally, therefore, which method, apart from avoiding or diminishing double taxation, will produce tax neutrality or economic efficiency.

ADAPTATION OF TAX SYSTEMS ACCORDING TO ECONOMIC EFFICIENCY

The economic effects of credit and exemption in international direct taxation have been described in terms of "capital export neutrality" and "capital import neutrality."[5] Worldwide taxation, in combination with foreign tax credit, is thought to produce capital export neutrality, whereas exemption of foreign income or assets is thought to result in capital import neutrality. According to the prevailing opinion, only capital export neutrality is in accordance with the efficiency goal.[6]

To the noneconomist, this dualism is difficult to comprehend,[7] and it has been competently criticized by economists, too.[8] The basic ideal of neutrality, so I understand, is that economic processes should not be affected by external influences (e.g., by taxation) or more realistically, that they should be affected as little as possible. If this interpretation is correct, how can the concept of neutrality be divided? Neutrality only with regard to particular influences, to a selection out of their totality, leaves other influences untouched. Therefore, it is nonneutrality. If a cup contains no milk but does contain coffee, it is not empty; and likewise, if it contains no coffee but does contain milk, it is not empty. Neutrality, like emptiness, is a negative concept; it is negated by admission of anything positive: milk, coffee—external influences. In other words, export as well as import neutrality only stand for the absence of particular influences; they are not neutrality properly speaking.

Moreover, the prevailing opinion of economic theory, according to which so-called export neutrality promotes efficient resource allocation, is not shared by many economic practitioners. In comparative research that I conducted on behalf of the International Fiscal Association (IFA) in 1984, reporters from industrial as well as developing countries were asked to specify tax obstacles to international investment resulting from the tax law of the investor's country of residence. To a considerable extent, they mentioned worldwide taxation and the tax credit method.[9]

The reporters pointed out, *inter alia,* that the tax credit method (as mentioned earlier) leads to absorption of tax advantages awarded by the state of the foreign investment, such as tax holidays granted by the foreign state, or it leads to a generally lower level of tax as compensation for lack of infrastructure or for a particular risk. If the effect of such incentives is consumed by a higher tax in the state of residence, a bias is introduced that favors investment in the residence state. IFA, upon discussion, supported this view and recommended that worldwide taxation be reconsidered and preference be given to "a system of territorial taxation or of exemption."[10] As early as 1955, the International Chamber of Commerce (ICC) adopted a resolution to the same effect, and it has since been consistently upheld.[11]

Although the ICC may be called a representation of interested parties, it was previously one of the primary advocates of worldwide taxation. Thus its 1955 resolution reflects a shift from Saul to Paul. What is more important, however, is that the IFA is a nonaligned organization of government agencies and their representatives as well as businessmen. However, most of these members of the IFA are, like the ICC, tax practitioners (accountants, lawyers, officials, etc.). It seems remarkable, therefore, that both the IFA and the ICC adopted a view in such disaccordance with the predominant view in economic theory.

This mainstream view has been challenged, however. Still adhering to the distinction of export and import neutrality, the German economist Otto Gandenberger has pointed out that, contrary to the arguments in favor of export neutrality, a reduced after-tax profit inevitably diminishes the chances for an enterprise to finance new investment.[12] Therefore, an enterprise that has to anticipate in its state of residence a higher tax burden than its competitors face in a low-tax country may be influenced against investing in that low-tax country. If so, even capital export neutrality is disturbed.

Gandenberger goes on to argue that the level of taxation in any country is likely to correspond to the degree to which public goods are provided; that is, in a developing country with a low infrastructure, the level of taxation often will be low. If this is the case, taxation according to the domestic level of the country of residence—in view of the fact that the enterprise receives less public goods than it would receive in its country of residence—again will affect its decision whether to invest in the low-tax country. Based on these and additional arguments, Gandenberger concludes that, contrary to the prevailing opinion in economic theory, preference should be given to capital import instead of export neutrality.

The American economist Norman Ture has gone a step further.[13] Rejecting the dualism of capital export and import neutrality, he has endeavored to redefine tax neutrality. In his words, tax neutrality means in general "that the taxation does not alter the (explicit or implicit) relative prices of goods, services, activities, production inputs, and so forth, in the private sector." At the international level, therefore, neutrality means that "neither country will attempt to use its fiscal powers to change relative prices in the other country, any more than it would in the absence of taxes." From this general presumption, Ture convincingly infers that worldwide taxation distorts neutrality and, therefore, impairs economic efficiency. He shows in detail that if secondary effects are considered, even from the point of view of the residence state, a source-based taxation is more advantageous than worldwide taxation.

Though his argument is conclusive, it can even be expanded. It can be shown that source-based taxation leaves a trace of nonneutrality, but one which, from the point of view of investment efficiency, is acceptable and even desirable. Source-based taxation gives an incentive toward investment in countries where the ratio of taxes to public goods provided is most beneficial to the investor; therefore, source-based taxation gives an incentive to governments to cut down inefficient spending.[14]

As far as I can see, Ture's considerations have not yet received as much attention and, in particular, discussion as they deserve. This may be attributable to a fact that has been demonstrated in the natural sciences and may exist in economic theory, too. Thoughts to which everyone is accustomed gain a weight of their own; thus a system that has been practiced for as long a time as worldwide taxation will only with utter reluctance be reappraised, let alone rejected, regardless of the weight of reasons brought forward against it.[15]

CONSIDERATIONS REGARDING EQUITY

Notwithstanding considerations of efficiency, there is a widespread conviction that worldwide taxation is at least demanded by equity.[16]

American law school professors like to refer to a taxpayer in Kansas (or Georgia, or Wisconsin) who would not understand if his neighbor, who receives exactly the same amount of income as he, but from foreign sources, has to pay less tax than he does on income earned at home. Basically, it is this very argument which has made the U.S. Senate reject tax sparing.

The current discussion of equity in international taxation is unsatisfactory, however, and a glance at legal traditions may be helpful in explaining why. Reasoning concerning equity—or concerning justice, which is the same—is a type of reasoning lawyers have had to apply and have been used to applying for more than 2000 years (even though some theorists, like the famous British legal theorist John Austin have denied their right to do it). Legal philosophers have analyzed their reasoning.[17] From this experience and analysis, we may infer that equity reasoning can never be based on a single set of presumptions. In a complex world, it is necessary to consider multiple aspects. Moreover, equity reasoning does not end in a clear-cut result like a logical inference; conflicting evaluations turn up, and they have to be weighed against each other. Reasoning concerning equity, therefore, can never be abbreviated to a single comparison, such as that of the Kansas taxpayer and his neighbor.

The various approaches[18] may be generally divided into those referring to individual equity and those referring to equity among nations.[19] On both levels, we can further distinguish the aspects of legitimation, equality, and integrity. Legitimation of taxes, in regard to the individual taxpayer, has traditionally been based on the two theories of sacrifice and benefit. Modern authors, such as the economist James M. Buchanan, have argued that taxes, though not the price for individual state services, may be viewed as consideration for the totality of state services.[20] As far as foreign income is concerned, there is no doubt that services by the state of source and their general level are of more importance to the taxpayer than services by the state of residence. Therefore, taxation by the state of source and according to its laws is more legitimate from the point of view of the taxpayer (as well as the source state) than taxation by the state of residence, though the latter is not totally unfounded.[21]

With regard to equality, it is not only the taxpayer's neighbor in his state of residence who must be considered. The taxpayer must be compared as well to his competitors in the foreign state where he earns his income. (Although this is acknowledged in principle, it is often neglected in discussions of the equality aspect.) If the taxpayer who has a foreign residence were subject to a lower tax burden than his competitors, it would be unequitable to them; and vice versa, it is unequitable to him if he is subject to higher tax rates. Moreover, foreign income cannot be fully equated to domestic income as long as it has not been remitted to the state of residence and is available for consumption or reinvestment. For during its stay in the source state, it is subject to particular risks; namely, it may be devaluated, or remittance may be prohibited by foreign exchange control law. Therefore, the equality argument can justify, if anything at all, only taxation of foreign income that has been remitted to the state of residence (as foreseen in some provisions of the tax law of the United Kingdom). There is no doubt that even the neighbor from Kansas will understand this distinction.

Finally, integrity must be considered. Integrity requires legislative decisions to be morally coherent with other equally binding legislative decisions. It "demands that the public standards of the community be both made and seen, so far as this is possible, to express a single coherent scheme of justice and fairness in right relation."[22] Thus it has been argued in favor of worldwide taxation that an income tax by its very nature is global, that it falls on all types of income indiscriminately, and therefore that it would be inconsistent to exempt foreign income alone. But this argument disregards the fact that the globality postulate presupposes a single national economy. It did not and does not consider that there are multiple national economies which must coexist. Consequently, leaving income produced in a foreign jurisdiction to be taxed only by that foreign state is not morally incoherent with the basically global character of income taxation. On the contrary, it can be argued that the present system is morally incoherent, because it combines two principles opposed to each other, worldwide and source-based taxation, instead of selecting just one of them.

On the level of inter-nations equity, the aspect of legitimation is paramount. Here again, it is decisive that the state of source contributes more to the production of income than the state of residence.

To sum up, then, it should be apparent that equity arguments favoring taxation exclusively by the state of source are by far predominant. However, equity reasoning by its very nature can never end in a result that excludes all other alternatives. Thus residence-state taxation of foreign income remitted into the residence state does not seem untenable, and there are even some, though less convincing, considerations that might argue for the worldwide taxation of citizens. Such legislation, even if equitable, however, would be adverse to economic reason, as previously shown. Therefore, another solution that is available, and which is both efficient and equitable, is preferable—source-based taxation.

CONCLUSION

Worldwide taxation, in contrast to what is generally believed, affects the international flow of investment. It impairs capital import, particularly into low-taxing states, which is detrimental to developing countries. It is also disadvantageous to the capital-exporting states that apply this type of taxation. Moreover, it is neither demanded by reasons of individual equity nor by inter-nations equity; rather, more convincing reasons can be brought forward in favor of source-based taxation. As a consequence, worldwide taxation should be abolished. Its elimination would considerably improve the interaction of tax systems.

For the United States, the best time to abolish worldwide taxation is now, because as long as tax rates remain low, there is not as much difference between tax credit and exemption. If such a change is postponed (and realistically we have to expect this), replacing worldwide with source-based taxation in domestic legislation and treaties will be one of the most urgent missions to be envisioned for the 21st century.

8

International Tax Law: The Need for Constructive Change

STANFORD G. ROSS

In highly political matters of government policy, such as taxation, the process is "bottom up," in the sense that local considerations influence the outcome of national policies. Similarly, national considerations influence positions taken on issues of international policies. Thus if one wants to understand where international tax law is likely to be in the 21st century, one must first look at where national policies on international tax matters are likely to be.

With regard to international tax law, the United States occupies a special position. For some time it has been the key player in worldwide governmental, business, and financial developments, and thus in taxation. In U.S. policy toward international tax matters, there is much to criticize. Yet we must recognize its great influence in order to understand fully developments outside the United States, since so many of them have been taken in response to U.S. actions.[1]

In adopting its modern income tax law in 1913, the United States decided to tax its citizens and domestic corporations on their worldwide income but to defer tax on the income of U.S.-owned foreign corporations until the earnings were distributed. This left unresolved a basic issue: How would U.S. jurisdictional rules be adjusted to the taxing rules of foreign governments?

In 1918, this question was answered when the United States became the first country to adopt a foreign tax credit mechanism. This was a pragmatic blending of theoretical and practical considerations, both recognizing the prior claim of the country of source (the place income is deemed to arise) to impose tax and allowing a credit for that source tax up to the amount of tax that otherwise would be imposed by the country of residence (the home country of the recipient of the income). Thus the country of residence did not relinquish tax jurisdiction on its taxpayers but reserved the right to impose tax if the source country taxed more lightly than the home country, while it recognized the priority of the country of source to tax income generated in its jurisdiction.[2]

Over the years, the foreign tax credit mechanism has been adopted by most countries and today stands as the basic building block for international tax treaty networks the world over. Theoretical arguments can be made that an exemption system is preferable in which a country only taxes income arising within its territory and does not tax income arising outside that country. However, such an exemption or territorial system involves a country broadly relinquishing its jurisdiction to tax and is generally considered impractical from the standpoint of preserving national revenues and preventing tax avoidance. Further, a tax credit system generally requires both the country of source and the country of residence to negotiate and accommodate their two systems, which is beneficial to both countries in harmonizing their tax relationships. Thus the foreign tax credit concept, in which countries retain a residual taxing power while agreeing that income should basically be taxed in the jurisdiction where it is earned, is likely to continue to be central to the development of international tax law into the 21st century.

Another conceptual innovation, implemented in the U.S. Revenue Act of 1962, was the current taxing of foreign income of foreign subsidiaries. Until then, U.S. tax was generally deferred until distributions were made to the U.S. parent company. This so-called elimination of deferral, or Subpart F development, was designed to prevent tax haven situations in which multinational corporations located income in low- or no-tax countries and thereby avoided tax in both source and residence countries with a legitimate claim to taxing such income. Subpart F-type provisions have subsequently been adopted by many other countries, including the United Kingdom, Canada, Australia, New Zealand, Japan, and Germany.

The importance of the elimination of tax deferral on the foreign earnings of foreign entities owned or controlled by a home country's taxpayers is that tax avoidance at the international level can be combatted. It is generally a goal of international tax rules to have tax imposed on all income currently by one or another country with a legitimate jurisdictional connection to the income or taxpayer. Deferral of tax for foreign income of foreign subsidiaries can often mean that no jurisdiction imposes tax currently, which translates into tax havens being allowed to flourish. Taxpayers who have deferral in their home country and who can manipulate their affairs so that their income does not fall in a country of source that imposes taxes can defeat the revenues in multiple jurisdictions. Postponement of tax may in effect become permanent exemption from tax by virtue of deferral continuing indefinitely. Subpart F developments have been a major tool in the never-ending struggle of national taxing authorities with multinational corporations.[3]

Presently, the United States is making another contribution to international tax law with respect to the corrective allocation of income and deductions, generally known as Section 482 adjustments. Multinational corporations often try to manipulate the source of income to achieve the lowest effective rate of tax on a worldwide basis. In response, an individual country seeks through its tax rules to specify the amount of income that is correctly subject to that country's jurisdiction. Here the goal of international tax law is to determine that the proper taxable income is being recognized in all jurisdictions with a claim to tax. The chief areas in which this corrective power is important are the pricing of goods and services by multinational corporations and the returns from transfers of technology and other intangibles developed in one country and exploited on a worldwide basis. Since these pricing decisions generally are internal corporate matters, they may not reflect arm's-length standards based on the outcome of a competitive market mechanism in comparable transactions. Indeed, because some products and especially intangible assets may be unique, there may well be no market-generated comparables.

The United States began to develop rules to address these problems in the aftermath of the 1962 Revenue Act and later in the 1960s produced the first detailed rules and regulations to govern the allocation of income and deductions. The United States has also developed on this subject a considerable jurisprudence, one that essentially strengthens the hand of the tax collector in disputes with multinational corporations.[4] As the United States has carried on this fight with its own taxpayers, other countries have begun to strengthen their corrective allocation provisions. Japan, alone among the major industrialized countries not to have enacted them into law and consequently at a handicap in dealing internationally on tax issues, has recently adopted such provisions.

Still another area in which the United States has demonstrated leadership is the pioneering in the last 20 years of so-called competent authority procedures under tax treaties. The competent authorities are a country's national taxing agency, like the Internal Revenue Service in the United States or Board of Inland Revenue in the United Kingdom, and the procedures here call for direct negotiation of countries by their authorized taxing authorities to reach an agreement on how to tax transactions in which both countries have a legitimate claim to tax. With these procedures national tax authorities may constructively resolve disputes in which there would otherwise be double taxation or the failure to impose proper taxation on multinational corporations. This development also started in the aftermath of the 1962 Revenue Act and a general increase in Internal Revenue Service auditing of international transactions. Other countries have begun to expand and to cooperate with the United States in competent authority proceedings, but this development is still in its rudimentary stages and will require far more resources and conceptual development in the years ahead if it is to achieve its goals.[5]

The provisions of the national tax laws affecting domestic taxpayers with foreign income and foreign taxpayers with domestic income are the main source of international tax law. These national taxing provisions are then harmonized in bilateral tax treaties, which are based on two nations agreeing to accommodate each other's national tax system. In a sense, international tax law is a misnomer since it suggests internationally applicable legal rules, and there are few binding legal arrangements that involve more than two nations at a time. The European Economic Community and other regional groupings have taken steps to harmonize their tax systems and to reach a substantial level of cooperation among taxing authorities, but the nations with market economies have continued to rely mainly on bilateral arrangements.

We are now beginning to see the development of multilateral treaties, as with the Multinational Convention on Mutual Assistance in Tax Matters developed by the Organization for Economic Cooperation and Development (OECD), which will become open to signature in 1988 and likely will be signed this year by a significant number of nations. But by the 21st century, we may well have multilateral arrangements in greater numbers and scope, perhaps even a General Agreement on Taxes on the order of the General Agreement on Tariffs and Trade (GATT). Before we look forward, however, consider some background on international tax agreements.[6]

The first modern tax convention is generally considered to have been that between France and Belgium in 1843. The developments most relevant today began after the First World War through the work of experts operating under the auspices of the League of Nations. Basic concepts to establish the source of income and the allocation of jurisdiction to tax were agreed upon and became the norms for national positions right up to the present day. Following the Second World War, as national economies recovered and international commerce grew, bilateral tax treaties were a natural outgrowth. Most advanced countries today have a full treaty network, generally including 30 or more bilateral treaties with all their major trading partners. Through the OECD and the United Nations, the rationalization of bilateral tax treaty networks is well advanced and likely to continue. For example, model conventions are used to standardize provisions to the extent practicable.

There are three basic functions of tax treaties, which, while interrelated, have distinctive roots and varying prospects for the 21st century. The first is to eliminate international double taxation of the same income, which is the reason why tax treaties were originally conceived and negotiated. Tax treaties are fundamentally intended to remove barriers to international trade and investment.

The second function is to ensure that at least one tax is imposed in most situations, that is, to avoid tax avoidance and the use of tax havens. This function, reflecting equitable concerns, turns out to have been the second major impetus guiding tax treaties beginning in the 1960s and is well advanced today. Most U.S. tax treaties now contain explicit provisions delineating the taxpayers entitled to the benefits of the treaty relief provisions and preventing other taxpayers (generally from countries not parties to the treaty) from use of the treaty. So-called anti-treaty shopping and other policies to protect national revenues are being written into more and more treaties.[7]

The third major function of tax treaties is to allocate revenues between nations. This aspect is currently receiving the most attention. The United States and Japan especially are looking closely at how traditional rules of accommodation work today and what level of taxation and tax revenues each country should fairly receive.

In many cases, because both countries impose a high level of tax and the burden is comparable whichever country's right to tax may prevail, the taxpayer is no more than a stakeholder. Provided the two countries agree on how to divide the taxes being paid, there is no double taxation and the taxpayer is unaffected by the process of two nations each seeking to tax the same income. This closer analysis of the revenue effects of tax treaties generally has not been explicitly acknowledged by governments but clearly will have to be so in the years ahead as the practice of multiple nations each seeking more revenues from the same transactions becomes more prevalent. This struggle by nations for taxing supremacy in particular situations may well be the principal force leading to multilateral agreements and even to a GATT-type arrangement on international tax issues.

A key in looking toward the 21st century is to see where the United States stands today on international tax matters and what this portends for the years ahead. In 1986, the United States had a massive tax reform, which in some respects signaled a new era of taxation. In basic respects, this reform reflected traditional liberal reform concepts, including opting for a strengthened corporate tax system in which a full corporate tax was to be paid by all corporations in all situations. There are two models here, one the so-called classical system dating back to the origins of the income tax in which individual and corporate taxes are deemed to be separate revenue-raising measures, and the other more modern system of integrating the individual and corporate tax systems so as to recognize the underlying economic reality that individuals ultimately bear the burden of all taxes and double taxes on the same income should be avoided. The United States rejected, after considerable debate, any move toward integration, largely for revenue-raising reasons and on populist political grounds that the public wanted corporations which are treated as independent juridical entities separate from their shareholders to pay substantial taxes. The bases of the individual and corporate taxes were broadened and rates were lowered, also reflecting traditional liberal reform concepts.

The 1986 Tax Reform Act is notable in that it renews the federal government's commitment to relying on income taxes as the major source of its revenues. While considerable economic thinking in the United States in the past ten years has suggested that the federal government should move more toward a consumption tax, or at least moderate the federal government's reliance on the income tax with a new tax, such as a value-added tax, the new act follows classic liberal reform philosophy by trying to restore a broad income tax base and attempting to renew public confidence in the income tax as the best way to finance government.[8]

Unfortunately, the treatment of international tax subjects in this tax reform was less than intelligent, perhaps even misguided. Instead of trying to think through what should happen, the deleterious tendencies of the last several tax bills in 1981, 1982, and 1984 were simply carried forward. The thrust in each of these recent acts has been to develop a multiplicity of detailed rules that raise revenues in specific situations and reflect policy objectives consistent with mistrust of multinational corporations and hostility to foreign taxpayers and foreign activities of U.S. taxpayers. Thus the United States is following a pattern that can best be described as micromanipulation of the rules, with the consequence that it is increasingly difficult for taxpayers to comply with the tax provisions governing international transactions.

It is generally agreed that the Internal Revenue Code rules affecting international transactions involve the greatest degree of complexity of any area of the tax laws, and this condition was exacerbated. To be specific, the foreign tax credit mechanism has been greatly complicated and weakened.[9] A "basket" system with entirely new concepts was put in to restrict the allowance of foreign tax credits by categories of income and thereby to raise U.S. revenues on foreign income earned by U.S. corporations. The new system requires taxpayers to undergo massive planning in order to salvage as many foreign tax credits as possible. Essentially the new provisions lead to an underrecognition of foreign jurisdictions' taxes. Subpart F was greatly expanded, simply as a way of increasing the number of situations in which foreign income is taxed currently. Section 482's arm's-length standards and conventional concepts of source were eroded by enacting provisions that allow the United States greater capacity to pull back on a source basis any income it believes belongs in its taxing jurisdiction.

Finally, most significantly, and to the great consternation of foreign governments, many provisions of the 1986 Tax Reform Act overrode tax treaties. As if all this were not enough, after the U.S. Treasury indicated it wanted to respond constructively to the protests of its foreign trading partners, the U.S. Congress put out a further statement interpreting the 1986 act and making explicit that in any unclear cases it intended to override tax treaties.

In sum, national concerns in the United States are totally dominating its international tax policies. The new restrictive changes, in combination with the new lower U.S. corporate tax rate, encourage domestic as opposed to foreign investment and are consistent with an increasingly protectionist philosophy. This fact takes us to the critical issue: What direction is the international taxing regime of the United States likely to take in the years ahead?

I think we can assume that income taxes will continue to be the principal revenue raiser and the U.S. corporate income tax will be more important than ever in taxing international transactions. This is consistent with the likelihood that multinational enterprises will continue to grow and markets will be increasingly exploited on a worldwide basis. The United States has reaffirmed the basic classical tax system, in contrast to most of the developed world, which uses some sort of imputation system (corporate and individual taxes are in some ways integrated), and thereby has created problems that require international negotiations. Although in the early stages of the tax reform the U.S. Treasury had advocated some steps toward integration, in the end it veered strongly in the opposite direction, and in all cases the United States will want to impose a full corporate tax as well as a full shareholder tax.

Because of this emphasis on corporate income taxes and the likelihood that tax rates will be raised in the post-Reagan years, it seems inevitable that the foreign tax credit mechanism will be reviewed and rationalized. The 1986 Tax Reform Act provisions may prove to be unadministerable, and in all events they will be the subject of manipulation by taxpayers. Some attempt at constructive change will have to be made, therefore, to assure that to the extent possible the right credit is allowed rather than a random credit based on arbitrary rules and uneven enforcement.

The same phenomenon of review and rationalization will probably have to take place in the deferral area. There will have to be revisions made to treat all foreign income of foreign subsidiaries on some basis that is grounded in traditional tax policy considerations of equity and efficiency. The time may finally be ripe for the so-called "big trade-off" in the foreign tax area, which is basically to eliminate deferral in exchange for a full foreign tax credit with fewer limitations.

In a sense, this kind of equitable taxing mechanism was offered to business in 1961 by the Kennedy administration and enacted in a primitive form in the minimum distributions provisions of the 1962 Revenue. The possibility for rationalizing the taxation of foreign income next existed in 1975 when the U.S. Senate voted to eliminate deferral of U.S. tax and the basic issues of proper international taxation were raised in the conference with the House of Representatives. However, the choice was made to pursue microregulation of various international tax situations as opposed to taking a comprehensive approach to the issues. With the additional globalization of business and the increasing complexity of the international tax world, it will become important in the 21st century to take a holistic view, which rationalizes deferral and the credit by the use of integrating mechanisms.

What accounts for the extraordinary complexity and present malaise of international tax policy in the United States? Part of the answer lies in the continuing difficulties of the U.S. economy. As the budget deficits persist, as the trade deficit grows and leads to a weakening of the dollar, the country has responded with quixotic policies that do not deal realistically with these fundamental economic problems. The United States has not yet confronted intelligently the realities of a changing world and adopted tax and other governmental policies that will further its true national interest and the worldwide interest in a strong and sound America. The political system has been deadlocked, and this in turn has led to inertia on major tax issues and too much change on secondary tax issues.[10]

Thus in resolving almost every international tax issue, a host of sometimes conflicting policy considerations must be balanced, and for each policy consideration there is a host of competing viewpoints. The first question that arises concerns what economic policies are being sought in the international tax area. Debate continues about whether the laws should reflect capital export neutrality (i.e., there should be no incentive or disincentive for a country's taxpayers to invest at home or abroad) or capital import neutrality (i.e., there should be no incentive or disincentive for foreign persons to invest in a country), or some nonneutral economic goal (e.g., a country's taxpayers should be encouraged to increase exports rather than to invest abroad). The relationship between foreign investment and foreign trade by American corporations and the relationship of foreign trade and investment to domestic investment, economic growth, and jobs also continue to be subjects of dispute. After almost 25 years of learned discussions by economists and others on these issues, remarkably little consensus has emerged.

A second policy consideration is that of equity and fairness. There are questions of equity between foreign and domestic investment and of what constitutes fairness in the applicable international tax regime. There are further questions of whether proper incentives are provided for certain kinds of desired activities, how to balance issues of neutrality and incentives, and how to deal equitably with a variety of industries and individuals in different circumstances.

Third, there is the ever-dominant consideration of tax avoidance and evasion. With more prejudice than reason, perhaps, Congress and the public have always felt that there are more opportunities for tax avoidance and evasion internationally than domestically. This prejudice is noticeable every time a major tax reform is undertaken and the question comes up of oil companies' tax credits, or banks' interest deductions, or the purchase of bearer instruments by Americans. The resolution is inevitably to circumscribe the activities of taxpayers with a panoply of detailed roles intended to protect U.S. revenues.

A fourth consideration is the accommodation of the U.S. tax system to other systems. While at times the United States has shown flexibility in accepting international norms, at other times it has insisted on its own national views. The continued insistence by the United States on taxing individuals on the basis of citizenship rather than residence, for example, and the problems this has caused for

Americans abroad are reflections of this nationalism. On the other hand, it should be noted that U.S. initiatives, such as Subpart F, have now been emulated in many countries and the American concern with international tax avoidance is now reflected in stronger Section 482 and other tax-avoidance measures in a variety of countries. Thus U.S. views often lead to changes in international norms.

Under the changing circumstances of the global economy and international commerce, no permanent resolutions will be found to all these concerns. The lack of consensus on these issues means that every time they come up, the debate will have to be replayed and temporary conclusions reached.

I believe that the key to sound international tax legislation is a prudent balancing of theory and reality. In the end, good international tax policy must be driven by the desire for constructive international economic and political developments. I expect that moment is coming and the 21st century will reflect a more enlightened international tax law than we now have.

In international issues, the emphasis in the United States today is on competitiveness and revenue raising, and these concerns may stimulate changes in national tax policy. Possibly they will lead to the introduction of a new tax on consumption, perhaps a value-added tax as has been adopted by most other developed countries because of its efficiency and effectiveness in raising revenues. If so, the international aspects of this tax will have to be looked at closely. As of today, too little work has been done in the United States on these issues to assure a constructive outcome if U.S. tax policy goes in this direction.

What are the implications for other countries of the tax developments in the United States? As stricter rules for taxing its multinationals and foreign taxpayers are adopted by the United States, other countries and tax collectors do the same. As long as the United States is wedded to the foreign tax credit system, and this seems inevitable, it will be the major mechanism other countries rely on. In general, there is a process of emulation among the developed countries, but only up to a point set by basic national differences.

The most important development may be a movement toward greater cooperation through exchanges of information, mutual enforcement actions, and expanded competent authority proceedings. One can anticipate that in the near future there will be multinational arrangements to increase pressure on countries to adhere to certain international norms on tax matters. The work of the OECD and the adoption of model conventions have been constructive, but in the future more coordinated attacks on tax havens and tax avoidance are in store. Countries with cultural backgrounds that condone or foster tax evasion or avoidance will be under increasing pressure to change their ways. Not all countries will agree to follow the same international tax rules, but the degree of disharmony will surely be reduced.

Finally, it seems likely that there will be fewer special tax preferences as the world economy becomes increasingly internationalized. Some countries considered part of the Third World have strengths that make them true competitors of developed countries. For example, Korea, Singapore, Hong Kong, and Taiwan compete favorably in some areas of business and finance with the United States, Japan, and other OECD countries. If nonmarket economies such as those in the USSR and China develop more economic ties with the West, evenhanded tax arrangements will have to be developed to reach them. It would seem that the international tax law will be more neutral in that it will attempt to treat everybody equally and raise required revenues as efficiently and fairly as possible.

What are the implications for taxpayers of these likely trends among governments? Taxpayers will try to avoid national taxes less than double taxation or inappropriately heavy taxation. There will likely be fewer tax havens and less ability to use them. The tax haven may well come to its well-earned demise by the early 21st century.

With the increasing internationalization of business and its importance to the economic health of all nations, taxation generally will be held to reasonable levels compatible with business growth and prosperity. Most taxpayers will be happy to see some level of stability and fairness in national and international tax matters. The constant and rapid change in the tax rules and the arbitrary nature of some of them are the most deleterious aspects for taxpayers here at the end of the 20th century.

I think that in international taxation, we may now be at the bottom of the valley. In 1986, the United States declared war on conventional concepts of international tax law; it will now have to work itself out of its present unfortunate position through negotiation with other nations and adaption of its national rules. I believe that just as the United States has led international tax law into the present state of disarray, it will take the lead into the 21st century when international tax rules will need to be truly neutral to allow international commerce to grow naturally with only a fair and reasonable level of taxation imposed. Only such an international taxing regime is compatible with a strong global economy.

9

International Cooperation *Is* Possible

ARNOLD H. WEISS AND FERENC E. MOLNAR

Business today is highly internationalized. Enterprises seeking to raise capital can do so at numerous financial markets scattered around the Western world. Multinational companies sell products to consumers on five continents, and even Asian peasants know such trademarks as Sony and Coca-Cola. Manufacturers produce goods that consist of components acquired in a myriad of countries, so an automobile assembled in the United States may well have a Japanese transmission, a Mexican or Brazilian motor, and tires from Canada. Services also cross borders routinely. A fish processing plant in Alaska may be erected by a Korean construction firm, or an advertising campaign in Europe for a Japanese product may be orchestrated by the subsidiary of an American public relations conglomerate.

The existence of these global commercial flows, however, does not mean that the world is one unified market or economy. We speak of

*The authors wish to acknowledge the contributions of their colleagues at the Washington, D.C. law firm of Arent, Fox, Kintner, Plotkin & Kahn; in particular, Edwin L. Kahn, Joel E. Bassett, John Harllee, Jr., and David J. Bardin.

international business precisely because these flows cross political borders dividing the world into more than 170 independent nations, each with its own culture, laws, and economic and social policies. These borders clearly affect, and at times even deflect or stop, global commercial flows in ways that would not arise were the world really one unified market. Most nations look upon international commerce as a beneficial force that can be harnessed to serve national social and economic goals, but the effect of harnessing commerce to these goals is to reduce its vitality, particularly if countries harness it differently.

In other words, there exists an interaction between international commerce and the national compartments through which it flows. These compartments can distort commerce, but at the same time, the individuality of each nation's policies is limited to the extent it wishes to profit from that commerce. Countries that choose to exclude international commerce as a factor in their economies—Albania comes to mind—are backward and lack a future. It follows that enlightened self-interest among nations should lead them to treat international commerce in such a way as to avoid killing the goose that lays the golden egg.

In a direct way, governments derive benefits from commerce through the imposition of taxes. In the international setting, taxation can be quite complex. Each country has different taxes, tax rules, and tax rates. A corporation planning an international transaction must take these differences into account and be aware that a number of countries may have jurisdiction to tax the same transaction simultaneously. Thus, the corporation faces the risk of double taxation, the possibility of tax avoidance, and the temptation to structure an operation in a manner that is less economically sensible than it would be if no tax considerations came into play. Indeed, sophisticated multinational corporations "play the game," at times pitting one potential host nation against another in an attempt to negotiate a special tax status. The need to solve such problems represents the motivation behind any attempt at tax coordination on the international level.

Precedents for such coordination are apparent today in a network of bilateral tax treaties designed to eliminate double taxation by the authorities in the signatory countries and also to reduce opportunities for tax avoidance. In the case of the value-added tax (V.A.T.), the members of the European Economic Community (EEC) have gone beyond bilateral tax coordination treaties. Pursuant to European Commission directives, they have harmonized basic value-added tax rules so that they are consistent among all EEC members. With these examples as models, it appears quite possible that by the middle of the 21st century the enlightened self-interest of nations will lead in the direction of multilateral international tax coordination. Such a step would complement present achievements, such as those of the General Agreement on Tariffs and Trade (GATT), in significantly reducing tariff barriers to trade, and it would in general serve to better accommodate and exploit the force of international business in the 21st century.

BASIC ASSUMPTIONS ABOUT THE 21ST CENTURY

Barring a cataclysm (natural or man-made) which would shatter historical continuity, we can make a number of basic assumptions about the world as it will exist in the year 2050:

National sovereignty will persist as the predominant structural factor in global politics. The division of the world into sovereign nation-states has been a central feature of Western and, to some extent, Asiatic history for at least the last four centuries. With the advent of such institutions as the United Nations after the Second World War, the concept of national sovereignty came increasingly into question. Nevertheless, the decolonization process of the postwar years created many new sovereign nations, while the tension between the superpowers highlighted the undeniable fact that national sovereignty had not lost its importance as a factor in global politics.

There is little reason today to believe that this state of affairs will change significantly by the year 2050. By then, there may well be fewer nations, or nations may form a number of economic blocs along the lines of the EEC, but independent nations will continue to exist as essentially sovereign entities. Economically speaking, however, the best guess is that none of these nations or economic unions will have significant predominance over all others. Therefore, we may assume a rough economic parity will exist among those nations or blocs that can be viewed as economically developed.

Some nations will remain economically underdeveloped, and there will be distinctions between net exporting and net importing nations, as well as between nations with market economies and those with centrally-planned economies.

Current population growth trends in the Third World, even if they begin to reverse, suggest that many developing nations are likely still to be underdeveloped in the middle of the 21st century. These nations may well become richer in absolute terms, but the gap between them and the developed world may increase, particularly if the speed of technological advances in the developed world outpaces the rate at which those advances are absorbed in less privileged countries. Some developing nations could close this gap through export-oriented industrialization. South Korea and other countries have done this, and they are now rapidly emerging from their underdevelopment.

Hand-in-hand with such industrialization would come the demographic transition toward lower population growth rates and eventually higher wage rates closer to those in the developed nations. Although we hope that such a process will be well under way by 2050, it is probable that many nations will still be far less developed than others. To the extent that the future of these poorer nations depends on their fruitful integration within the global economy, they should be eager participants in international tax coordination schemes, albeit on terms that recognize their less advanced economic status.

It is equally unrealistic to expect that trade or capital flows among countries will be roughly balanced by 2050. On the contrary, those flows can be expected to be out of balance at any time, with some nations being net merchandise and/or capital exporters and others naturally being net importers. Trade and capital imbalances will probably tend to shift so that no particular nation will constantly occupy a favored position.

Furthermore, as a corollary to the existence of national sovereignty, there will also be distinctions between nations with market economies and those with state-controlled economies. In the West, it is fashionable to see the state-controlled economy as being in decline, and, indeed, recent economic reforms in China and the Soviet Union point the way toward greater economic liberalization in such settings. But in many countries, the model retains strength. Even countries with a market economy retain important sectors of state control, such as the control of natural resources in Latin American nations and of electric utilities in many countries.

National governments will continue to need to generate revenue through taxation, and they will continue to use taxation as an important tool in economic and social policy making.

The need of governments for funds to finance their operations could conceivably be proportionately greater than it is at present. Additional funds will be needed as developing countries try to build a solid infrastructure or as developed countries feel compelled to take on expanded social welfare responsibilities to cover an increasingly mature population or to increase defense expenditures to keep armed forces at the cutting edge of advancing technology. On the other hand, at least for the developed world, it is also conceivable that the need for revenue could decline as the population's wealth grows, enabling people to provide for more of their own needs. Regardless of whether revenue requirements decrease or increase, however, governments will continue to need revenues.

Taxation will be the major source of those revenues, and each nation will rely on a different mix of tax types and tax rates, as is best suited to its circumstances and policies. The most common forms of tax may well be those least susceptible to evasion, such as payroll taxes (as a way to collect income tax on employees) and a V.A.T. Indeed, in certain countries where a significant portion of the economy might be underground, such as Peru, the only reliable method of official taxation might be a V.A.T. by virtue of its "self-enforcing" feature. The V.A.T. works fairly for any enterprise in a manufacturing/distribution chain only to the extent that all other links in that chain respect the rules of the tax regime. If one link in the chain charges the tax, it is in the self-interest of all subsequent links in the chain to do likewise (otherwise they will not be reimbursed for taxes paid on goods of which they were not the ultimate consumer). Thus a tax system can theoretically draw an underground economy into the open, an important factor to consider in light of the fact that the economies of many underdeveloped countries today are becoming more and more of an underground market.

The critical point is that each nation will consider itself entitled to orchestrate its taxes to serve its budgetary, economic, and social needs. If a nation wishes to finance a Strategic Defensive Initiative ("Star Wars"), it might raise taxes. If it wishes to stimulate or slow down the national economy, it might lower or raise taxes accordingly. If it wishes to encourage pollution reduction, it might manipulate taxes to that end. Taxation as a key policy tool for governments will still be with us in 2050. (The U.S. Tax Reform Act of 1986, interestingly enough, represents both a use of taxation as a policy tool through across-the-board reductions in tax rates and a reaction against such use through the reduction or elimination of numerous tax preferences. This tax reform may presage a trend to use tax only as a macroeconomic policy tool rather than as a policy tool aimed at a specific sector, which is more distortive.)

The world will have fewer barriers to the international flow of people, capital, goods, services, and communication.

It is a cliche to say that technological advances are making the world smaller. Nonetheless, it is undeniable that with telephones, telecopiers, telexes, and overnight couriers, distances and borders are no longer obstacles to the instantaneous transmission of information. Such technology is being used more and more frequently by more and more people and enterprises. It is safe to say that the transmission of data and the transportation of goods and people will only become easier and less expensive with time. The psychological impact of these advanced technologies is perhaps more important. Rare is the hamlet where there is no radio or where nobody has ever heard of Nestle. As a result, rare is the citizenry that does not have heightened economic aspirations.

Nations could conceivably try to isolate themselves from these influences, but isolation would be possible only at the cost of severe repression and, in essence, by resigning from the 21st century. Therefore, any such isolationist policies would likely be the exception rather than the norm. As a result, we predict that global commerce will flow relatively unimpeded by 2050, not only because of the economic logic of comparative advantage, but also for the more pragmatic reason that those flows simply cannot be stopped without incurring staggering sacrifices. Even today those who express protectionist sentiments claim that they are not against trade, but rather they are in favor of "fair trade." They also claim that the trade barriers they espouse are merely designed as incentives to encourage other countries to open their borders wider. Such rhetoric reflects the underlying strength of concepts favoring the free flow of global commerce.

Given the expected pervasiveness of global commercial flows, we predict that nations will increasingly use tax incentives to enhance the international competitiveness of their domestic enterprises and to attract foreign investment.

Taxes are by no means the most important factor in determining a nation's attractiveness for business; a developed infrastructure, an educated labor force, and political stability are typically more important. Yet tax regimes must be taken into account by business planners and can be decisive when other factors are nearly equal between two countries competing for the same investment. Most importantly, tax changes and manipulations can be effected much more quickly than raising literacy rates or stabilizing a political system.

INTERNATIONAL TAX CONSEQUENCES OF BASIC ASSUMPTIONS ABOUT THE 21ST CENTURY

Consequences for international taxation will derive from efforts to resolve the tension between our two primary assumptions about the next century: (1) the persistence of national sovereignty, with its compartmentalizing influence and (2) the fall of barriers to global commerce, which will tend to unify the world of commerce. Emerging from the clash between these two trends should be a harmonious international tax structure that allows commerce and, therefore, nations to prosper. Such a result may not be achieved by the year 2050, but its eventual realization is not unrealistic because it represents the product of nations' enlightened self-interest.

Commerce is the best development engine and source of prosperity known to man. Consequently, national governments will have to listen when commercial enterprises complain that their international activities are impeded by the differing requirements of overlapping national tax jurisdictions with their mix of tax types and tax rates. At least three negative consequences can result from such a tax patchwork:

- The administrative costs required to adapt to and comply with overlapping national tax regimes could become quite high for multinational enterprises.
- Commercial flows could be so distorted that multinational enterprises might be tempted to structure international transactions or investments in a less rational manner than they would if tax consideration did not exist.
- The risk or reality of double taxation could stifle beneficial international transactions.

It would be in the self-interest of nations to resolve these problems. Without a measure of uniformity and predictability in the tax treatment of international operations, such operations will fail to achieve their maximum potential, and to a parallel extent, the potential prosperity of nations will be tempered.

On the other hand, it is understandable that individual nations wili be extremely reluctant to yield much, if any, of their taxing sovereignty. A nation's ability to tax according to its own criteria is a key ingredient of its autonomy, and it will not voluntarily limit itself without strong motivation. Even if the need to limit national taxing sovereignty were recognized in principle, it would still be difficult to agree on the precise terms of such a limitation. For example, net capital-importing countries and poor developing countries would favor taxing income on the basis of its source rather than on the basis of the residence of the party earning that income. Net capital-exporting countries would tend to favor the exact opposite.

Nevertheless, as the network of bilateral tax treaties existing between countries today attests, nations have seen the wisdom of bridging these differences for the sake of preserving the vitality of international commerce. The motivations underlying such treaties should grow even stronger as the internationalization of business grows. It is already apparent that the economic fate of one nation is linked to that of others, so there really is no such thing as absolute fiscal autonomy or sovereignty. Witness the periodic economic summits among Western allies. Europe and Japan encourage the United States to reduce its budget deficit; the United States asks Germany to stimulate its economy in order to become more of a market for U.S. exports; for the same reason the United States wishes savings rates would be lower and consumption rates higher in Japan. Developing countries need open markets for their products in the developed world, and loans or aid are extended to them on condition, as commonly imposed by the International Monetary Fund, that they rationalize their fiscal policies. These webs of interdependence impinge upon fiscal sovereignty and point toward greater international harmonization, not only through an expansion of the bilateral tax treaty network, but also through other more dramatic mechanisms.

The expected proliferation of national tax incentives to attract international business or make local enterprises more internationally competitive is another factor that should lead logically to greater international tax harmonization. Lower tax rates for business, tax holidays, generous depreciation rules—all of these have costs to the governments that allow them. Each of these tax breaks represents a revenue loss that can be recaptured only if the multiplier effect generated by the industries enjoying the benefit is enough at least to compensate for that initial loss. Presumably, this multiplier rationale is what motivates jurisdictions such as Ireland and Puerto Rico to rely on tax incentives as a development tool.

However, it is relatively easy for other nations to copy such tax incentives, and they will be tempted to do so if incentives in other countries attract enough business to have a negative impact on their neighbors. But competition of this sort among nations quickly becomes a counterproductive zero-sum game, and the situation would become ripe for a multilateral effort to control such practices. In fact, such multilateral controls are already in place to discourage tax incentives for injurious exports. These controls are spelled out in the GATT Subsidies Code.

In short, given the increasing internationalization of business and despite the continuing existence of national sovereignty, existing forces and precedents suggest that a degree of multilateral international tax coordination is possible, and perhaps even likely, by the year 2050. The question is, what form will the new international tax regime take?

POSSIBLE MODELS FOR A FUTURE INTERNATIONAL TAX ORDER

The rise of a coordinated multilateral international tax regime could occur along a three-step progression. Models for each of these three steps exist today:

The first step: negotiation (the tax treaty model). The current network of tax treaties is designed to solve problems, such as double taxation, arising from the contact between two countries' different tax systems. These bilateral treaties are the logical first step in the coordination of international taxation. A number of generic models exist, such as the U.S. model treaty, the United Nations model treaty, and the Organization for Economic Cooperation and Development (OECD) model treaty, none of which is radically different from the others. These treaties have the practical virtue of leaving each signatory's tax system largely intact: their provisions merely regulate the contact between two tax systems, and these provisions can be flexibly molded to the particular circumstances of the commercial relationship between the parties involved. Therefore, such treaties do not represent a significant departure from the concept of national fiscal sovereignty. Yet they succeed in rationalizing the tax effects of a transaction that touches the jurisdiction of both signatories.

In the future, this bilateral treaty network could easily expand, not only by the addition of new country pairings, but also by the expansion of the scope of the treaties to cover more types of taxes and different types of problems. For example, the income tax treaties to which the United States is a party do not deal with such issues as the international implications of taxation by state governments. However, with the enforcement by California and other states of a unitary tax system with significant international repercussions, these issues may soon be relevant in the negotiation of tax treaties. At least in the case of the United States, there appears to be no constitutional impediment to regulating by treaty the international effects of a state's taxation regime.

Treaty provisions could also be crafted to allow the poorest of nations to use tax incentives as a development tool. Given the present workings of the U.S. foreign tax credit and the fact that the U.S. taxes its corporations on their worldwide income, a tax holiday offered by an African country to a U.S. corporation would do nothing to reduce that corporation's overall tax burden. Since the corporation would have received a foreign tax credit for the African tax, eliminating that tax in turn eliminates the credit, so the net effect is that the company bears the same tax burden but pays all of it to the United States. Therefore, if tax incentives by nations are to have any effect on U.S. companies, the foreign tax credit should be awarded even for taxes spared in other countries, or foreign-source income should be exempt from U.S. taxation. By applying such mechanisms reciprocally through bilateral treaties, authorities could carefully control them in order to benefit only the poorest of nations, thus preventing the counterproductive spread of tax incentives.

The second step: harmonization (the EEC model). This much more difficult step would involve the ambitious task of making the tax systems, and even the tax rates, of different countries more similar in order to reduce tax-based distortions in commerce between the countries. Such harmonization would have obvious economic advantages, but national fiscal sovereignty would be greatly curtailed as a result.

The EEC has already taken great strides in this direction with the V.A.T. The underlying motivation for this tax harmonization lies in the 1957 Treaty of Rome. This treaty reflects an aspiration for the attainment of a united Europe without internal frontiers, thus enabling Europe to more effectively compete politically and economically with the other world powers.

An important step in the elimination of internal frontiers is the reduction of disparities between the tax systems of EEC members. Beginning with the First Council Directive in 1967 and culminating with the Sixth Council Directive ten years later, the EEC nations have instituted a common V.A.T., with uniform rules defining what constitutes a taxable person and a taxable transaction and generally uniform rules establishing the basis for tax assessment. Internal frontiers still affect the V.A.T, however. Exports are immune from the V.A.T., but imports are not; therefore, border checks are still necessary to collect on imports, and exporters have the administrative burden of demonstrating that their export transactions have indeed taken place in order to claim a credit for taxes paid to their suppliers.

Therefore, the next goal for V.A.T. harmonization in the EEC is to eliminate export drawbacks and taxation of imports, so international commercial transactions within the EEC are treated like purely domestic ones. Such a change is heralded by the 1985 European Commission White Paper, "Completing the Internal Market," as well as by proposals adopted by the Commission in July 1987. The Commission recognizes, however, that the elimination of fiscal frontiers cannot be accomplished without an approximation of tax rates as well as of tax systems. Otherwise, the result would be that residents of high-tax countries would go to low-tax countries to purchase goods they would then take back home.

Consequently, the Commission has proposed that by 1992, all EEC members impose a standard V.A.T. rate of 14 percent to 20 percent and a reduced V.A.T. rate for food and other basic items of 4 percent to 9 percent. Although the current rates of many members fall within these bands, the fiscal consequences would be dramatic for some. Denmark and Ireland, for example, would lose substantial revenues because their V.A.T. rates are now higher than the proposed Commission target, and Luxembourg would gain revenues at the expense of some of its businesses because its V.A.T. rates are now lower than the target.

These results point out the delicate nature of tax-rate harmonization in an atmosphere of national sovereignty. To the extent that a nation commits itself to a tax rate pegged to that for other nations, it limits its ability to use that tax rate as a tool of fiscal, economic, and social policy. Such a sacrifice represents a commitment to the collectivity that may be possible only among like-minded nations with ties as strong as those linking the EEC members. It also represents a yielding of power to the collectivity, for if anyone is to use harmonized tax rates as a fiscal policy tool, it will have to be that collectivity.

In a sense, the EEC's V.A.T. harmonization proposal is modest. For example, it does not encompass individual and corporate income taxes, which thus remain as a purely national tool of fiscal policy. Furthermore, it provides the opportunity for "derogations," whereby individual nations could obtain exemptions from the proposal's application. Whether or not the proposal succeeds by 1992, the fact that it has been formally presented is a significant testament to the force of international business as a catalyst for tax coordination. As Lord Arthur Cockfield, vice president of the European Commission, has stated in defense of the proposal, "the people of Europe have embarked on the long march to European unity—not simply from idealism but from hard economic necessity. There is no way that process can be stopped."

The third step: integration (the Law of the Sea model). The EEC tax-harmonization proposal does not go so far as to eliminate each member nation's taxing authority and to create a centralized, multinational tax and budgetary institution—although an extreme, long-term extrapolation of the proposal's effects would seem to point in that direction. However, in regard to the future exploitation of resources in areas where nations have yet to carve out proprietary claims, such as space and the deep seabed, complete multilateral tax integration may well result.

Today's model for such a development is Part XI (Articles 133 through 191) as well as Annex III of the United Nations Convention on the Law of the Sea. The final draft of the convention was approved in 1982 by a vote of 130 nations in favor, 4 against (United States, Israel, Turkey, and Venezuela), and 17 abstentions. More than 30 of the 60 nations necessary to bring it into force have already ratified the convention.

The convention provides that mineral resources in the deep seabed be exploited only under the regulation of an International Sea-Bed Authority comprised of all the convention signatories. Parties wishing to exploit these resources would have to seek permission from and make financial contributions to the authority, which in essence becomes a tax collecting body. A party has a choice of paying that contribution in the form of a production charge, representing a percentage of the market value of the processed metals produced, or of a combination of production charge plus a share of net proceeds. Revenues obtained by the authority will be shared equitably on a nondiscriminatory basis, "taking into particular consideration the interests and needs of developing States and peoples who have not attained full independence or other self-governing status."

It is precisely this deep seabed regime which prompted the United States to vote against the convention. Nevertheless, when deep seabed mining becomes technically and economically feasible, there will have to be some ground rules to regulate such activity, and it would be politically implausible not to give some recognition to the concept that the resources are part of the "common heritage of mankind." In fiscal terms, that concept translates into at least some kind of international revenue sharing.

Multilateral tax integration might also be used in the future as a tool to combat the deterioration of international resources, such as the high ozone layer. A tax could be imposed on the sources of contaminants, and the revenues could be used by an international body to compensate areas suffering from damaged ecologies or to promote research in pollution abatement and control.

ADMINISTRATIVE AND ACCOUNTING CONSIDERATIONS

Whatever tax coordination is achieved among nations by the year 2050 will have to be accompanied by heightened cooperation among national taxing authorities and by the development of uniformity in accounting principles. Such principles would represent a kind of accounting "metric system," without which tax coordination would be seriously hampered. In particular, the accounting treatment of matters such as inflation, depreciation, and inventories would have to be homogenized. It is also important to develop universally accepted cost-accounting principles (to permit identification of costs and value added at each step of a production and distribution chain) as well as income recognition rules (to avoid year-to-year "management" of income).

The UN Convention on the Law of the Sea already foreshadows such needs by providing detailed definitions for concepts such as "net proceeds," "development costs," "gross proceeds," "operating costs," and "return on investment" for purposes of calculating the revenues to be collected from deep seabed mining activities. More generally, the convention specifies that the International Sea-Bed Authority shall establish "uniform and non-discriminatory costing and accounting rules." To establish such accounting principles acceptable to nations coordinating their taxes, special provisions could be written into bilateral tax treaties between them.

Bilateral tax treaties also foreshadow the need for greater cooperation between national tax authorities if increased international tax coordination is to become a reality. It will be necessary to establish procedures by which authorities will meet regularly, exchange information, and ensure its confidentiality appropriately. These procedures will be necessary not just for purposes of coordination (as in the reapportionment of multinational corporation profits), but also for preventing tax evasion. Such administrative cooperation already exists to some extent, but it will undoubtedly expand. Under the V.A.T. harmonization proposed by the European Commission in 1987, for example, there would be a "clearinghouse" mechanism to compensate for the elimination of fiscal frontiers. Through this mechanism, net importing nations would receive compensation to make up for the fact that they must pay a V.A.T. credit to an importer for a tax it paid to a foreign exporter and, therefore, indirectly to the exporter's national taxing authority. In this way, the destination principle of the V.A.T. (whereby the tax ultimately only enriches the coffers of the nation wherein final consumption of a good occurs) is preserved even with the abolition of fiscal borders.

It is in the area of tax administration that technological advances may have the greatest impact. The computers of one nation's tax authority might routinely "talk" with those of another country's fiscal bureaucracy. With the increased use of credit cards, greater numbers of transactions will be recorded in computer data banks. Such developments could permit easier tracking of global economic activities and country-by-country comparisons of positions taken by individuals and multinational corporations. It will thus be harder to hide from the tax collector and perhaps easier for tax authorities to cope with the growing complexity of tax laws. It is already technically feasible to apply such computer techniques. The question remains whether or not it would be politically feasible to implement these advances both domestically and across national borders.

CONCLUSION

Although a uniform, multilateral, international taxation regime is quite appealing in the abstract, its complete realization by the year

2050 is unlikely, given the basic assumption of unabated national sovereignty. Nevertheless, the advantages to nations of promoting the global commercial flows that result from the internationalization of business should lead to increased international tax coordination by 2050. Models already exist for the progressive phases through which such coordination might develop. Exactly how far along in that progression we shall be in the 21st century is anyone's guess. However, the aspiration for significant international tax coordination is by no means unrealistic for the Western free-market nations, their currently less developed neighbors, and even the economies that are centrally planned to the extent they have to interact with the global economy.

10

Developing Countries' Delicate Balances

MARIO S. BRODERSOHN

In the mid-1950s, if we in the developing world had asked ourselves what tax structure we should adopt for our countries in the coming years, the answer would have been relatively simple: Design a system with minumum bureaucratic costs and a certain progressiveness in order to collect the funds necessary to finance a state destined to play a leading role in assuring economic development and social equity.

However, in subsequent years, the public sector has expanded tremendously, resulting in the inefficiencies and distortions that seem to be common to many countries. As a consequence, the answer to our question involves dramatic changes of emphasis. Present-day realities provide us with other restrictions, other needs regarding the role of the state, and induce us to consider other directions to be followed for tax policy in the future:

- Although governments have made great efforts to collect taxes, revenues have steadily lagged behind budgetary needs. Inflationary pressure has become chronic, and foreign debt has been used on an unprecedented scale to deal with fiscal deficits.

- At present, the tax structures of many countries are the chaotic residues of successive emergencies and momentary crises. They have evolved into complex encumbrances that collect relatively little revenue at exceptionally high costs, have lost any sense of equity, and permit widespread tax evasion. As a result, tax collection has become increasingly problematic.
- The huge foreign debts that have been accrued in recent years aggravate budgetary stress.
- The great development of the world's capital market in the past two decades, which has virtually erased the financial borders between countries, has placed serious restrictions on domestic economic policies, particularly tax policy. Clearly, national tax policies cannot be fully independent in a world characterized by strong mobility of resources, such as financial capital and highly trained manpower.
- The growth of the informal economy has affected tax collection. We believe that there is a clear signal here of the direction that public preferences are taking as to relations between the Treasury and the private economy.
- Social demands for material growth, which are as deeply rooted today as ever, put additional demands on tax revenues.

We believe that a correct understanding of these trends and restrictions calls for a whole new set of philosophic outlines and practical guidelines for the necessary task of reformulating the tax system not only for the 21st century but also for the more immediate and pressing 1990s.

The contemporary tax problem is not how to finance the expansion of a public sector that functions as the engine of economic development. Instead, the mission is to meet—without resorting to inflationary financing—the budgetary needs of a more prudent, rational, and efficient state, and one that has suddenly been required to face strong foreign obligations even as it confronts a growing demand for greater equality in income distribution. This objective must be accomplished within the framework of a notoriously interdependent world economy.

In my opinion, the ideal tax system would respect three basic principles:

1. It should be based on small assessments, simple legislation, a wide tax base, and low rates. The basic condition is that it be implemented by tax collection bodies that have adopted technological advances in data processing in order to exert steady and equitable pressure on the taxpayers.
2. It should favor taxes of low economic cost.
3. It should concern itself not only with the regressiveness of a particular tax but should also consider the degree of progressiveness of the public expenditure and revenue system as a whole. The appropriate way to evaluate public finances lies not through any single tax but rather from the perspective of the entire national budget.

Consequently, I believe that the tax structure for the coming decades should be supported on the following pillars:

A value-added tax (V.A.T.), if possible of the consumption type, that reaches the fringes of the private economy and assesses them uniformly at a rate that will depend on the size of national public expenditures. The advantageous neutrality of such a tax is well known. Moreover, by permitting the deduction of 100 percent of investment costs, the V.A.T. would also prevent the double assessment of capital. For developing countries in a world of growing international financial integration, this last feature has particular attraction.

Because the V.A.T. affects a very broad group of taxpayers, high costs for collection and inspection have been traditionally attributed to it. Thus it was thought to be impractical. At present, however, these problems can be mitigated so as to allow the use of the V.A.T. in relatively impoverished countries. The tremendous advance of computer technology has brought about a dramatic drop in the costs of checking and processing information. The same development makes the evasion of other taxes more costly and improbable. And finally, the regressiveness of the V.A.T. may be mitigated either by exempting from it the basic consumptions of the population or by returning its equivalent in the broad context of the national budget.

In other words, as an instrument for affecting income distribution, expenditures are as suitable, transparent, and precise an instrument as taxation. By increasing or reducing the general rate of the V.A.T., it will be possible to satisfy momentary needs for funds with flexibility and promptness.

A tax on real estate, not including industrial or agricultural improvements. This tax, which in most countries does not exceed 2 percent of the market value of the property affected, offers considerable advantages. It involves minimum administrative costs and is very hard to evade. Given its high visibility, however, this tax generally arouses great political resistance. This resistance can be mitigated by clearly defining the tax base and the tax rate once and for all, by reappraising properties flexibly in the event of natural catastrophes or acute changes in relative prices, especially those that affect agriculture, and by refraining from overusing the tax.

A subsystem of domestic consumption taxes (excise taxes) with a per-industry variable rate. This is a form of taxation that countries such as England, the United States, and Canada have historically adopted (as opposed to the countries of continental Europe, which have tended toward sales taxes—"turnover"—with more equal rates). As a component of a tax structure generating significant funds, this tax imparts flexible progressiveness to the system. It falls on luxury consumption and penalizes consumption that is considered socially negative—alcohol, tobacco, gambling, etc. The historic widespread adoption of this type of tax is precisely what led to the formulation of the well-known Ramsey rule, which holds a central position in public finance theory. The rule suggests that the level of the tax rate affecting each product should be inversely proportional to the price elasticity of the demand for the product. The application of this principle can assure substantial income for treasuries with minimum costs of resource allocation.

Corporate and personal income taxes with moderately progressive rates, which maintain a relationship of equilibrium with rates and tax systems in effect in other countries, such as the United States, Canada, and those in Western Europe. The strong international mobility of capital and highly trained manpower resources—human capital—which characterizes modern economies make it indispensable to proceed with caution and a sense of proportion. We must bear in mind the steady flight of capital that has devastated countries that abused corporate and personal taxes. It must also be pointed out that the capital emigrating from developing countries has found refuge in tax havens protected by the developed countries. They use these tax havens to capture greater capital to solve their own budgetary imbalances.

A tax or levy that captures the income from such natural resources as hydrocarbons and minerals. In one form or another, this is already applied in all developing countries. It is worth mentioning the desirability for any country to bring the relative prices of these products near international levels. This involves taxing the revenue without causing distortions in economically optimal production levels.

Tariffs involving public companies and services. Although such tariffs are not strictly taxation, they often implicitly bear a tax component and are a truly important part of total tax resources. The resource-allocation advantages of establishing tariffs, following the marginal cost principle, are also worth noting. Moreover, the assessments incorporated in the tariffs offer the advantage of low evasion and low collection cost.

Finally, a tax we should avoid: inflation, or assessment on real cash balances. The impact of this tax on the public finances of many countries—such as Argentina, Israel, and Brazil—has often outweighed the other components of the tax system. Inflation most directly affects the poorer sectors of the population, individuals who maintain a greater proportion of their income in the form of cash, so that the existence of chronically high rates of inflation has fatally upset in a visible way the goal of a progressive tax system. In addition, inflation exerts hidden effects upon the tax structure. For example, the loss of the government's purchasing power experienced through direct taxes by corporations and high-income groups is maximized in view of the fact that the time elapsed between the determination of the tax and the actual payment to the Treasury is the longest for those assessments.

In conclusion, let us link the principal fiscal phenomenon of our time—foreign debt—to the public budget. The eminently public nature of debt gives it a rough and profound influence on the size and structure of national budgets. In the countries of the southern cone of Latin America, the cost of servicing the debt is by itself roughly 6 percent of the national income, and a quick look is enough to tell us how it has been financed since the time that the curtain first opened on the debt drama: mainly through reductions in public investment and the salaries paid by the public sector. Private salaries, in turn, have also fallen considerably, thanks to the real depreciation in domestic currencies that was necessary to sustain a certain equilibrium in international accounts. For many reasons, an important portion of budgetary needs has been and continues to be financed by the inflationary tax and through a decrease of expenditures on public infrastructure and in such social areas as education and public health.

However, expenditures on education and health have a fundamental role in promoting economic growth, since they are the principal instruments in the process of accumulating human capital. Coming, as many of us have, from countries of recent and massive immigration, we can assert that there is no faster and more effective vehicle than broad education of the popular classes for promoting upward social mobility, renewing the ruling classes, and once and for all democratizing and strengthening the stability of the political institutions of nations.

What should be done in the face of so many obligations arising from current reality and contending with each other for the national budget? Beyond the medium- and long-term arrangements that we may arrive at in foreign debt negotiations, we should take note of some clear lessons about economic efficiency and social equity.

It is essential to bring about budgetary change toward greater tax progressivity, so seriously injured in recent years. We believe that the first step in this direction is the substitution of the inflationary tax with a broad-based, reduced-rate V.A.T. It is also essential to create a privileged place in our budgets for expenditures on primary and secondary education and health to enable us to grow with increasing social equality. There should be more efficient collection of taxes imposed on wealth-indicative consumption and taxes imposed on estates and high incomes from capital and labor, bearing in mind another piece of real information: The growing internationalization of national economies requires us, above all, to be moderate and cautious.

11

Day of Reckoning Approaches for the European Community

SIJBREN CNOSSEN

There is an old story in an old book. The book is the Bible, and the story is about high tax burdens. As Chronicles tells us, when Rehoboam sought to succeed his father, Solomon, as king of the 12 tribes of Israel, he went to be crowned in Shechem. However, before accepting him as their leader, the spokesmen for the various tribes put him to the test: Was Rehoboam prepared to lighten the grievous tax burdens, mainly in the form of forced labor, imposed on them by his father?

As the story goes, Rehoboam did not listen to the elders counseling kindness and moderation. Instead, he lent his ear to the younger men and told the assembled tribes: "My little finger is thicker than my father's waist. My father laid on you a heavy yoke; I will make it even heavier. My father scourged you with whips; I will scourge you with scorpions."

Ten tribes did not like the message. They stoned the chief tax collector, Adoniram, who was in charge of forced labor, and went to their tents to arm themselves against Rehoboam. The chronicler concludes dramatically: "So Israel has been in rebellion against the house of David to this day."

Is there a message in this story for the member states of the European Community (EC), who are also 12 in number, and who have tax burdens that are unprecedented in history and are not found in their major competitors and trading partners, the United States and Japan? The answer is no and yes.

It is unlikely that the high levels of taxation in EC countries, which have been imposed by democratically elected governments and which the public at large apparently consents to, will lead to the disestablishment of the Community. But what is likely, as manifested by the growing underground economies, is that the high tax burdens, if maintained, will weaken citizens' allegiance to government.

Competitive individualism and the influence of market forces, both indispensable counterweights to excessive bureaucratic government, will also suffer. The appropriate balance between the public sector and the private sector will probably emerge as a crucial issue affecting the direction and rate of economic progress. Economic growth, while probably positive as the EC moves closer to becoming a single large domestic market, may not be sufficient initially to reduce unemployment to more tolerable levels; and later, as populations age, it may fail to provide sufficient funding for income-maintenance programs.

My focus is on the high levels of taxation, spending, and deficits presently found in the EC and likely to prevail in the foreseeable future. Their detrimental effects on economic growth, employment, saving, and investment are highlighted. A review of the underlying political cultures leads me to this conclusion: Closer political and economic integration, in any case a slow and tortuous process, will not change the public finance picture in the EC very much. Generally, as we move into the 21st century and beyond, governments will continue to buy time: They will reduce expenditure by, say, two percentage points of gross domestic product (GDP), increase revenue by one percentage point, and muddle on much as before.

A market-oriented economist may not see this as conducive to promoting the welfare (broadly defined to include the undeniable benefits of basic social expenditure and income-maintenance programs), but governments and people have their own perceptions about what is in their interest and what is not. If change is to be brought about, it will probably have to be achieved through some kill-or-cure remedy, a dose of Reaganomics—that is, cuts in taxation to increase the pressure on expenditure reductions. Institutional changes may also help, such as more transparent forms of taxation, as well as greater use of direct rather than indirect forms of political representation—more use of the ballot box rather than the tit-for-tat dealings in the corridors of government.

While the total level of taxation should be the primary policy concern, the structure of taxation is also relevant. In my opinion, moves to broaden tax bases or to increase the reliance on consumption taxes should be resisted. If history is a guide, such moves will only lead to further increases in the total tax burden. I believe that the playing field should not be leveled. Rather, incentive schemes to promote saving and investment should continue to be used to shore up the market regime. To eliminate the distortion between present and future consumption (inherent to the income tax that taxes savings twice) and, more generally, to counterbalance the disincentives on saving and investment emanating from reductions in income inequalities, it would be desirable to replace the income tax with an expenditure tax.

HIGH LEVELS OF EXPENDITURE, REVENUE, AND DEFICITS

Government operations in the EC are characterized by an explosion of expenditure, insufficient revenue, high deficits, and a lack of budget discipline.

Explosion of Expenditure

High taxes are required to finance high expenditures. High taxes financed a large army and an opulent royal household in Rehoboam's days. In modern times, high expenditures are required to fuel a large public sector engaged in redistributing resources to the old, the poor, the sick, and the unemployed (the distribution branch of government); to minimize cyclically induced fluctuations of the economy (the stabilization branch); and to provide protection, justice, roads, and other goods and services (the allocation branch).

The size of general government in EC countries has risen to daunting levels: from some 20 percent of GDP in the 1920s, to 30 percent in the late 1950s, and to some 50 percent in the middle 1980s, only a quarter of a century later. These levels are found in Germany, France, Britain, and Italy, four member states which together account for 80 percent of the EC's combined gross domestic product (see Table 1). General government expenditure is higher still in the smaller EC countries. In the Netherlands, Belgium, Denmark, and Ireland, levels of 60 percent of GDP have been reached. However, government spending is much lower, although growing faster, in Spain, Portugal, and Greece. But then these countries are distinctly less industrialized than their fellow member states.

The enormous increase in government spending is largely the consequence of the growth of social expenditure. Final consumption expenditure on the traditional functions of government, as a proportion of GDP, rose from 14 percent in 1960 to 19 percent in 1983, or by 40 percent. In sharp contrast, social expenditure and transfers on pensions, education, health services, unemployment compensation, and other income-maintenance and welfare services increased twice as fast: from 16 percent of GDP in 1960 to about 30 percent in 1981 (see Table 2).[1] Such programs, imposed in the 1960s and early 1970s when economies were booming and the immediate cost of social programs was relatively small, are difficult to deny under changed economic conditions. Increases in coverage and real benefits have literally led to an explosion of expenditure.

In 1984, government spending in the EC as a percentage of GDP was nearly 40 percent higher than government spending in the United States, while revenue was 35 percent higher. The difference in the relative levels of expenditure must be attributed largely to the difference in social expenditure. The EC and the United States both spend the same relative amount on final consumption of government, but social expenditure is 42 percent higher in the EC compared to the U.S. level (see Tables 1 and 2).

Table 1
European Community: General Government Operations
(as Percent of Gross Domestic Product at Current Prices)

Member State	GDP as Percent of Combined GDP (1984)	Expenditure 1960	Expenditure 1984	Revenue 1960	Revenue 1984	Surplus/Deficit (–) 1960	Surplus/Deficit (–) 1984
Germany	26.0	32.5	48.7	35.1	45.8	2.6	−2.9
France	20.7	34.6	51.0	34.9	47.1	0.3	−3.8
United Kingdom	17.9	32.6	47.3	30.3	44.2	−2.3	−3.2
Italy[a]	14.7	30.1	57.4	28.8	41.0	−1.3	−15.6
Total/Weighted Average	*79.3*	*32.6*	*50.6*	*32.8*	*44.9*	*0.2*	*−5.7*
Netherlands	5.2	33.7	60.5	33.9	54.4	0.2	−6.1
Belgium	3.2	30.3	60.0	27.5	48.9	−2.8	−11.1
Denmark (1960–83)	2.3	24.8	60.7	27.3	54.1	2.5	−6.6
Ireland	0.8	28.0	57.5	24.8	46.3	−3.2	−11.1
Luxembourg (1960–83)	0.1	30.5	47.3	32.5	43.8	2.0	−3.5
Total/Weighted Average	*11.6*	*30.6*	*60.0*	*30.2*	*52.2*	*−0.4*	*−7.8*
Spain (1960–83)	6.8	18.8	37.3	18.8	30.7	—	−6.6
Greece (1960–81)[b]	1.4	17.4	41.4	21.1	30.4	3.7	−10.9
Portugal (1960–81)[a]	0.8	17.0	34.1	17.6	30.6	0.6	−3.5
Total/Weighted Average	*9.1*	*18.4*	*37.7*	*19.1*	*30.6*	*0.7*	*−7.1*
European Community	100.0	31.1	50.5	31.3	44.4	0.2	−6.1
United States		27.6	36.5	27.3	33.0	−0.3	−3.5
Japan (1960–83)		18.3	34.8	20.7	32.4	2.4	−2.4

Sources: GDP percentages, OECD (1986): 18–19; 1960 expenditure and revenue figures, Saunders and Klau (1985): 29; 1984 expenditure and revenue figures, IMF (1986): 84–87, 96–97. Figures may not tally because of rounding.

[a]Central government operations only.

[b]Current disbursements only.

Table 2
European Community: Composition of Expenditure[a]
(as Percent of Gross Domestic Product at Current Prices)

Member State	Final Consumption 1960	Final Consumption 1983	Social Expenditure 1960	Social Expenditure 1981	Interest Payments 1970	Interest Payments 1985
Germany	13.4	20.0	20.5	31.5	1.0	3.0
France	13.0	16.3	13.4[b]	29.5	1.0	3.0
United Kingdom	16.4	22.0	13.9	23.7	3.9	5.0
Italy	12.8	19.5	16.8	29.1	1.8	9.7
Weighted Average	*13.9*	*19.4*	*16.5*	*28.8*	*1.8*	*4.7*
Netherlands	12.8	17.7	16.2	36.1	3.0	6.4
Belgium	12.4	17.7	17.4	37.6[c]	3.4	10.9
Denmark	13.3	27.2	NA	33.3[d]	1.3	9.6
Ireland	12.5	20.2	11.7	28.4	NA	10.9
Luxembourg	9.8	17.3	NA	NA	1.2	1.2
Weighted Average	*12.7*	*19.7*	*16.3*	*34.9*	*2.6*	*8.5*
European Community	13.7	19.4	16.5	29.6	1.9	5.2
United States	16.9	19.3	10.9	20.8	NA	NA
Japan	8.0	10.2	8.0	17.5	NA	NA

Sources: Final Consumption, OECD, as reported in Tanzi (1986): 21; Social Expenditure, OECD (1985): 21; Interest Payments, EC, as reported in Tanzi (1986): 27.

Note: NA = figures are not available

[a]Excluding Spain, Greece, and Portugal for which figures are not available.

[b]Excluding education.

[c]1980.

[d]1979.

Insufficient Revenue

In the 1960s and early 1970s, the revenues to finance the rapidly growing outlays on social expenditure came in almost automatically. Initially, high economic growth rates pushed taxpayers into higher nominal income tax brackets, resulting in higher real-tax payments. Later, this effect was exacerbated by inflation, the ideal "silent tax," which can be levied without appropriate representation. Potential resistance to the income tax and social security contributions was greatly reduced by the introduction of withholding schemes. The growth in the size of production and distribution establishments and their use of modern business accounting methods, to which the schemes could easily be attached, also assisted in raising taxes. At the same time, a whole new government money machine was invented: the value-added tax which spreads the burden of the tax on consumer prices in a nondistortionary fashion over the whole of commerce and industry. This new tax was much easier to collect than previous broad-based consumption taxes.

Later, however, as income tax brackets and exemptions were indexed for inflation, and while economic growth slowed down and unemployment increased, revenue could not keep up with expenditure (also indexed) on government wages and transfer payments. In 1984, overall revenue levels reached 45 percent of GDP in the big member states and 52 percent in the small member states (see Table 1), considerably short of spending requirements. According to Carolyn Webber and Aaron Wildavsky (in *A History of Taxation and Expenditure in the Western World*), this "scissors crisis"—a term they attribute to Daniel Tarschys—has created a structural budgetary fault "with demands that cannot be reduced and supplies of revenue that cannot be raised sufficiently to satisfy them."

High Deficits and Lack of Budget Discipline

The basic statistic for the budgetary fault is the budget deficit, expressed as a percentage of GDP. In 1984, the weighted, cyclically unadjusted deficit was nearly 6 percent of GDP in the big member states and 8 percent in the small member states (see Table 1). If budget deficits are not to be inflationary, they must be financed by borrowing. As a result, an increasing proportion of the budget must be allocated to interest payments: 5 percent of GDP in the big member states and nearly 9 percent in the small member states (see Table 2). In other words, to meet the cost of government borrowing, Germany, France, Britain, and Italy on average spend 9 percent of total public expenditure on interest and small member states spend 14 percent. In a few years, the increase in interest payments exceeded the growth of revenue, and they have now driven out new spending. In 1984, all member states had a deficit on their government operations. In 1960, seven of them still had a surplus, as did the EC as a whole.

Along with the increase in spending, taxing, and borrowing, there has been a profound transformation of the budgetary norms that are applied. The traditional budgetary process of estimation, authorization, appropriation, and execution has given way to "entitlements," "backdoor financing," "mandatory items," and other gimmicks that signify lack of comprehensiveness and accountability. Webber and Wildavsky sum up their analysis of the situation as follows:

> As things now stand . . . the inner discipline that kept the budget battle within tolerable limits gives way [and] budgetary control has deteriorated into a free-for-all. No longer can governments control spending by controlling departments; most spending is outside departments. No longer is it possible to control departments by controlling spending; most spending in which departments are interested is subject neither to annual review nor to central control. No longer are the participants clear about whether control is desirable or feasible.

So we are living through the *Dies Irae* of public finance, and it is going to be a long day of reckoning.

DETRIMENTAL EFFECTS ON ECONOMIC PERFORMANCE

High tax burdens appear to slow economic growth, which in turn affects employment.

Welfare Losses

The phenomenal increase in the size of the public sector in EC member states has made it a formidable economic agent in its own right; it exercises a pervasive influence on incentives in the economy as a whole. Government spending, particularly on income transfers, alters incentives to work, save, and invest. So do its taxing activities. The empirical evidence on the size of the incentive effects of transfer payments and tax burdens is scarce, but as the Organization for Economic Cooperation and Development (OECD) notes (in *Structural Adjustment and Economic Performance*): ". . . it is through the concomitant rise in the burden of taxation that the growth of public spending probably imposed its greatest economic costs." While magnitudes differ from country to country, "estimates suggest that $1 raised through taxes may, at the margin, reduce national income by 10 to 15 cents and possibly considerably more, depending on the tax measures used, while the net overall cost of present tax systems could be in the order of 3 to 5 percent of GNP."

Taxes impair economic performance by creating or widening wedges between the social and the private rate of return on economic activities. Taxes impose burdens over and above the amount of revenue that is raised. Labor and capital are diverted from highly taxed to lightly taxed activities: from work to leisure, do-it-yourself jobs, and barter; from occupations with fully taxable monetary rewards to occupations with a higher nontaxable in-kind content of the gross remuneration or with greater opportunities to reduce taxable income through deductible costs; from conventional saving (taxed twice under the income tax) to consumption or (qualitatively different) institutional forms of saving; and from assets with high taxable returns to assets (housing, yachts) with no or low taxable returns. The widening of the difference between gross and net-of-tax returns will also reduce labor and capital mobility and makes emigration and capital flight more attractive. These substitution effects, which induce people to do things they would not have done in the absence of the tax, are an economic waste.[2]

Assar Lindbeck has pointed out (in *The Limits of the Welfare State*) that over time changes in preferences and attitudes induced by taxes may be reflected in, for instance, wage contracts that stress benefits related to leisure. Moreover, the concomitant effect of high government spending and taxing may have detrimental effects on the role of the family. Thus he notes that the care of things (for instance, home and car maintenance) is shifted from the market to the household, while the care of persons (education, nursing) has been monopolized by the state through a system that essentially limits the freedom of choice of the family. High taxes and transfer payments are also major factors contributing to the high levels of tax evasion and avoidance and benefit cheating found in most welfare states. Honesty toward government is taxed away, with possible repercussions on the integrity of the relationships among private agents. Efforts by government to stem the tide may mean that privacy will also be taxed away.

High Taxes and High Unemployment

Average and marginal tax rates on labor use in the EC are extraordinarily high (see Table 3). In 1983, a married couple with two children and only one spouse employed, earning the wages of an average production worker, had on average a tax liability equivalent to 42 percent of total compensation, while it faced a marginal tax rate of 60 percent. In comparison, the average and marginal tax rates in the United States were 28 percent and 43 percent, respectively, while the corresponding figures for Japan were 19 percent and 40 percent. What matters most in this context is the relative spread between the average tax rate and the marginal tax rate. This spread is smallest by far in the EC—which implies that a reduction of the marginal tax rate without a change in the average tax rate (to maintain tax yield) would have little, if any, effect on the elimination of excess burdens.

Table 3 also shows that a double-digit unemployment rate of 11 percent of the labor force in the EC is nearly twice as high as the unemployment rate in the United States and nearly four times as high as the unemployment rate in Japan. It is not clear how much of the difference should be attributed to the disincentive effects of the higher tax rates in the EC. More generous unemployment benefits

Table 3
European Community: Tax Rates (1983);
Unemployment and Economic Growth (1987)

Member State	Tax Rates on Labor Use[1] (as Percent of Total Compensation) Average	Marginal	Unemployment (as Percent of the Labor Force)	Economic Growth (as Percent of GDP)
Germany	36.6	57.0	8	1 1/2
France	47.6	59.7	11 1/4	1 1/4
United Kingdom	39.0	54.5	11 1/4	3 1/4
Italy	48.9	62.7	11 1/2	3
Unweighted Average	*43.0*	*58.5*	*10 1/2*	*2 1/4*
Netherlands	37.5	73.5	12 3/4	1 1/2
Belgium	48.1	61.7	11 3/4	1 1/4
Denmark	53.4	71.2	8 1/2	− 3/4
Ireland	44.9	63.8	18 3/4	3/4
Luxembourg	32.6	50.6	1 1/4	2 1/2
Unweighted Average	*46.0*	*67.6*	*13*	*1 1/4*
Spain	35.5	46.7	21	3
Portugal	37.1	44.3	8 3/4	3 1/2
Greece	NA	NA	8 3/4	−1
Unweighted Average	*36.3*	*45.5*	*13*	2
European Community	41.9	59.5	11 1/2	2
United States	28.2	42.6	6 3/4	2 1/2
Japan	19.1	39.9	3	2

Sources: OECD (1987): 14 and (1987a): 2, 28, and 29.

[1]Comprising payroll taxes, employer and employee contributions for social insurance, personal income taxes, and general consumption taxes and excise taxes.

and looser eligibility requirements in most EC member states probably play a more important role. The unemployment rate may drop in the years ahead, perhaps more on account of demographic factors (aging populations) than on structural improvements in the labor market.

Economic growth in the EC would have to be 3 percent a year for the jobless rate to start dropping, but in 1987 it is estimated at only 2 percent (see Table 3). This is less than half the average annual growth rate prevailing in the third quarter of this century (which may have been unusually high). To be sure, lackadaisical economic performance cannot be blamed on the growth and size of the public sector alone but must also be attributed to pervasive interventions in product markets—in large part agricultural products, but also many manufactured products—as well as factor markets. In labor markets, occupational and industrial wage differentials are artificially compressed, legislative and regulatory restrictions are imposed on retrenchments, and restrictive work practices greatly reduce the flexibility and mobility of the market (see *Structural Adjustment and Economic Performance,* OECD).

In analyzing these factors, however, it should be borne in mind that the public sector, simply because of its size, strongly influences the functioning of product and factor markets through its purchasing, spending, and taxing activities, as well as its involvement in wage bargaining.

This is what has been called Eurosclerosis, an ailment characterized by large public sectors, strong influence of unions, overregulation of business, and lack of an entrepreneurial spirit. The picture for 1988 is not much better: 2.3 percent growth and 11.7 percent unemployment, as reported from the European Commission by *The New York Times* in October 1987. The OECD has proposed a broad range of measures to improve the responsiveness of factor markets and the efficiency and effectiveness of the public sectors in the EC (and other OECD member countries), but whether the measures will be accepted and implemented depends largely on the nature of the political regimes in the various member states.

BUDGETS: A MANIFESTATION OF THE SOCIAL ORDER

We need to examine budgets as an expression of the social order to explain the high levels of expenditure and revenue in the EC and to understand why governments have walked the tightrope of public sector solvency in recent years, and also why the private sector has been neglected. Understanding these issues offers some inkling of what the future portends, and most importantly, helps us to learn how we might do something positive in the present to affect that future.

Public Choice Aspects

Dennis C. Mueller (in "The Growth of Government: A Public Choice Perspective") has examined five sets of hypotheses about the size of government, based essentially on two different conceptualizations of the state. In the citizen-over-state view of the polity, three hypotheses explaining the size and growth of government have been tested: (1) the demand for and the price of public goods have gone up, and the quest to eliminate externalities has been intensified; (2) the demand for redistributing income and wealth through the budget has increased; and (3) the influence of interest groups, with their special programs and plans, has grown disproportionately. The other two hypotheses may be associated with the state-rules-citizen view of politics, which allows government to grow beyond the level citizens prefer: (4) bureaucracies "manufacture" their own demands independent of the citizens; and (5) tax burdens are disguised. Mueller concludes that all five hypotheses may help to explain the size and growth of government.

However, the underlying conceptualizations of the state may represent more fundamental influences. As political scientists, such as Harley H. Hinrichs, tell us, budgets are a manifestation of the prevailing social order. Budget size and, by implication, the tax burden are most likely not determined by structural needs but by ideological commitments to the political regimes in which they are imbedded.

The political cultures in most EC member states are characterized by the state-rules-citizen view of the polity, relatively weak market regimes, and strong egalitarian influences. In combination, these factors shed light on the ever larger proportion of national product absorbed by government. The prominent position of the state explains the preference for regulation, the inclination toward mercantilistic policies, and the subsidization of enterprises for social reasons or to maintain employment. The weak market regime is mirrored in the concern with large economic and social differences, as well as with economic growth itself. In perspective, it is probably the pervasive rise of egalitarianism, with its passion for equality of condition, that best explains the continuous increase in the size of government. When faced with the choice, European countries, conditioned by the unsettling effects of two world wars and a great depression, appear to prefer equality of result over equality of opportunity and the preservation of individual economic freedom. Equal shares are favored even if this means that everyone receives less than under an alternative regime.

What budgets will look like when we move into the 21st century, therefore, depends on our assessment of the political regimes most likely to prevail. Without a change in institutions—that is, forms of political representation—that help shape the social order, I find it difficult to believe that attitudes and preferences in the EC will change much in the years ahead. Equality seems a self-generating condition of which there is never enough and which always finds shades of difference to bicker about.

Moreover, as we move into the 21st century, most industrial countries will have to cope with the problems of an aging population. The share in the total population of those 65 and older is projected to rise, on average, from 12.5 percent to 20.5 percent in the period 1980–2025. Since the elderly also vote, pressures to keep pensions in line with the development of real wages or the consumer price index will be strong, implying an increase in income-maintenance payments to the population of 65 and over.

If this happens, expenditure levels will probably remain very high, revenue insufficient, and deficits a perennial problem. At best, spending may be reduced by a few GDP-percentage points and revenue increased somewhat. As a result, the threat of financial insolvency will have been staved off, and governments can muddle on much as before.

However, we may also wish to reject or modify the present political regime in favor of a regime that places greater emphasis on market-oriented policies. Three factors may influence events: the economic and political integration of the EC, the introduction of institutional changes to forge closer participation of voters in taxing and spending decisions, and changes in the structure of taxation to emphasize incentives to work, save, and invest.

THE COMMUNITY'S TAX PROGRAM

Interestingly, tax burdens in federal systems of government, such as the United States, Canada, and Australia, are considerably lower than those in the unitary systems prevalent in EC member states. If the EC would move toward an Economic and Monetary Union, as envisaged in the Treaty of Rome, through a closer approximation of the economic policies of the member states, would this imply that tax burdens imposed by the various member states (and Brussels) would come down? A review of the EC's tax program may provide a tentative answer.

Indirect Taxes and Nontariff Barriers

As is well known, the Treaty of Rome, which came into force at the beginning of 1958, aims at the creation of a single, integrated market free of restrictions on the movement of goods, services, persons, and capital, and the institution of a system ensuring that competition is not distorted. These goals have, among other things, a number of consequences for the tax systems of the member states, including the abolition of customs duties, the coordination of the major indirect taxes, and the approximation of some direct laws as required for the proper functioning of the Common Market.[3] In short, while competition is the allocating mechanism in the EC, tax coordination is its corollary insofar as it aims at ensuring that equal conditions for competitors are not distorted.

First, in 1968, customs duties imposed on goods moving from one member state to another were abolished, and a common customs tariff was established with respect to imports from third countries. However, if different product regulations and standards for health or safety reasons and environmental protection—the new tricks of the trade that effectively impede entry—are permitted to remain in place under Article 36 of the treaty, related costs will have the same effect as customs duties in continuing to divide the EC.

To remove these technical, nontariff barriers, the Commission of the EC (in a wide-ranging White Paper of 1985) proposed to accept this guiding principle: If a product is lawfully manufactured and marketed in one member state, it will be allowed to be sold freely throughout the EC. Furthermore, essential health and safety requirements, as well as industrial standards in important fields of production, are to be harmonized. Also, the procedures for public procurement, a sizable part of each member state's GDP, are to be liberalized, and the EC's restrictive policies on state aids are to be vigorously enforced.

Second, the aim of instituting a system ensuring that competition is not distorted required that the consumption taxes of the member states be revamped in such a way that precise rebates are given upon export of goods from one member state to another and that precise compensating taxes are levied on imports by one member state from another. These rebates and compensating taxes, called border tax adjustments, were made uniform throughout the EC with the introduction of a destination-based, value-added tax of the consumption type. Perhaps the most notable achievement to come out of this development was the adoption and implementation of the Sixth Directive on Value-Added Tax in 1977 which prescribes a uniform basis of assessment for member states.

To shift border tax adjustments from borders to books of account (obviating the need for border controls), the White Paper envisaged a tax credit clearance system for the value-added tax relating to intra-Community transactions. Under this system, suppliers exporting to other member states would charge the full value-added tax of their own country, while the customer in the importing member state would take credit for that tax in his return filed with his own administration. In turn, the importing country's tax administration would collate and tabulate the various foreign tax credits and present them for payment to the exporting state under a clearing-house mechanism for all EC members to be administered by the Commission. Net balances would be payable by member states that are net exporters.[4]

Third, approximation is required of effective tax rates on the use of capital. Substantial coordination has already been achieved through unilateral exemptions and tax credits and bilateral tax treaties, but harmonization, particularly of corporation taxes, is essential if free movement of capital is to occur without distortion of the structure of production. In line with its philosophy that agreement on the type of tax should precede agreement on the basis of assessment and the rate structure, the Council of Ministers of the EC, upon recommendation of the Commission, adopted in 1975 a draft directive on the interstate integration of corporation and individual income taxes, as well as on a harmonized system of withholding taxes on dividends.

However, the draft directive became stranded in the European Parliament which argued that it made little sense to harmonize corporation tax rates and the tax treatment of profit distributions as long as possibly large differences in the rules for computing taxable company income continued to exist among member states. This issue is not dealt with in the Commission's White Paper (but it intends to publish a separate paper on the subject). Finally, coordination of the personal income tax and social security systems, which represent the bulk of the tax revenue collected in the member states, has not been viewed as being urgent, although continuing efforts are made to further the freedom of labor by ensuring that double taxation, especially of frontier and migrant workers, does not occur.

The Commission believes that the economies of scale offered by a large common market cannot be reaped fully if various obstacles to industrial cooperation remain in place. National laws and administrative practices hamper the development of cross-border activities by companies of different member states. For this purpose, the

European Interest Grouping, governed by EC legislation, is being set up, and a proposed statute for a European company has been put up for a Council decision. Furthermore, national legislation on limited companies will be coordinated, and the legal position of branches and subsidiaries clarified. The acquisition of holdings in companies in other member states and cross-border mergers are also to be facilitated. In turn, these proposals have tax aspects that may well be the most important obstacle to eventual agreement. So far anyway, fear of revenue loss, either directly or through the emigration of companies to lower-tax member states, has stalled progress.

Quo Vadimus?

This is an ambitious program for moving closer to the ideal of an integrated market with all the characteristics of a single domestic market. The Commission has proposed the end of 1992 as the date at which all these physical, technical, and fiscal barriers among member states should be removed. It should be possible to eliminate physical barriers, which, in my opinion, should be accompanied by much closer integration of external customs and police controls, but the Commission proposes no such change. The shifting of border tax adjustments for the value-added taxes to books of account and coming to an agreement on the harmonization of the excises, further tax coordination, and removal of technical barriers may take us well into the 21st century. As the experience in federal systems, such as those of the United States and Canada, shows, tax coordination between subordinate units of government is an ongoing process even after a single domestic market has been created.

More importantly, perhaps, the Commission appears to attach more significance to the process and the fact of harmonization than to which issues are ultimately harmonized. At least this may be gauged from the Commission's insistence on tax convergence "by reference to the points of departure rather than to a point of arrival" (in its "Report on the Scope of Convergence of Tax Systems in the Community"). The emphasis on tax equalization in the EC appears to imply that tax burdens should be maintained at their present high levels so as not to distort competitive conditions. Tax equalization is certainly not conducive to fostering tax competition, which might bring these levels down to more tolerable levels and result in leaner, more efficient public sectors. The European Council wishes to create "a more favourable environment for stimulating enterprise, competition and trade,"[5] but equalizing extremely high tax burdens may not bring this about if such burdens involve costs that harm the EC's competitive position in world markets.

REDUCING HIGH TAX LEVELS

The initiative for a reduction of the high tax levels in EC countries will have to come from the countries themselves. Without adopting the much exaggerated claims of the new supply-side economists, there seems little doubt that a reduction of the very high tax levels will have a favorable effect on the rate of technological progress, on employment, and on economic growth. Tax reduction may not have much effect on demand, but the available evidence indicates that there are substantial positive effects on supply as well as other benefits, such as a decrease in the size of underground economies.

No Leveling of the Playing Field

Attention from the issue of the detrimental effects of high tax levels on economic performance is diverted by a fairly strong movement to level the playing field, that is, to broaden tax bases, particularly of the income tax, by removing exemptions, reliefs, and special concessions.[6] Specifically, it advocates taxing capital income and gains more widely (and preferably at the same rates that are applicable to other income); abolishing investment incentives, such as accelerated depreciation and tax credits; reviewing the deductibility of premiums for private pension and life insurance schemes, and with respect to private investment in equities; taxing fringe benefits and reviewing deductible costs in earning income with a view to eliminating most of them. Generally, income tax reform is proposed in a revenue-neutral context: Additional revenues would be used to reduce high marginal tax rates; in other words, rate schedules would be flattened.

While the flattening of rate schedules in effect focuses primarily on the taxation of income from labor, the arguments for widening the tax base, which are given more attention, aim at a more comprehensive taxation of income from business and capital. It is doubtful, however, whether the latter move is desirable. Lawrence H. Summers (at the 1986 Annual Conference of the National Tax Association of America) forcefully argued that "leveling the playing field is an issue of little economic importance and that efforts [in that direction] are likely to create more economic nonneutralities than those they eliminate." On the basis of a careful review of the literature. Summers concludes (1) that the costs of nonneutrality or deadweight loss are likely to be very small: on the order of 0.3 percent of GNP, comparable to the typical statistical discrepancy in national accounts; (2) that effective tax rates do not adequately reflect actual tax burdens because depreciation is not properly measured, the effects of different leverage opportunities are left out of account, and tax benefits are inadequately discounted; and (3) that other nonneutralities should also be taken into consideration, such as the immediate expensing of intangible assets, the favorable treatment of owner-occupied housing, and the discrimination against new capital.

In my opinion, the focus of attention, particularly in the EC, should remain on the detrimental effects of high tax levels. It is unlikely that a reduction of marginal tax rates that leaves the extremely high average rates of tax unaffected will have an appreciable effect on saving, investment, or work effort. An important conclusion of a 1985 conference on the effects of U.S. proposals (Treasury I and Treasury II) for improving the fairness, efficiency, and simplicity of the income tax was that "no revenue-neutral tax change will affect economic growth significantly."[7]

I believe that this dictum is also true with respect to proposals to shift the tax burden from taxes on income to taxes on consumption.

Politically, there is ample precedence in the history of taxation that such moves leave the income tax burden at the prevailing level while increasing the burden of consumption taxes. At the same time, available evidence suggests that the elimination of taxes on business income and on capital would produce significant, steady-state welfare gains. This points toward considering the introduction of an expenditure tax, which would eliminate the large intertemporal and intersectoral distortions of the income tax.

How can total levels of taxation in the EC be contained or, better still, be brought down? The best approach, of course, would be to reduce government spending, particularly on income transfers and social services, to more tolerable levels, but I doubt whether a consensus on such a move can be reached in EC countries. Another way to reduce tax levels would be a kind of kill-or-cure remedy, a dose of Reaganomics—that is, a reduction of tax burdens to increase the pressure on expenditure cuts. This has been done in the United States, and the example is now being followed in Belgium.[8] However, this all-or-nothing prescription is a rather questionable policy measure.

Greater Tax Transparency and Direct Representation

The outcome of the game, however, may also be affected by its rules. People's awareness of the taxes they pay may be heightened by the form in which such taxes are levied. Taxpayer resistance, for instance, to property taxes, for which they must save and which they must remit themselves, is much stronger than against, say, income and payroll withholding taxes of which they are largely oblivious, or against consumption taxes which are paid in "installments" on purchases throughout the year.

The transparency of the value-added tax would be improved if countries that do not yet do so would require retailers to list the tax separately on invoices rather than permit them to "hide" it in the price. The same might be done with respect to the excise on purchases of alcohol, tobacco, and gasoline. Receipts for wages and other forms of income subject to withholding might explicitly state the marginal tax rate (the percentage of the last dollar of income paid in taxes) and the average tax rate (by denoting, for example, the number of days per annum an employee has worked for the government). It might also be useful to express income tax rates as a percentage of net-of-tax income, particularly since it is the latter magnitude that drives taxpayer behavior. Thus in the Netherlands, the 72-percent tax-inclusive top income tax rate would translate into a tax-exclusive rate of 257 percent.

There may also be another route. While political attitudes and preferences shape the institutions through which they are expressed, it is also true that institutions affect attitudes and preferences toward public spending and taxation. This is forcefully demonstrated by the economists Werner Pommerehne and Friedrich Schneider who (in *Public Finance and Public Employment*) confront the size of the public sector in 48 Swiss municipalities that have direct representation with the size of the public sector in 62 other municipalities that have indirect representation. They find that the municipalities with indirect representation on average spent 28 percent more on public sector outlays than the municipalities with direct representation. In other words, if citizens are able to influence outcomes directly (e.g., through referenda tying benefits and costs), the size of the public sector is considerably smaller than if there is a layer of representative government between them and the political outcomes. In my opinion, there is a message here that should not be lost on the body politic in EC countries.

For those who believe that more use of direct representation would diminish society's concern for its fellow man, it is worth quoting from a recent paper by Vito Tanzi, entitled "Public Expenditure and Public Debt":

> When we compare some of the countries in which the level of public spending has recently approached 60 percent of GDP with, say, Switzerland, where it is still around 30 percent, can we identify the social goods that those countries have purchased with the extra 30 percentage points of spending? Are the indexes of life expectancy, health, literacy, job security, unemployment, etc., that we try to

manipulate through spending clearly better in those countries than in Switzerland? If the answer is no, then, perhaps, there is scope for a reassessment of the spending categories.

CONCLUSION

I end with an attempt to put the foregoing observations in a balanced perspective. Economic growth and competitive individualism are not the only factors, as economist Herbert Stein points out (in *Washington Bedtime Stories: The Politics of Money and Jobs*). Neither is egalitarianism, with its goal of economic equality of condition. I do not wish to advocate that the social welfare state should be dismantled. The quality of life is high, very high, in the EC, and the care for our fellow men, in Europe and elsewhere, should always be a central concern. Modern, complex societies require strong and fairly large governments to do things the market, however efficient, is simply incapable of doing. But there are limits to the welfare state beyond which lie treacherous territories not merely of economic waste but more fundamentally of insuperable difficulties in maintaining the integrity of the relationships between government and citizens and between private agents.

Pluralistic democracies have always thrived and benefited from a precious but also precarious balance between an economic order that gives the forces of competition full reign and a political order that seeks to maintain and reinforce cultural values in counterbalance to the centrifugal forces of a free market. At the same time, the market and competitive individualism have a vital function in checking excessive and intrusive bureaucratic government. It is the search for the appropriate balance between government power and market power, rather than the size of the public sector as such, that should be the guiding principle in evaluating the role and scope of government as we move into the 21st century.

12
Outlook for Japan*

HIROSHI KANEKO
YUJI GOMI

I. THE TAX SYSTEM OF POSTWAR JAPAN AND RECENT BASIC TAX REFORM

The Development of the Tax System

Japan's tax system was extensively revised in 1950. This reform was based on the Report of the Shoup Mission from the United States, which was headed by Professor Carl Shoup of Columbia University and included such eminent scholars as Professors Stanley Surrey, William Warren, and William Vickrey.

The most important points of the report were the following:

1. It strongly recommended that the direct tax, especially the income tax, should be the primary tax in the system for two reasons: The direct tax is much superior to the indirect tax from the viewpoints of equity and the ability to pay; and

* Parts I through IV were written by Hiroshi Kaneko. Part V was written by Yuji Gomi.

second, taxpayers pay the direct tax with a consciousness of their burden and, as a result, are interested in how tax revenues are used by the government (that is, there is democratic control of public finance). Therefore, the report said, the consumption tax should be imposed only on luxuries and some nonnecessities.

2. The report emphasized the importance of the comprehensive income tax. A broad-based, progressive income tax had already been adopted in 1947 as a part of the reform legislation after the Second World War. The Shoup Report recommended full development of the system. In particular, it emphasized the importance of fully taxing capital gains by an averaging method.
3. The report further recommended a reduction in the rates of the individual income tax. At that time, there were 14 income tax brackets, with the highest rate at 85 percent. The report recommended a rate schedule of eight brackets, with the highest rate being 55 percent. The reasons cited for reducing the highest rate were to aid in the prevention of tax evasion and avoidance and to make tax administration easier.
4. The report suggested the adoption of a net wealth tax with four progressive rates, ranging from 0.5 percent to 3 percent. This was a substitute for the reduction in the individual income tax rates.
5. Finally, the report recommended further promotion of the self-assessment system, which had been adopted in 1947 and replaced a system in which the National Tax Authority would calculate and assess taxes. The report suggested various measures and devices to improve the standard of compliance and enforcement.

Especially noteworthy was the "blue-return" system. For the success of a self-assessment system, it is necessary that businesses keep books and records, make entries of all transactions, calculate profit and loss accurately, and complete their returns honestly. However, since at that time it was not common for Japanese businesses—both individual and corporate—to keep books, it was thought to be too early to impose bookkeeping duties. Therefore, as an inducement, the report recommended that the Ministry of Finance establish standards of satisfactory bookkeeping, and businesses that kept their books satisfactorily could, with the permission of the director of the district office, file their tax returns using a blue form. And only the "blue-returners" could use certain tax advantages, such as loss carry-back and carry-over.

The Shoup recommendations were adopted in the reform legislation of 1950, and the system continued in its original form for some years. However, amendments of two kinds followed.

First, the highest rate of individual income tax was again gradually raised to a very high level in an effort to increase revenue. At its peak, the highest rate was 93 percent (if prefectural and local community inhabitants taxes, which are income tax by nature, were included). The rate of corporate income taxes also rose.

Second, the erosion of the comprehensive income tax began with the introduction of various preferential tax treatments for the purpose of encouraging capital formation and economic growth. In individual income taxation, for example, income from the sale of securities was soon exempted for the reason that such exemption was necessary to prevent the lock-in effect and to vitalize the stock market. In addition, the scope of the exemption of interest income was tremendously enlarged. Furthermore, interest income was given the option of being taxed separately at a low flat rate. In both individual and corporate income taxation, various kinds of special depreciations and special reserves were introduced. The Special Tax Measures Act is now one of the most complicated statutes.

It could be said, therefore, that in the period of postwar reform, equity and ability to pay were the most important maxims of taxation. However, in the period of economic growth since around 1955, the tax system was extensively utilized for various nonrevenue policy purposes, such as encouraging capital formation, foreign trade, technological innovation, and so on. Since the size of the pie and, accordingly, the share of individuals had increased rather rapidly, taxpayers generally did not feel their tax burden to be heavy and thus did not much criticize these preferential treatments. In this period, economic growth was as important as equity and ability to pay.

However, now the tide is changing again. With the oil shocks, the age of high economic growth has come to an end. On account of smaller increases (or perhaps even decreases) in their income caused by the slowdown in economic growth, individuals and corporations have started to feel their tax burdens to be much heavier than before, and as a result, they are increasingly concerned with tax equity. In other words, they are now severely dissatisfied with the tax system and call for a drastic tax cut and tax reform.

Due to the recent slowdown in economic growth, the rate of increase in tax revenue has also stagnated. At the same time, the demand for government expenditure has been rapidly expanding. Therefore, the government has begun to suffer from a gap between revenues and expenditures. For these two reasons, Japan, like many other countries, now needs a basic tax reform. Before discussing recent developments, let us take a look at the present situation of public finance in Japan.

The Public Finance Situation

The gross national product (GNP) of Japan in fiscal year 1986 was approximately 335 trillion yen and the total tax revenue, including both national and local taxes, amounted to nearly 64.9 trillion yen, or about 19.4 percent of the GNP. Direct taxes (income tax, corporation tax, inhabitants tax) have the dominant weight, and the indirect tax is relatively less important.

The most serious problem for public finance in Japan is the gap between tax revenues and government expenditures, which is heavily financed by debt. The accumulated amount of debt was more than 145 trillion yen at the end of fiscal 1986. This amount is more than 2.6 times the national government's general account budget for the year. Both the absolute amount and the ratio of debt service also have been constantly increasing.

Table 1
Trend of Expenditures
(National Government General Account Original Budget)
(Billion Yen)*

	1973	1974	1975	1976	1977	1978
General	**10,799**	**12,855**	**15,841**	**18,822**	**21,544**	**25,676**
Expenditure	% 75.6	75.2	74.4	77.5	75.6	74.9
(Sum of 1–6)	100.0	119.0	146.7	174.3	199.5	237.8
(1) Social	2,115	2,892	3,928	4,808	5,692	6,781
Security	% 14.8	16.9	18.5	19.8	20.0	19.8
	100.0	136.7	185.7	227.3	269.1	320.6
(2) Education &	1,532	1,924	2,589	2,965	3,353	3,846
Science	% 10.7	11.3	12.2	12.2	11.8	11.2
	100.0	125.6	169.0	193.6	218.9	251.1
(3) Public Works	2,842	2,843	2,912	3,530	4,285	5,455
	% 19.9	116.6	13.7	14.5	15.0	15.9
	100.0	100.0	102.4	124.2	150.7	191.9
(4) Defense	936	1,093	1,327	1,512	1,691	1,901
	% 6.5	6.4	6.2	6.2	5.9	5.5
	100.0	116.8	141.9	161.7	180.7	203.2
(5) Economic	140	180	193	201	216	263
Cooperation	% 1.0	1.1	0.9	0.8	0.8	0.8
	100.0	129.3	138.1	144.2	154.7	188.8
(6) Others	3,234	3,923	4,892	5,805	6,307	7,429
	% 22.6	22.9	23.0	23.9	22.1	21.7
	100.0	121.3	151.3	179.5	195.0	229.7
Local Allocation	**2,781**	**3,382**	**4,409**	**3,810**	**4,622**	**5,397**
Grant	% 19.5	19.9	20.7	15.7	16.2	15.7
	100.0	121.6	158.5	137.0	166.2	194.1
Debt Service	**705**	**862**	**1,039**	**1,665**	**2,349**	**3,223**
	% 4.9	5.0	4.9	6.9	8.2	9.4
	100.0	122.4	147.5	236.3	333.4	457.4
Total	**14,284**	**17,099**	**21,289**	**24,296**	**28,514**	**34,295**
	% 100.0	100.0	100.0	100.0	100.0	100.0
	100.0	119.7	149.0	170.1	199.6	240.1

*For each item, first line shows amount of expenditure, the second line shows the percent of the amount to total expenditure, and third line shows expansion on rate.

1979	1980	1981	1982	1983	1984	1985	1986
29,234	**30,733**	**32,050**	**32,620**	**32,620**	**32,586**	**32,585**	**32,584**
75.7	72.2	68.5	65.7	64.7	64.4	62.1	60.2
270.7	284.6	296.8	302.1	302.1	301.8	301.8	301.7
7,627	8,212	8,837	9,085	9,140	9,321	9,574	9,835
19.8	19.3	18.9	18.3	18.1	18.4	18.2	18.2
360.5	388.2	417.7	429.5	432.1	440.6	452.6	464.9
4,294	4,519	4,735	4,853	4,797	4,832	4,841	4,845
11.1	10.6	10.1	9.8	9.5	9.5	9.2	9.0
280.4	295.0	309.1	316.8	313.2	315.5	316.0	316.3
6,547	6,655	6,655	6,655	6,655	6,520	6,369	6,223
17.0	15.6	14.2	13.4	13.2	12.9	12.1	11.5
230.3	234.1	234.1	234.1	234.1	229.4	224.1	218.9
2,095	2,230	2,400	2,586	2,754	2,935	3,137	3,344
5.4	5.2	5.1	5.2	5.5	5.8	6.0	6.2
223.9	238.4	256.5	276.4	294.4	313.7	335.3	357.4
325	383	425	471	504	544	586	623
0.9	0.9	0.9	0.9	1.0	1.1	1.1	1.2
233.3	274.2	304.9	337.7	361.5	390.0	420.3	446.7
8,346	8,734	8,998	8,970	8,769	8,434	8,079	7,715
21.6	20.5	19.2	18.1	17.4	16.7	15.4	14.
258.1	270.1	278.2	277.4	271.1	260.8	249.8	238.
5,288	**6,545**	**8,084**	**9,231**	**7,315**	**8,886**	**9,690**	**10,185**
13.7	15.4	17.3	18.6	14.5	17.6	18.5	18.
190.1	235.3	290.7	331.9	263.0	319.5	348.4	366.
4,078	**5,310**	**6,654**	**7,830**	**8,193**	**9,155**	**10,224**	**11,320**
10.6	12.5	14.2	15.8	16.3	18.1	19.5	20.
578.9	753.8	944.5	1,111.4	1,162.9	1,299.5	1,451.3	1,606.
38,600	**42,589**	**46,788**	**49,681**	**50,380**	**50,627**	**52,500**	**54,089**
100.0	100.0	100.0	100.0	100.0	100.0	100.0	100.
270.2	298.2	327.6	347.8	352.7	354.4	367.5	378.

This gap has been caused because there has been only a slightly increased rate of tax revenue (as mentioned earlier) but a much larger increase in the rate of expenditure (see Table 1, pp. 152–153). For the 14 years of the table, while tax revenues have increased 3.37 times, expenditures have increased about 3.79 times. The reason for the high growth in outlays is the magnitude and rapid expansion in social security expenditures (medical care, pensions, subsistence maintenance, etc.).

As Table 1 shows, while total expenditures have expanded about 3.79 times, social security expenditures have expanded about 4.65 times, and their ratio to total expenditure has risen from 14.8 percent to 18.2 percent in this period. In 1980, the ratio of social security expenditures to gross national income was about 14 percent. However, it is estimated that it will increase to somewhere from 24.5 percent to 27 percent in 2010. On the other hand, the incremental growth in tax revenue will be small if the economy continues to be sluggish and the present tax system is not amended.

Accordingly, it is quite possible that the gap between tax revenues and expenditures will continue to widen into the 21st century. This is a serious situation and should be resolved before it is too late. As it is impossible to cut expenditures substantially, the tax burden should be increased. As shown in Chart 1, the ratios of the total tax burden and total social security contribution to the amount of gross national income is lower for the Japanese than for other developed countries. The tax burden per capita is also lower in Japan than in other countries. Therefore, it would not be impossible to increase the tax burden considerably.

It is impossible, however, to increase the burden of income tax. Rather, in view of the various problems to be described later, a sizable tax cut is necessary. The only alternative is to increase the indirect tax by introducing some kind of general consumption tax. The Japanese system of indirect taxation is a single-stage, selective consumption tax. If the system were to be transformed into a general consumption tax, the increased indirect tax revenues would

Chart 1
Comparison of Tax Burden and Burden of Social Security Contributions as Percent of National Income

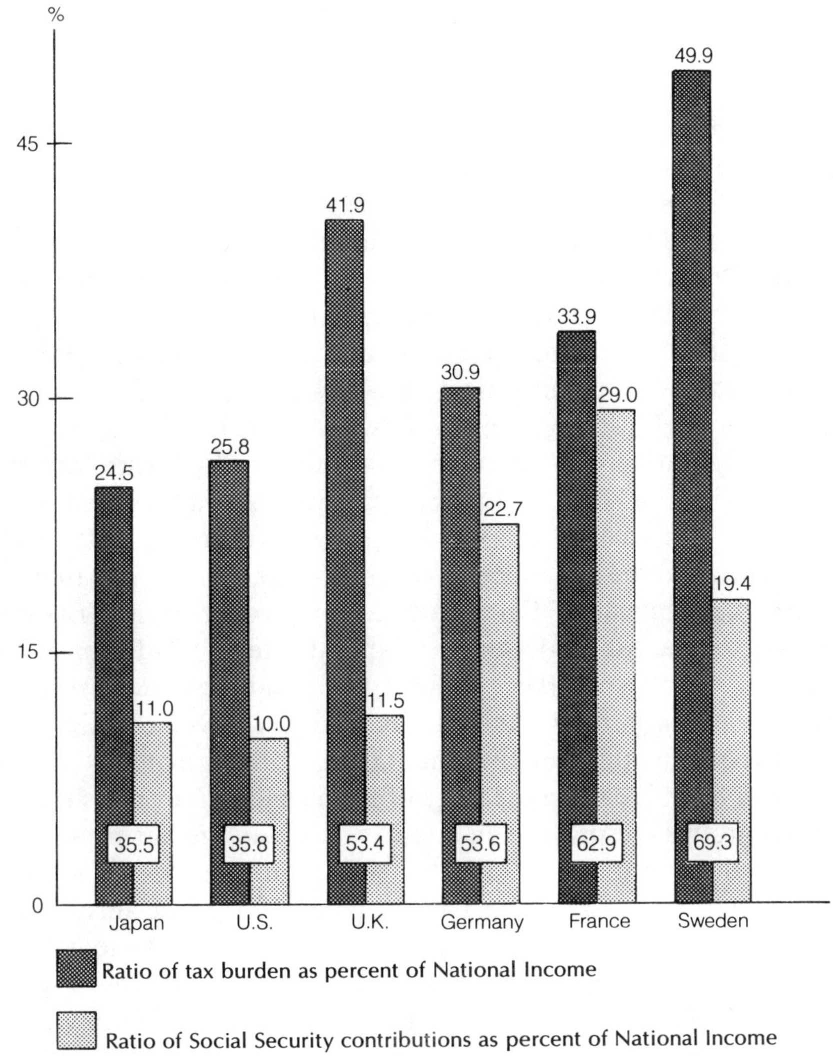

Sources: Japan 1986 budget; U.S. 1983 actuals; Other countries 1984 actuals.

greatly improve the situation. Furthermore, it may be possible to reduce the burden of income tax without causing a new deficit.

A Recent Development: Tax Reform

Given this background, the necessity for basic reform has been generally recognized since the 1970s.

A first attempt at basic tax reform was made by Prime Minister Ohira in 1978. He wanted to help close the gap by introducing a general consumption tax similar in substance to the value-added tax (V.A.T.) levied by the European Community (EC). On the advice of the Tax Policy Committee of the government, Mr. Ohira officially declared his support for the general consumption tax and announced that his cabinet would attempt to introduce it. However, on account of this commitment, he was badly defeated in the general election. His attempt failed even before the bill was drafted.

A second attempt at tax reform was initiated by Prime Minister Nakasone in 1985. Mr. Nakasone's reform plan was different from Mr. Ohira's in that he proposed a package of drastic cuts in the income tax and the introduction of an EC-type V.A.T., with the idea of "revenue neutrality." On the advice of the government's Tax Policy Committee, Mr. Nakasone's cabinet drafted a bill for basic tax reform (the Nakasone Basic Reform Plan) and introduced it in the Diet in February 1987. As Nakasone's Liberal-Democratic party had a predominant majority in the Diet, the bill was expected to pass sooner or later. However, because of strong and fierce opposition by various groups—especially medium- and small-size businesses—to the introduction of the V.A.T., the entire bill was aborted without any deliberation. Instead, the Diet took up a bill for the amendment of the Individual Income Tax Act, which includes a tax reduction, but one that is much smaller than that proposed in the original reform bill. This bill became law in September 1987. But in view of the bitter antagonism that many Japanese showed against the basic reform bill, drastic tax reform will take many years to be realized and should be now considered only as a long-run policy matter.

Assumptions for Long-Run Tax Policy

Though it is difficult to make any definite prediction about what kind of society, economy, and culture we will have in the 21st century, the following three factors should be pointed out as the decisive elements for designing the future tax policy of Japan:

1. The economy will grow very slowly. The growth rate will be low and sometimes may even be negative. Incidentally, the structure of the economy will continue to change, with the service and information industries having relatively greater weight as opposed to manufacturing.
2. The ratio of the aged will be very high in the population as a whole. Needless to say, this will be caused mainly by continuing advances in medical science and health care programs. As is shown in Table 2 and Chart 2 (see p. 158) nearly one-fourth of the population in 2020 will be people over the age of 65.
3. Internationalization will continue in every field of human endeavor, and the national economy will be integrated into the international economic order.

Table 2

Ratio of Population Over 65 for Five Countries

	1950	1970	1985	2000	2020
1. Japan	4.9	7.1	10.3	16.3	23.6
2. W. Germany	9.4	13.2	14.5	16.7	21.2
3. France	11.4	12.9	12.4	14.7	18.0
4. United Kingdom	10.7	12.9	15.1	15.3	17.8
5. United States	8.1	9.8	11.7	12.0	15.4

Sources: Based on National Census (Japan) and U.N. Statistics (Other Countries)

Chart 2
Ratio of Aged People (Over 65)

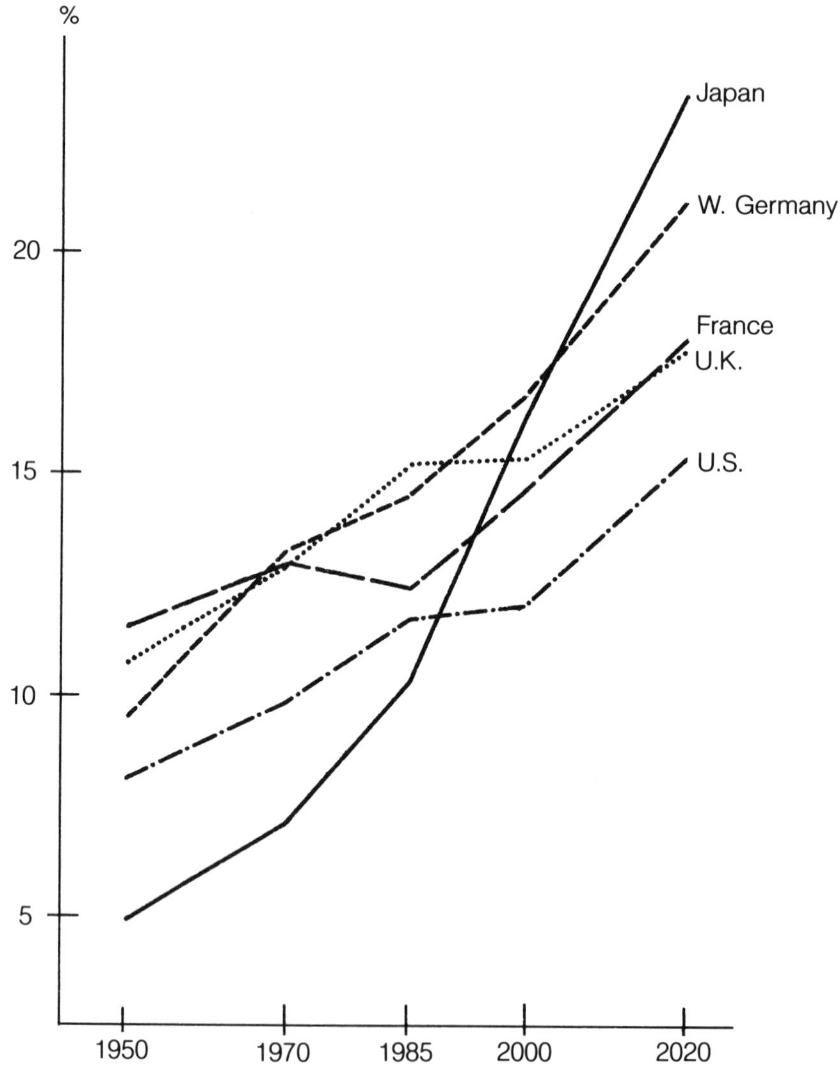

Source: Based on National Census (Japan) and U.N. Statistics (Other Countries)

II. INDIVIDUAL INCOME TAX REFORM

The General Direction of Reform of the Income Tax System

More than 40 percent of total national tax revenue in Japan comes from the individual income tax. The individual income tax system still maintains the basic structure of the broad-based progressive tax recommended by the Shoup Report. The level of minimum taxable income is rather high (in the case of a married salary earner with two dependent children, 2.619 million yen, about $20,952 by the exchange rate at the end of 1987). And the rates are highly progressive (as is shown on the first and second columns of Table 3, p. 160). If the local income tax is included, the highest rate was 88 percent until September 1987.

However, this highly progressive rate structure causes various problems, as the Shoup Report warned. Among these problems are inequality, complexity, disincentive to work, tax base erosion, lack of neutrality, inefficient resource allocation, distortion of private decision making, and so forth. As a result of this highly progressive rate structure, various preferential tax treatments for business and property incomes have been introduced. Because of this, the Japanese income tax system has departed considerably from the objective of a broad-based, progressive income tax and in substance has become a hybrid of the broad-based income tax and the consumption-type income tax. The problem is whether in the long run the Japanese system will or should be transformed into a consumption-type income tax system.

The theory of the consumption-type income tax is rather popular among Japanese economists. Theoretically, it has various merits relative to the traditional income tax. But for two reasons it is not likely that the Japanese will move in this direction.

First, under the consumption-type income tax, labor income will be more heavily taxed than business and property incomes because most of the former will be consumed sooner or later, but a considerable part of the latter will be saved and will continue to be saved,

Table 3
Comparison of Three Income Tax Rate Schedules
(Hundred Thousand Yen)

Previous Schedule[1] (Until September 1987)		Present Schedule[2]		Nakasone's Plan[3] (Aborted)	
Up to 5	10.5%	Up to	%	Up to	%
12	12	15	10.5	12	10
20	14	20	12		
30	17	30	16		
40	21	50	20	50	15
60	25	60	25		
80	30	80	30	70	20
100	35	100	35		
120	40	120	40	100	30
150	45	150	45		
200	50			150	40
300	55	300	50	Over 150	50
500	60	500	55		
800	65	Over 500	60		
Over 800	70				

[1] Prefectural Inhabitants Tax: 2 brackets, rates 2–4%; Local Communities Inhabitants Tax: 13 brackets, rates 2.5–14%

[2] Prefectural Inhabitants Tax: 3 brackets, rates 2–4%; Local Communities Inhabitants Tax: 7 brackets, rates 3–12%

[3] Prefectural Inhabitants Tax: 2 brackets, rates 2–4%; Local Communities Inhabitants Tax: 4 brackets, rates 3–11%

without being used for consumption. Therefore, the consumption-type income tax will violate tax equality between labor income and business and property incomes.

In Japan, to recover this equality is considered to be one of the most important goals of tax reform. If a heavy net wealth tax and/or a heavy inheritance tax is adopted together with the consumption-type income tax, the tax equality problem will be mitigated. However, the possibility of adoption of the net wealth tax is not great in Japan. In addition, it is generally accepted in Japan that the income tax and the inheritance tax should go together in both tax increases and tax reductions.

Second, the propensity to save is very high in Japan. At present, the total amount of accumulated savings by individuals is more than 400 trillion yen. The Japanese population will continue to save in the future without need for encouragement through the adoption of a consumption-type income tax.

For these reasons, the long-run tax policy of Japan will be to maintain the broad-based income tax and to improve it by eliminating various elements of erosion and distortion.

Reform of the Rate Structure

Because Japanese taxpayers, especially employees, feel their tax burden to be very heavy, they are greatly dissatisfied with the present income tax structure. In addition, as mentioned before, the present highly progressive rate structure has caused various problems. Therefore, it should be a goal of tax reform to reexamine the present rate structure in order to reduce the income tax burden generally and to mitigate or eliminate the various problems caused by the current framework.

First, it will be necessary to drastically reduce rates. As is shown in Table 3, the highest rate before the amendment of September 1987 was 70 percent. This rate is exceptionally high when compared to the rate structures of other countries.

Next, the number of brackets should be reduced, and the width of the brackets broadened. As can be seen from Table 3, there were 15 rather narrow brackets before the amendment. This structure was very unpopular among taxpayers, especially employees, because of the bracket creeping it caused.

At the request of Prime Minister Nakasone, the Tax Policy Committee examined the rate structure and concluded that the highest rate should be cut to 50 percent and the number of brackets reduced to six much broader ones. Under this change, adopted in the Nakasone Basic Reform Plan, the tax burden would be considerably reduced at all levels of income, and the problem of bracket creeping would be less severe. The first two brackets (see Table 3, third column) would be 10 percent and 15 percent and would have a rather wide span. According to the statistics, most salary earners would be in one of these two brackets throughout their lives. Therefore, for the majority of wage earners, this rate schedule would almost result in a flat income tax.

Unfortunately, as the Nakasone Basic Reform Plan was aborted, this income tax cut was not realized. The rate schedule in the amendment to the September 1987 Individual Income Tax Act is less drastic, as is shown in the second column of Table 3. It is likely that this amendment will not mitigate much of the dissatisfaction felt by taxpayers and will not eliminate the problems that have been caused by the high progressive rates.

It may be impossible to make the rates as flat as those in the U.S. Tax Reform Act of 1986 because economic democracy is considered very important in Japan and the income tax is expected to have a considerable redistributive function. Nevertheless, it is my prediction that in the long run the highest rate will be gradually reduced to around 50 percent, including the local income tax.

Reform of the Tax Base

As mentioned before, preferential treatments for business and property income have produced inequality between these and salary income. Though employees are granted a rather large "salary income deduction," they are quite dissatisfied with this inequality, and their dissatisfaction could disturb the stability of Japanese society in the future.

In fiscal year 1986, the estimated revenue loss resulting from preferential measures amounted to 1,081 billion yen, or about 6.4 percent of the total estimated individual income tax revenue of 16,819 billion yen (see Table 4). At first glance, this ratio looks small. However, according to my estimate, about 9,845 billion yen (or about 60 percent) of the total individual income tax revenue comes from salary income, and 6,974 billion yen (or 40 percent) comes from other incomes. Therefore, the ratio of the revenue loss to the revenue from other incomes is 15.5 percent, which is rather substantial. The

Table 4
Estimated Revenue Loss from
Preferential Measures of Individual Income Tax
(FY 1986)

Preferential Measures	Amount (Billion Yen)
Exempted Savings	507
Separate Taxation of Interest	15
Separate Taxation of Dividends	44
Life Insurance Premium Deduction	237
Property Insurance Premium Deduction	16
Credit for Purchase of Residence	67
Special Depreciation	6
Special Deduction for Blue-Returns	34
Deemed Corporation Taxation	21
Special Deduction for Doctors & Dentists	99
Special Dependents Deduction	35
Total	*1,080*

preferential treatments enjoyed by business include many kinds of special depreciation and special reserves. Self-employed people are permitted to deduct salaries paid to family members if they are employed full time. However, it is difficult for the tax administration to check whether the family members really worked full time and if the amount of salary paid is appropriate. This is not a preferential treatment per se, but a matter of compliance and enforcement. However, in practice, this deduction for salary paid to family members works like a preferential treatment for the splitting of business income among family members.

In addition, self-employed persons can easily split their business income among family members by incorporating the business and making themselves and their family members executives or employees of the corporation. The salaries paid to relatives who work only part-time are also deductible. Again, this is not a preferential treatment, but it results in tax inequality between salary earners and business people. Finally, more than ten years ago, a "deemed corporation" measure was adopted as a preferential treatment. Under this system, individual business owners may treat their business as a corporation and their deemed salary as salary income on which a substantial salary income deduction is granted. Therefore, in computing business income, business owners may deduct necessary expenses and get a salary income deduction, too.

Also in the area of property income, many preferential treatments have been available. For instance, capital gains from the sale of securities are tax exempt if certain requirements are satisfied. But the most infamous favorable treatment has been that of interest income. There were three kinds of tax-exempted savings in Japan until the amendment of September 1987. The first was the exemption of interest from Post Office deposits of up to 3 million yen. The second was the exemption of interest from small savings accounts, also of up to 3 million yen. The third was the exemption of interest from public bonds savings accounts, again of 3 million yen per individual. Therefore, a family with two dependent children could have tax-exempt savings up to 36 million yen. Since the savings of the average Japanese household in Japan are less than 5 million yen, these exemptions were really extravagant. In addition, the interest from long-term savings was—and continues to be—taxed separately at a flat rate of 35 percent.

These measures had originally been adopted and enlarged to encourage savings. However, the propensity of the Japanese to save has traditionally been very pronounced, and it is likely they would have continued to do so without these measures.

An additional point is that Japan now has enough savings. At the end of March 1986, the total amount of savings and deposits by individuals amounted to 406 trillion yen, of which 287 trillion yen was the aggregate amount of the exempted savings. Therefore, there was no justification for maintaining these preferential measures. The Tax Policy Committee had repeatedly asserted that they should be repealed. However, it had been impossible to do so because of various pressures. Recently, a compromise was reached under which all interest income is to be taxed separately at a flat 20-percent rate, with the exception that the exemption measures already in place would be maintained for the aged and the physically and socially handicapped, such as widows with dependent children.

This compromise was adopted in the amendment of the Individual Income Tax Act of September 1987.

Yet it should be noted that the separate taxation of interest income with a flat rate is still another preferential treatment. To restore tax equality between salary income and business and property incomes, it is necessary to strictly scrutinize the indispensability of all preferential treatments, to repeal as many preferential treatments as possible, and to tax all business and property income in the same manner as salary income. If the highly progressive rates were drastically reduced in the future, most of these measures would lose their justification, and politically it would be less difficult to repeal them. Therefore, the direction of long-run tax policy will be to gradually abolish these preferential treatments and bring all business and property incomes under the application of a drastically reduced progressive rate schedule.

The tax exemption for capital gains from the sale of securities will be abolished sooner or later. The separate taxation of interest income will also be abolished eventually, and interest income will be brought under the application of the progressive rate schedule.

Improvement of the Compliance Standard

The blue-return system has contributed greatly to the improvement of the compliance standard in Japan. At present, more than 90 percent of corporations and about 55 percent of individual businesses are blue returners. The system has also served to modernize the management of business.

Nevertheless, the standard of compliance has not yet reached a satisfactory level. First of all, there are still many businesses ("white returners") that do not keep books and records that meet the standards. And even among blue returners the compliance standard is not satisfactory.

The Japanese expression "kuroyon," meaning literally "nine-six-four," refers to the compliance problem. It implies that while about 90 percent of salary income is collected by the tax administration, only about 60 percent of business income and 40 percent of agricultural income are caught. In fact, no one knows how much the compliance standard, or the rate of "being caught," differs among the various kinds of income. Nevertheless, it cannot be denied that on average there is much difference between salary income and other incomes.

On the one hand, the differences exist because of a very elaborate and efficient system of withholding applied to salary income. On the other hand, since the tax administration does not have enough manpower to make sufficient audits, it is difficult to capture business income and property income accurately. Although there is a withholding system on interest and dividends, it is often difficult to ascertain to whom the interest and dividends belong. Since the income that evades being taxed is often saved at financial institutions or invested in securities under false names, it is necessary to identify the owners of these savings and securities in order to discover tax evasion.

Japan has no taxpayers' identification system. If one were adopted, it would be much easier to detect tax evasion. Therefore, two measures must be taken to improve the compliance standard in Japan:

1. The government must endeavor to encourage more corporations and individual business owners to become blue returners.
2. A system of taxpayers' identification numbers is indispensable for the efficient enforcement of tax law despite the general public's continuing resistance. It is quite possible that the Japanese people will be more responsible taxpayers in the 21st century.

III. REFORM OF THE CORPORATE INCOME TAX

Unlike other developed countries, Japan relies on the corporate income tax as an important source of revenue. It amounted to more than 30 percent of the total tax revenue in fiscal year 1986. Three factors explain this difference: (1) the corporate tax rate is rather high when compared to that of other nations, (2) the profit rate of Japanese corporations is on average higher than that of other countries, and (3) corporate profits before taxes in 1986 were 6.3 percent of Japan's GNP for that year.

There are three problem areas involved in reforming the corporate income tax: (1) the level of the corporate tax burden, (2) the corporate tax base, and (3) the integration of corporate and individual income taxes.

The Level of the Corporate Tax Burden

Corporations are taxed on their income by national, prefectural, and local governments. The aggregate statutory rate is higher than that of the other developed countries except Germany. Since the statutory rate was subsequently reduced in the United States, the United Kingdom, and France, there is little question that the effective rate is highest in Japan.

Because of this heavy burden, Japanese economists and businesspeople have been expressing their concern that not only capital but also manufacturing industries are fleeing from Japan to countries where the effective corporate tax rate is lower. This evacuation of manufacturing industries is contrary to the policy of encouraging and enlarging domestic demands, which the Japanese government has been pursuing to avoid trade conflicts with other countries. Furthermore, this high corporate tax burden will adversely affect the competitiveness of Japanese corporations.

For these reasons, business leaders and economists in Japan have been insisting that the statutory rate has to be substantially reduced. Perhaps it will be a goal of Japan's long-run tax policy to reduce the corporate tax rate to the level of other developed countries.

Incidentally, in this age of rapid internationalization, it is necessary to bring harmony to the corporate tax system in order to eliminate inefficiency in trade and the flow of capital and to maintain international tax equity. Therefore, the harmonization of the corporate tax system should be a long-run policy goal of the whole world. The first step will be the harmonization of the tax rate, which will not be easy and will take a long time. The second step will be the harmonization of the tax base, which will be even more difficult and take a longer period of time because the tax base in each country is the combined result of such various factors as economic policy, political pressures, accounting principles, and so forth. However, I believe that the harmonization of the corporate income tax system should be realized in the early years of the 21st century.

The Corporate Tax Base

The difference between the statutory rate and the average effective rate is very small in Japan compared to that of other countries for two reasons.

First, in computing their taxable incomes, Japanese corporations are severely restricted in the deduction of entertainment expenses. Corporations with a paid-in capital of more than 50 million yen are not permitted to deduct entertainment expenses at all. Corporations with a paid-in capital of 50 million yen or less are permitted to deduct entertainment expenses only to a maximum amount fixed by law. The estimated amount of the revenue increase attributable to this measure was about 783 billion yen in fiscal 1986 (see Table 5).

Second, despite many preferential treatments for corporations in Japan, on average the tax benefits arising from them are very small and have been declining in recent years. There are 19 kinds of special depreciations and 19 kinds of special reserves. In periods of high economic growth, there were even more, and the resulting tax benefits were even larger. However, some of these preferential treatments have been abolished, and the tax benefits resulting from the remaining preferences have been reduced in recent years. Therefore, the loss of corporate tax revenue due to preferential treatments has been decreasing.

As is shown in Table 5, the estimated revenue loss in fiscal 1986 was about 406 billion yen, which was only about 3.2 percent of the total estimated corporate tax revenue. Therefore, the revenue

Table 5
Estimated Revenue Increase and Loss from Preferential Treatments of Corporate Income Tax (FY 1986)

Preferential Treatments	Amount (Billion Yen)
Special Depreciations	154
Special Reserves	35
Special Depreciations and Credits	217
Total	406
Adverse Measure for Entertainment Expense Deduction	+783
Total	*+377*

increase related to the limited deduction available for entertainment expenses exceeded the revenue loss as a result of the various preferential treatments, and accordingly, the average effective corporate tax rate exceeded the statutory rate in 1986.

Apart from the macroeconomic viewpoint, the tax benefits enjoyed by the corporate taxpayer due to these preferential treatments could be substantial for corporations that utilize these measures to the full extent. Therefore, to keep equality among corporations, it is necessary to abolish these treatments or reduce the benefits arising from them.

Since these treatments were introduced under pressure from various interest groups and organizations, it is often quite difficult to revoke them. Moreover, some people think they were adopted to promote justifiable policy objectives and that when equality and efficiency are the trade-off, the former should give way to the latter. However, with a reduction in corporate tax rates, these treatments will be gradually abolished in the long run. It is quite possible that in the 21st century people will think equality promotes efficiency.

IV. Reform of the Indirect Tax

Among the various kinds of indirect tax in Japan, consumption taxes are the most prominent, although they are a rather insignificant source of revenue. The Japanese system of consumption tax is one of single-stage, selective excises, most of which are levied at the manufacturer's level.

The present system of selective excises is based on the traditional philosophy of ability to pay; that is, only luxury and quasi-luxury items should be taxed, and the necessities and quasi-necessities should be excluded from taxation. However, this philosophy has been becoming rapidly old fashioned on account of changing lifestyles, equalization of income, the increasing weight of the service industries, and so forth.

The most glaring defect of the present system is that it lacks neutrality and equality. First, services are generally not taxed. However, the weight of services has been rapidly increasing in recent years. The estimated level of total final consumption by individuals was about 186 trillion yen in 1985, and about 51 percent of that amount was expended for services. Therefore, it is against neutrality and equality to exclude services from taxation.

Second, the choice of the tax object is difficult and sometimes arbitrary. For instance, furs are taxed, but expensive kimono textiles are not; maple chests are taxed, but not poulownia-wood chests.

Third, lifestyles are changing. An often cited example is a wealthy young person who buys ten cheap, fashionable watches that are untaxed instead of one expensive watch that is taxed.

To make the consumption tax system more neutral and equal, therefore, a general consumption tax is more appropriate. Also, in order to drastically reduce the income tax burden, a substitute revenue source is necessary, and adoption of a general consumption tax is thought to be the best alternative.

Furthermore, as previously discussed, public finance in Japan is heavily dependent on debt, and the situation is worsening because of the rapid increase in social security expenditures. To solve this problem and to take care of the future, some kind of new tax with a substantial revenue potential should be introduced. A general consumption tax would be the most suitable alternative.

Failed Passage of the Nakasone Plan and Future Prospects

In 1985, the Tax Policy Committee was asked by Prime Minister Nakasone to examine, under the principle of revenue neutrality, what should be the substitute revenue source to permit a drastic reduction in both individual and corporate income taxes. The opinion of the majority was that a general consumption tax would be the best alternative, and the EC-type value-added tax would be the best type of general consumption tax. The reasons are as follows:

- Since its base is broad, it satisfies the requirement of neutrality and equality.
- For the same reason, the tax rate can be low and still raise the desired revenue without an undue increase in price.
- The forward shifting of the tax will be easily realized through its invoice requirement. The border tax adjustment will be easily effected.
- The possibility of tax avoidance and evasion is relatively small.
- As an added benefit, the "kuroyon" phenomenon could be mitigated.

This majority opinion was accepted by Mr. Nakasone and adopted into his basic tax reform bill (the statutory name of the tax is "Sales Tax"). However, the plan failed to pass in the Diet for several reasons. Small and medium-size businesses strongly opposed the tax and very efficiently organized political opposition. And the government very hastily drafted the bill and sent it to the Diet without polling public opinion. Since there is a general perception in Japan that direct taxes are fair and equal but that indirect taxes are not, such a process was indispensable. Furthermore, in the process of drafting the bill, the content of the system was eroded and distorted under various political pressures. For instance, exemptions were introduced one by one, to the point where the whole bill became complicated and difficult to understand. And for technical reasons, the full details of the system were not made clear.

In view of the strong opposition that the public has shown toward the value-added tax, it may take several more years to adopt it. However, the factors that necessitated considering it will continue to exist. In fact, they will become even more pressing in the future. It is certain that the public attitude must change gradually, and sooner or later the time will come when the Japanese will accept the value-added tax.

V. INTERNATIONAL TAX

Tax Reform, Past and Present

From the early 1950s to the early 1970s in Japan, the emphasis of tax reform was in three areas: the elimination of double taxation, rationalization of nonresident taxation to encourage capital investment from abroad, and economic assistance to developing countries through tax-sparing credits incorporated into tax treaties.

The most notable changes to occur during this period were as follows:

- In 1953: A foreign tax credit scheme applicable to Japanese residents was passed into the domestic tax law. Earlier, foreign taxes were deductible only from taxable income.
- In 1960: In an international tax treaty with India, a tax-sparing credit was first introduced.
- In 1962: With respect to the foreign tax credit, the overall limitation method was introduced in addition to the per country limitation method. The indirect foreign tax credit scheme was introduced. Local taxes as well as the national tax were included in the foreign tax credit scheme.

- In 1964: Japan adopted the Organization for Economic Cooperation and Development (OECD) model tax convention and at the same time entered the OECD.
- From 1965: Japan has concluded many tax treaties that are substantively in accord with the OECD model convention and has included tax credit provisions in all tax treaties with developing countries.

Since the end of the 1970s, tax reform in Japan has emphasized the fair and proper taxation of multinational enterprises that avail themselves of the advantages of tax haven countries. The objectives have been to ensure equity of taxation among taxpayers, including those engaged in international business, and to secure Japan's share of the taxes paid by Japanese multinationals. The principal changes that occurred were these:

- In 1978: Anti-tax haven legislation was passed to prevent unfair and insufficient taxation of international businesses taking advantage of tax haven countries.
- In 1985: The method of computation of the foreign tax credit limitation was improved in an effort to secure tax revenue attributable to Japan.
- In 1986: Transfer pricing legislation on international transactions among associated enterprises was introduced to capture the proper tax due and to maintain the fair taxation of enterprises taking advantage of tax haven countries.
- In 1988: Curtailment of the limitation amount (i.e., a lower ceiling for tax credits) and exclusion of foreign taxes in excess of a maximum tax rate may be introduced in a further effort to ensure Japan's share of the taxes paid by Japanese multinationals.

The Economic and Social Backgrounds of the Reforms

The Japanese economy was not internationalized between the early 1950s and the early 1970s. In this period, tax policy was focused only on the introduction of an ideal international tax system.

Then an increasing number of Japanese companies extended their businesses abroad, and some of them utilized tax haven countries to avoid their full tax burden.

In the early 1980s, many countries tended to intensify the taxation of foreign-controlled domestic firms and foreign branches in their countries. Japanese domestic corporations paid more tax to foreign countries and less tax to Japan on account of foreign tax credits and the transfer pricing mechanism. In fact, some of Japan's biggest corporations in banking, trading, and the oil industry paid no tax or very little to the Japanese government in this period. The reason, in part, was the generosity of the foreign tax scheme, such as the overall limitation on foreign tax credits (as opposed to the per country limitation), the expanded definition of foreign-source income in the computation of the limitation, and the extensive application of tax credits in tax treaties.

Furthermore, those Japanese companies that should have tried through legal appeals to amend the heavy tax burdens to which they were subject abroad, did nothing about the problem themselves. They had no motivation to act since any foreign taxes paid were deducted from their Japanese tax liability and their total tax burden would remain unchanged.

In more recent times of budget deficits throughout the world, tax increases are generally not acceptable to most people as a means of raising revenues. Therefore, efforts are made to collect existing taxes more efficiently through stricter application of current laws. Foreign controlled subsidiaries and the branches of foreign corporations have become particular targets for this intensified tax scrutiny, in part because they are not well supported politically in the host country.

One example of this intensified scrutiny is the aggressive application of the transfer pricing tax. Another such strong weapon might be the Tax Equity and Fiscal Responsibility Act (TEFRA) in the United States.

On the other hand, tax authorities also try to collect a larger share of the tax on domestic enterprises engaging in international business. Good examples of this trend are a strict application or even curtailment of the foreign tax credit scheme and an unwillingness to accept correlative adjustments with respect to transfer pricing.

If these tendencies intensify and spread, disputes among tax authorities to obtain a greater portion of the taxes from multinational enterprises may occur. This could lead to international tax friction and could also give business a heavy international tax burden as well as double taxation. The result could be unfavorable to the international free economy.

Current Problems in International Taxation

The two most pressing tasks in international taxation today are these:

1. Tax equality among enterprises without regard to their activities either abroad or at home must be assured. To achieve this goal, anti-tax haven measures were introduced in the late 1970s, and transfer pricing legislation was written into domestic law in 1986. In an effort to better administer this legislation, the tax authorities of many countries have exchanged information and jointly studied the international activities of industry. To formalize such cooperation, conventions for mutual assistance in tax matters are being drawn up.

2. A fair allocation of the tax on enterprises or groups of enterprises engaged in international business must be secured. This problem is the most difficult, and it is complicated by the conflict of interest among the countries involved. Many steps have been taken, among them increased withholding taxes on nonresident corporations, stricter treatment of foreign tax credit schemes, and an aggressive attitude toward transfer pricing adjustments applied to foreign-controlled subsidiaries. Financial deficits intensify this situation, as do the stricter application of current tax laws, the lack of any concrete, established principle of taxation for nonresident companies, and the absence of an agreement on arm's-length pricing.

In fact, there is yet to be universal agreement concerning the preeminence of the tax treaty over domestic laws. Some countries contend that domestic law supersedes treaty law: One such case is the U.S. approach to tax amendments regarding branch level taxation and second withholding of taxes on interest and dividends; another is the proposed Japanese tax amendment covering foreign tax credits.

The Final Target of International Taxation

In an economic sense, the final target of international taxation is to reach tax neutrality for domestic corporations in every country. If the same tax burden is imposed on the same amount of income earned by a resident corporation without regard to the country in which the income is made, a maximization of welfare is realized worldwide through the most efficient and reasonable allocation of resources.

In the current and, no doubt, continuing economic situation in which a corporation can choose almost any country as its base, and as foreign exchange control is abolished in major countries, it is desirable that the same tax burden be imposed on the same amount of income derived by any country's corporation without regard to the country in which the income is produced.

This goal will require the harmonization of tax systems, tax accounting methods, and tax administration methods of many countries. At present, we are far from this final objective. Yet if historical development follows the fundamental process of dialectic, thesis, antithesis, and synthesis, then international tax development, in my opinion, is in the stage of antithesis.

Eager for a greater share of the tax on international corporations, many countries have introduced aggressive policies of taxing income. The dangerous weapons in this respect are the withholding tax, taxation by estimate, transfer pricing measures, disregard for correlative adjustments, and strict treatment of the foreign tax credit system. If continued, this tendency will result in the so-called bulldog case, in which countries fight for the right to a larger piece of an unchanging pie. In so doing, they may nullify long-standing efforts by many countries and international organizations to avoid double taxation.

The unitary tax in California is a good example of the problem of tax allocation among countries. Yet even if the unitary method of computing taxable income via a specific formula were completely abolished, the problem of determination of arm's-length pricing would remain an issue in the computation of taxable income by means of a separate accounting method.

The difficulty of solving the tax-allocation problem may best be met if it can be studied jointly by many different tax authorities and resolved in an international context in a spirit of mutual concession.

I contend that the tax authorities of most countries have the wisdom to avoid a bullying attitude which would intensify international tax friction and lead to chaos. They should maintain close communication internationally, make their best effort to establish some common standards in determining taxable income, and strive for harmonization within the tax system, as has been accomplished in the EC with the imputation system and the V.A.T.

The road to harmonization will only become longer and more difficult if the burden of direct taxation continues to be heavy. So it is very important to shift from direct taxes to indirect taxes, especially in Japan and the United States. With this shift, tax resources will be secured in proportion to the consumption of the population in each country.

In the 21st century, international tax policy must reach, or at least come closer to, the objective of international tax neutrality, which will lead to the maximization of our economic and social welfare.

13

A Plea for Stable Principles

JACK F. BENNETT

After reflecting from the point of view of an international businessman on how tax policy is likely to change during the next 50 years, I have reached three conclusions:

1. While there will be many—in all probability too many—changes in specific tax rules, the net result will be a tax system still so complex and unprincipled that in the mid-21st century an unconscionably large number of folk like us will still be devoting to the subject a great amount of what might otherwise be useful labor.

2. Measured against what should and could be in place by the end of this period, the national systems of taxation will still be highly unsatisfactory for corporate business and even more unsatisfactory for international ventures.

3. There will not have developed, even among the governments of the larger economies, anything remotely approaching

universal adoption of a common principle as to what proportion of the fruits of enterprise taken by governments should go to the governments of the territories where the ideas and the capital for an enterprise originate, and what proportion should go to the governments of the territories where the enterprise's physical production takes place.

These three lugubrious conclusions are leavened by one more consideration. Despite the fear I sense among economists that continuing international economic integration will intensify competition among tax authorities, I expect that such competition will be the salvation of international business in what would otherwise be a grim world of taxes. Such competition will be the only effective restraint on the rapaciousness of the preparers of tax laws and regulations toward those who, by their nature, are not likely to have the political clout, for example, of the "small" local businessman.

These 50-year predictions are, of course, influenced by my own experience, which over the past 35 years has involved spending a larger part of my time than it is pleasant to recall, trying to educate legislators and officials about the influence of taxation on international business.

This had not been my plan when I left Harvard with my doctor's degree in 1951 and went to work for the new agency set up to implement President Truman's "Point Four" program of technical assistance to developing nations. But I soon became convinced that a greater flow of U.S. private investment to these countries would be of even greater help than direct technical assistance from the many U.S. government agencies that were competing for the agency's funds. This perception quickly led me to recognize the importance of taxation. And yet, to my chagrin, I realized that in four years of graduate study of international economics, I had not heard one reference to the taxation of the movements of international capital. (Perhaps I am living evidence of the old observation that there must be a lot of knowledge at Harvard, since each year those arriving bring in a lot of knowledge, and those leaving never seem to take any away!)

Under the circumstances, I applied myself to trying to become an expert in the public policy aspects of international taxation. I quickly found that it was not a crowded field, so much so that not long thereafter, when President Eisenhower and the leaders of Congress appointed a joint commission on international economic policy, I found myself appointed to the staff and lecturing the senior members of the tax-writing committees on international taxation. And many times since, as a corporate official, I have testified on the subject before Congressional committees.

One might expect that I would have found myself over time before more understanding audiences as the percentage of the U.S. economy directly involved in international trade has grown. Yet the Lord seems to have created in the United States an inexhaustible supply of new legislators with little background or particular interest in international business, with the result that even today, drafting the international provisions of new U.S. tax legislation is often delegated by the Congressional committees at the last minute to inexperienced, short-service staff members—such as I once was. The result is not a structure pleasant to behold. Each year has added idiosyncrasies and complexities which may provide employment to lawyers but deter international capital movements.

Moreover, basic anomalies remain. Income from U.S. investment abroad is often taxed at higher total effective rates than income from investment in the United States, even when the foreign tax rate is lower than the U.S. rate. And the United States seeks to collect considerably more tax on income generated in a less developed country, whose government has rightfully concluded that it does not have the physical and managerial infrastructure to justify a high income tax rate, than on income from a mature country, such as West Germany.

Reinforcing my pessimism about the specific international tax provisions is a lack of optimism about the basic structures of domestic taxation of business income in the future. I do not expect any system of taxation of international business to be set up entirely apart from the domestic systems. Possibly I am being unduly influenced by recent experience, but my hopes were painfully dashed by the so-called Tax Reform Act of 1986, which not only raised the already discriminatorily high total U.S. tax burden on income from corporate endeavor, but also roundly rebuffed proposals to introduce some timid, first steps toward phasing out the double taxation of corporate income and toward reducing the taxation of inflationary increases in revenue as if they were true income.

With respect to what should be, it seems to me that in a really intelligent 21st century there would not be a separate form of taxation of business. Taxes would be applied to individuals, including shareholders and bondholders, and the drafters of tax laws would have recognized in practice what most of them probably already recognize in principle, that there is no justification for the present forms of separate and additional taxation of income earned through corporate investment, and that these present tax rules hamper economic growth and restrain standards of living. One would think that acknowledgment of these tax effects would be particularly appropriate in the United States, where the relative performance in savings and productivity in recent decades has been so miserable.

Nevertheless, my guess is that in 2037, most governments will still be relying on corporate income taxes for a large part of their revenue from corporate investment projects. I acknowledge that some governments, including those of Germany and the United Kingdom, have introduced measures to alleviate the burdens of corporate double taxation at home. Naturally, I hope that someday competition will force similar common sense to flower in the United States. But I am not sanguine.

Moreover, those foreign measures to reduce double taxation at home provide considerably less than complete relief and could well be circumscribed, rather than extended, in the next frantic search for revenue. Even where relief is granted, or continued, in most cases it will probably be in the context of a high-percentage corporate tax rate with a partial credit to the shareholder against some part of his individual tax, if any. In this way, governments are likely to feel that they can still derive revenue from income destined for exempt, eleemosynary, and foreign entities without the necessity of overtly legislating special taxes on these recipients.

I hope I shall not be understood to be arguing for tax subsidies, incentives, or even encouragement for investment either at home or abroad. As long as there are taxes that vary with income, there will be a disincentive for earning income that is reportable. I have not seen a persuasive case arguing that all this disincentive should be focused on earnings from labor and that none of it should apply to earnings from investment.

I recognize that I am thus rejecting the proposals for replacing the income tax with some form of taxation of income minus savings. I also realize that a tax system that treats labor income and investment income equally is likely to create a different amount and pattern of investment (and labor) than might exist in a theoretical world in which investment income were totally free of tax. But I do suggest that in the future tax systems that discriminate, as they do today, against investment income and favor the other types of income should be considered unreasonable, whether that income originates at home or abroad.

It also seems to me unreasonable for taxes on income from an investment within either of two countries with similar domestic tax systems and rates to be less than the total taxes on a similar investment between the countries.

At first glance, it might appear that the present U.S. tax system is based on a principle that avoids discrimination in taxing investment income from abroad, namely, the principle that the government of the territory where income is produced has the priority right to tax. And if that principle is accepted by the United States today, the question might be asked: Can it reasonably be expected to be accepted by the United States in the future and to serve as the basis for a harmonious interlocking of national tax systems?

However, there are serious qualifications to those first-glance appearances. It is true that the U.S. tax system generally allows U.S. corporations to take foreign income tax as a credit against U.S. corporate income tax which would otherwise be due on income from abroad. But credit for foreign taxes is not permitted to the individual shareholder of a U.S. corporation, who must still pay full U.S. individual income tax on his portion of the income generated by the projects in which his funds have been invested abroad. As a result, substantial U.S. tax is imposed in most cases on income earned abroad. This is the result even when the foreign income tax exceeds the total double tax in the United States.

Furthermore, credit is given in the United States only for foreign income taxes, but not for other forms of tax a foreign government may use. In addition, governments do not always agree on where and when income is produced, particularly when royalties for intangible assets and payments for services are provided.

Finally, there are significant exceptions in the foreign tax credit provisions of U.S. law. Just four are mentioned here:

1. A portion of the credit for foreign income taxes is disallowed when calculating a corporation's possible liability under U.S. alternative minimum tax provisions.
2. Even when a corporation's foreign subsidiaries are soundly financed by foreign borrowing and the domestic subsidiaries are soundly financed by domestic borrowing, a portion of any interest paid by the parent company and subsidiaries in its consolidated U.S. tax return is effectively used to deny credit for foreign income taxes paid.
3. When a foreign tax credit cannot be used in a particular year because there is a domestic loss to offset the foreign income in that year, use of that foreign tax credit is permanently denied, in effect, since the next year's domestic income will be fully taxed with no offset by the prior year's U.S. domestic loss.
4. On some occasions, credit for foreign taxes is effectively lost by special provisions introduced to "protect" particular domestic producers from "runaway" plants and the competition in general of U.S. plants abroad. U.S. refineries abroad, for example, if they export in any direction from the countries where they are located, are discriminatorily made subject to current U.S. income tax, even though in the eyes of the foreign tax collector they have not yet earned taxable income and

> have not yet paid any dividends. The result can be the loss of credit for the taxes paid later in the foreign jurisdictions.

For completeness, I should probably mention that under present U.S. tax laws there are cases in which income from corporate investment abroad is effectively taxed at a lower rate than income from a comparable corporate investment in the United States. This can happen when the foreign jurisdiction has a lower corporate tax rate than that of the United States and the foreign investment is made by a foreign incorporated subsidiary that reinvests its earnings for some period before distributing them as dividends to the U.S. parent. Taxes that bring payments up to the full U.S. income tax rate are paid when dividends are paid, but the delay in the U.S. portion of those taxes can lower the effective rate of total tax on the foreign income below the U.S. standard.

Many cases that seem to be of this nature are not, however, since the calculations leave out of account the non-income taxes collected by the foreign government, and sometimes also omit the fact that an apparently low rate of foreign tax in a particular year results only from a different way of scheduling depreciation over the years of a project's life. For U.S. tax purposes, the rate of depreciation permitted by U.S. law is lower on foreign projects than on domestic projects. Moreover, even when the effective rate of corporate tax on a foreign investment is less than that on a U.S. investment, the total corporate plus individual tax on that foreign income is probably more than that on the same amount of U.S. income from laboring.

Our present system resembles a crazy quilt. It not only double taxes purely domestic corporate income at two levels, but it also leads to a considerable degree of double taxation in the form of both foreign and U.S. taxes on the same income. In spite of this, it might be hoped that over the next 50 years, negotiations among nations will bring about some purer system for sharing taxation of the income from international investment. Particularly since the United States may have become—or may soon become—the world's largest international debtor, it might be hoped that the United States would now find it easier to take a balanced look at the taxation of international capital flows in all directions rather than considering the subject just from the point of view of a provider of capital. It might be hoped that a broad and persistent effort in treaty negotiation would lead to a more rational structure of the taxation of international business.

Yet for several reasons, the outlook is not this promising. First of all, there will probably always be academics who point out that, while a pure system based on full credit for foreign taxes might leave an investor undeterred from placing his investment in the physically most promising location, under that system the capital-exporting country would get less from an investment abroad than from a less productive investment at home. From the latter investment, the home economy would receive both the private investor's returns and the government share, while on the investment abroad the home government might receive no revenue.

In rebuttal to this line of reasoning, it can be pointed out that in a large proportion of cases an investment in the United States is not really a likely alternative to a foreign investment and that blocking a foreign investment would just deprive a country of additional earnings. Even when domestic and foreign investments are alternative possibilities, a country whose export and import of capital are in balance would probably still come out ahead from the universal adoption of a pure and comprehensive foreign tax credit system. But a country's capital accounts are rarely in balance, and even when they are, the spokesmen for industries suffering from foreign competition will not be easily persuaded by the argument for global balance.

Recent events have also not been promising for a broad new international tax treaty program. In announcing the cancellation of the tax treaty between the United States and the Netherlands Antilles in 1987, the U.S. Treasury evidenced no concern that the action would cause severe losses to a large number of foreign investors. The Treasury revised its proposed action only after a number of vocal U.S. bondholders pointed out that they would also be harmed. Despite the massive extent to which the United States is now relying on foreigners to provide the funds, which U.S. net savings are not providing, there are currently in Congress a number of serious proposals to place barriers in the way of both direct and portfolio-equity investment in the United States by foreigners, and the current draft of the technical corrections tax bill contains broad provisions overriding all existing tax treaties.

Fortunately, on the other hand, some counterweight to this type of xenophobia is provided by those who recognize that, whether we like it or not, we are in serious competition with foreigners and our nation's tax system can severely handicap us. The effect of such competitive pressures on tax provisions can be seen both in general ways and in ways that are more narrowly focused. An example of the general type was the 1987 decision by a number of governments to reconsider their corporate tax structures. They did so because the U.S. Tax Reform Act of 1986, while raising the overall tax burden on corporations, gave the impression—in many cases unwarranted—that marginal corporate tax rates were being effectively lowered.

A more specific illustration of the counterweight of competition appeared in the 1970s when the United States perceived that the world's financial services business was rapidly shifting from New York to London. This realization finally led to abandonment of the interest equalization tax and other measures that had been introduced in the 1960s to limit U.S. international capital outflows. More recently, the complaints of U.S. firms facing financing disadvantage relative to their foreign competitors led to removal of U.S. withholding taxes on the interest paid on U.S. firms' borrowing abroad. (Removal of that tax could be considered another departure from the principle of priority for the taxing authority of the territory where income is earned, and there are those in Congress today who urge a new U.S. tax on interest paid abroad.)

The effects of competitive pressure are also clear at the state level in provisions relating to the taxation of direct investment from abroad. Florida abandoned its high effective rate of tax on foreign subsidiaries in the state—the result of the application of a so-called "unitary" tax to the worldwide earnings of the foreign investing company—when it became evident that Florida was losing business to other states. (The U.S. Treasury has made clear that unitary tax provisions are not needed to avoid abuse of international transfer prices between related companies. The Treasury has offered to share with the state collectors the extensive and adequate information already available to the Treasury on the bulk of U.S. trade, which has been gathered through its audit programs and agreements for interchange of data with foreign tax collectors.)

I can cite episodes that illustrate the restraining influence of competitive tax systems on the petroleum industry in which I am involved. In the mid-1970s, the Malaysian government, after substantial oil reserves had been discovered on its eastern coast, abruptly decreed a substantial increase in government "take" from oil production. The result was a nearly complete shutdown in further development and exploration. Only after the rules were revised again so that the effective rate of taxation, while still much higher than on other forms of investment income, was more in line with practices in other producing areas did foreign investment in Malaysia's oil industry resume.

In the United Kingdom, a special and additional Petroleum Revenue Tax was introduced in 1975, and subsequent increases took the marginal rate of tax on petroleum extraction to more than 90 percent by the early 1980s. With reason, industry's attitude became cautious. Exploratory drilling was cut in half, and applications for new field developments virtually stopped. The government, faced with concerns about construction jobs, balance of payments, and petroleum self-sufficiency, scaled back the high level of taxes on oil income starting in 1983. The improvements were principally designed to reduce the deterrents to new exploration and small field development projects. The impact was almost instantaneous. Exploration activities surged to record levels in 1984–1985, with a 40-percent increase over the prior two years. The largest number of companies ever, some 130, filed applications for new offshore exploration acreage in the government's next licensing round.

In Canada, additional taxes were imposed on petroleum production revenue in 1980, and subsequently, drilling activity decreased by almost 30 percent. Following the phaseout of these taxes in

1985–1986, drilling activity markedly increased and now exceeds pre-1981 levels.

More recently, other major oil- and gas-producing countries have also felt a competitive need for steps to moderate high effective rates of tax. In 1986, Norway made several significant improvements to its fiscal regime to prevent a major decline in exploration, development activity, and related jobs. Australia, faced with production cutbacks and new project deferrals on account of unacceptable profitability at lower oil prices, has taken what the industry hopes are only the initial steps in improving the fiscal regime and the investment environment. As a result, oil production is expected to be significantly higher in 1987–1988, and project development activities have been accelerated.

The present complex array of tax provisions affecting international capital movements is the result of conflicting pressures. On the one hand, there have usually been pressures for more government revenue, populist preference for loading the tax burden onto "unearned" income and big business, pleas from various unions and firms for "protection" from the competition of plants abroad owned by U.S. investors, and just plain general prejudice against foreigners. On the other hand, there have been pressures from communities and nations wishing to attract investments that generate employment and revenue from firms wishing to remain financially competitive and to have economic access to sources of foreign supply, and from national governments wishing to borrow cheaply and to avoid the embarrassment of extreme decline in the foreign exchange value of their currencies.

I see no reason why any of these pressures will disappear in the future, even though the relative strength of the pressures will vary over time. For this reason, I do not have any great hopes for a one-way progression over the next 50 years toward some simple and principled worldwide structure for the taxing of international business. I recognize that the international integration of business has been increasing, but the importance of international investment is really nothing new.

On balance, the United States has probably slipped backward in its tax treatment of international business in recent years. Looking ahead from present circumstances, I am inclined to feel that the best the international businessman can hope for in the coming decades is that the tax writers will come to realize the damage done by constant change in the rules. This damage comes not only from the effect of uncertainty in hindering economic choices, but also from the vast amount of manpower necessarily employed in trying to influence proposed changes in tax rules and in trying to comprehend and adapt to them once they are adopted. A little stability even in the present, very imperfect tax system would make a considerable contribution to mankind.

14

Political Realities in a New Century

ALAN A. WALTERS

In conjecturing about what will be the main problems and issues of government and the financing of government activities in the 2000s, it would be misleading simply to extrapolate present trends. Extrapolation is useful only in showing the pressures inherent in political and economic processes. They should be regarded as parables rather than revelations. Nevertheless, the order of magnitude of government spending as a fraction of gross national product (GNP) gives a target of sorts for the performance of the revenue-raising authorities.

One must make optimistic assumptions about the retention of degrees of openness of the major countries of the world in the future. It would be easy to assume that the world will degenerate into protectionism and autarky; we have rather depressing models of such "beggar thy neighbor" systems from the miserable 1930s. But in spite of the rash of protectionism now sweeping through the U.S. Congress, I shall suppose, perhaps implausibly, that the absurdities of protection will soon be revealed and the protectionists soundly thrashed in legislatures. Nevertheless, any assessment would be seriously incomplete without some sketch about the consequences of autarky.

THE POLITICAL REALITIES OF PUBLIC SPENDING

Perhaps the most notable feature of the 1980s is that governments of all political colors, consciously and as a matter of responding to electoral pressure, have embarked on programs designed to curb the expansion of public spending. The most remarkable result is their failure.

No one doubts the earnest attempts by such towering statespersons as President Reagan and Mrs. Thatcher to curtail public expenditure, and in some respects they were successful. Nondefense and nonentitlement expenditures in both the United States and Britain have been actually reduced in real terms. But political realities have prevented any substantial check on the growth of entitlements. Of course, some of the gross waste has been eliminated —while much of it has not—but not even the most partisan can claim a success in arresting the growth of entitlement spending. And President Reagan and Mrs. Thatcher are politicians who are most disposed, personally and politically, to cutting spending. Mrs. Thatcher may continue in office to 2000—she would be only 75— but realistically, one must deal with the successors if one is to get some idea of the path of public spending.

From all the signs, it is clear that, under new leaders, the inherent pressures for additional public expenditure will appear again, unchecked by Reagan-Thatcher disciplines. The demographics, which indicate a growing fraction of retirees, particularly in Japan, and the increased cost of the higher standards of medical care point to a rate of growth of the "caring" expenditures considerably greater than gross domestic product (GDP). The only realistic hope for modification of the growth in public spending arises from some reduction in defense expenditure engendered by an enforceable arms agreement. But I fear that to rely on any such development would be cocking a snoot at history.

In sum, there is no sign of escaping the progressive increase of government spending, particularly the caring expenditures, as a fraction of GDP. However, this cannot go on forever. It is bound to be contained, at least in part, by squeezing other expenditure categories. But the basic restraint is the reluctance to levy and, more powerfully, to pay increased taxes in the form of either overt taxes or inflation. The critical determinant is the development of more "painless" taxes, which are unobtrusive, difficult to avoid or evade, and economically efficient.

TAXES IN THE 21ST CENTURY

In the long run, increased expenditures must be financed by increases in taxes. (Inflationary finance is another form of taxation, and borrowings must be repaid sometime.) Tax burdens have increased in all countries of the Organization for Economic Cooperation and Development (OECD)—and most other countries—since the 1960s. Furthermore, in spite of tax revolts, conservative tax cutters, and so forth, the burden as measured in terms of the percentage of GDP taken in tax receipts has increased during the first half of the 1980s. The exceptions are illuminating. The United States is the outstanding example—because of the use of borrowing rather than tax increases to finance the burgeoning spending (see Chart 1). Britain, on the other hand, although increasing public spending about as fast as the United States, has dramatically reduced her dependence on borrowing and thus shown a sharp increase in taxes as a fraction of GDP.

The first point to settle is whether or not there is a natural ceiling to the fraction of income taken in taxes. Many decades ago, Colin Clark averred that there was such a ceiling, of 25 percent, and that any country attempting to exceed such taxation would suffer inhibitions to its growth and development. A glance at Table 1 (p. 194) shows that it is dangerous to try to formulate such rules, at least from the foundation of economic analysis alone. There is, however, a political case to be made for some sort of ceiling. There is some

Chart 1 Overall Tax Burdens as Percent of GDP for OECD Member Countries.

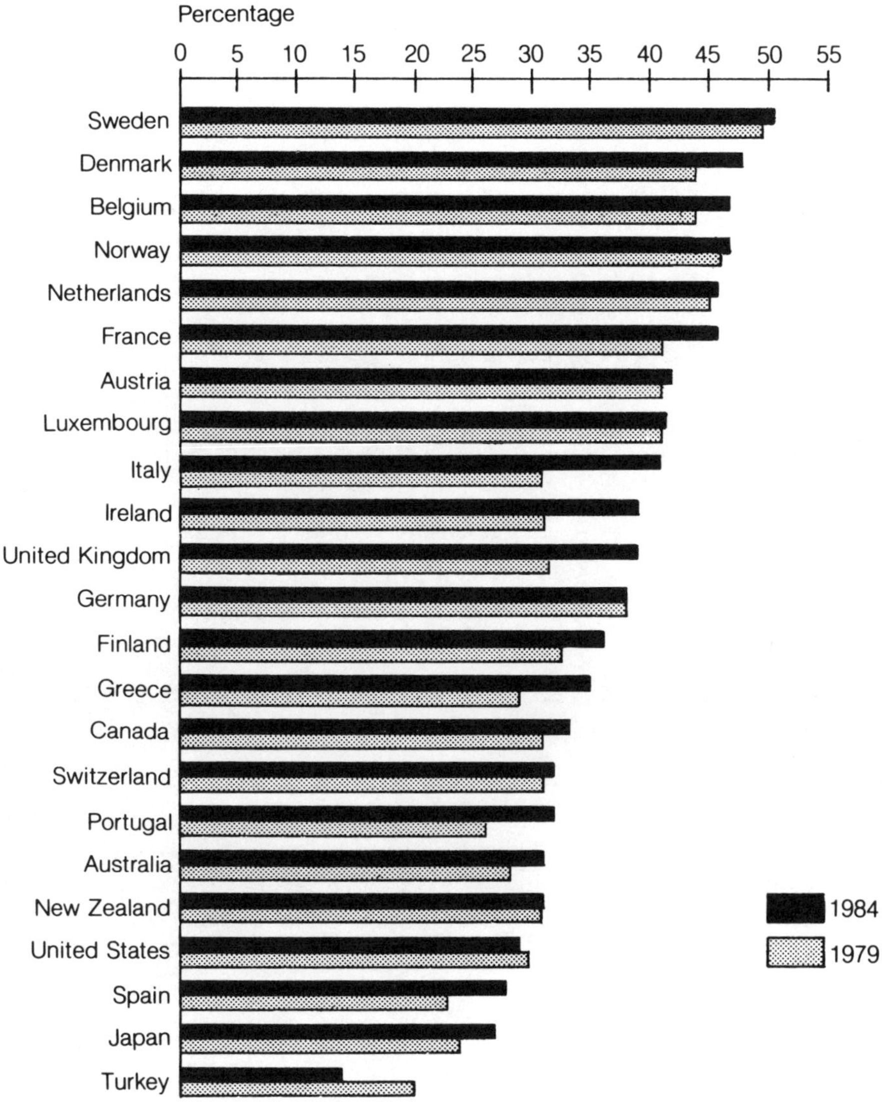

Source: Revenue Statistics of OECD Member Countries, OECD, Paris, (1986).

Table 1
Tax Revenues Expressed as a Percent of GDP at Market Prices

	Total Tax Revenue			Personal Income Taxes			Social Security Contributions						All Other Taxes		
							Employees			Employers					
	1981	1984	1985	1981	1984	1985	1981	1984	1985	1981	1984	1985	1981	1984	1985
Australia	31	31	NA	14	14	NA	—	—	—	—	—	—	17	17	NA
Austria	42	42	42	10	9	10	5	5	6	7	7	7	20	20	20
Belgium	44	47	NA	16	16	NA	4	6	NA	8	8	NA	16	17	NA
Canada	34	34	34	12	11	11	1	1	2	3	3	3	19	18	18
Denmark	45	48	49	24	24	25	1	1	1	0	1	1	21	22	23
Finland	35	36	37	16	16	17	—	—	—	3	3	3	16	16	17
France	43	45	46	6	6	6	5	6	6	12	13	13	20	21	21
Germany	38	38	38	11	11	11	6	6	6	7	7	7	14	14	14
Greece	29	35	NA	4	5	NA	4	5	NA	4	5	NA	16	20	NA
Ireland	35	39	38	11	12	12	2	2	2	3	4	4	19	22	21
Italy	36	41	NA	9	11	NA	2	3	NA	10	10	NA	15	18	NA
Japan	26	27	NA	7	7	NA	3	3	NA	4	4	NA	13	14	NA
Luxembourg	43	41	NA	12	11	NA	5	4	NA	7	6	NA	19	20	NA
Netherlands	45	46	45	11	9	9	8	8	8	8	8	8	18	19	20
New Zealand	32	31	NA	20	18	NA	—	—	—	—	—	—	12	14	NA
Norway	49	46	48	13	11	11	2	3	3	7	7	7	26	26	28
Portugal	31	32	31	NA	NA	NA	3	3	NA	5	5	NA	22	24	NA
Spain	25	28	28	5	6	6	2	2	2	9	9	9	8	11	11
Sweden	51	50	51	20	19	20	—	—	—	14	13	12	16	18	19
Switzerland	31	32	32	11	12	11	3	3	NA	3	3	NA	13	14	21
Turkey	20	14	16	10	6	5	—	—	—	1	1	1	10	7	10
United Kingdom	37	39	39	11	10	10	2	3	3	3	4	4	20	21	22
United States	31	29	NA	12	10	NA	3	3	NA	5	5	NA	11	11	NA

Source: National Westminster Bank Quarterly Review, May 1987.

level of taxation at which additional taxation becomes "politically impossible" and the pressure for reductions difficult to resist.

What determines this level? I would conjecture that it tends to increase with the level of income per capita but diminishes with the growth rate. (I am not claiming any cause and effect in these relationships.) Moreover, it depends critically on the form of public spending and the efficiency of the public sector. For example, the efficiency of the Swedish public sector gives a much higher tolerance level than the case of the United Kingdom or the United States.

I suspect that for the Western industrial countries the pressure for tax containment becomes particularly severe as the percentage rises above 40 percent (as measured during recession periods). Poujadistes take to the streets, and even respectable people are tempted from the bright paths of rectitude into the underground economy. Although the shady statistics of the underground economy are notoriously vague, I would conjecture that when it rises over 7 percent of the GDP, there is clear evidence of the impossibility of raising further taxes.

In short, I suspect that between the political pressures for spending, particularly in the caring category, and the political constraints of taxation, the tax rates of most Western industrialized countries will decline slightly from their present high values of 46 to 50 percent, and those of Japan and the United States will increase from their low figures of 27 to 30 percent. I envisage a "regression to mediocracy" on the part of the industrialized Western countries.

As for the developing countries, as their incomes per capita increase they, too, will boost, even overboost, their caring expenditures. Countries such as Taiwan will find that the government can no longer resist the call for social security, unemployment benefits, and so forth, and the long climb will begin.

An Equalization Process?

With my major premise of reductions in protectionism and increased freedom for the mobility of capital, one might expect that there would be considerable market pressure for the equalization of tax rates, both marginal and average. Countries that maintain high rates of tax on capital, for example, would find that there was a leaching away of capital to other countries that maintain more propitious rates of tax. During the last five years, we have observed massive capital flight from many developing countries—Argentina, Mexico, and Venezuela are the most publicized examples—but one can observe similar effects in many other countries, such as the United Kingdom in 1974–1979. With more opening of capital markets and advances in information technology, the ultimate sanction of capital flight is likely to put persistent pressure on countries to move toward a central tax role.

So far, the theory goes; but political realities suggest that even the governments of Western democracies will find this a difficult pill to swallow. Expropriating savers has been a popular policy in many countries for these many years since the Second World War, and effectively, the mobility of capital denies that opportunity. This will mean a considerable pressure to return to exchange and capital controls for those few countries that do not now exercise such controls—the United States, the United Kingdom, and the Federal Republic of Germany are the main ones in the industrialized West. An intensification of controls is called for in France, Italy, Japan, and others, where capital controls are still intact.

A sure sign that capital controls are creeping back into fashion is the fact that many "liberal" economists are advocating them as the only way to check the so-called destabilizing movements of "hot money" that are said to cause exchange rates to deviate markedly from the levels that such economists deem appropriate. James Tobin, for example, has called for more "friction in the system," and Rudiger Dornbusch has asserted that capital controls should be considered an ordinary policy instrument of public finance. The impatience of economists with a market reality that does not conform to their models has increased their entirely natural animosity toward free contractual arrangements. (My guess is that the development of information technology will enable capital owners to outwit the regulators. The bureaucracy will always lag behind the private sector in the use of new methods and techniques of avoiding the network of controls.)

With this most important reservation on the return of capital controls, one may ask how this equality, or near equality, of the tax treatment of capital is to be achieved. In extreme form, shall we go down to the lowest common denominator, up to the highest, or perhaps somewhere in the middle? Or will the world be dragged along to the levels of its largest economy, which may still be the United States? Nor is equality strictly a matter of the level of capital taxation: There is also the issue of the form of the capital taxes. The basis and the base, the rates and the progression are all under a similar equalizing pressure.

In my view, the world is likely in the future to act more rationally in taxing owners of capital than it did from the 1940s to the 1970s. It is widely recognized that high tax rates, and particularly the double taxation of savings, have inhibited thrift and capital formation. The attempt to expropriate the capitalist failed, of course, but it did an enormous amount of harm in the process. Thus it is more likely that the modest rates of tax, such as those exacted by the United States, will be the model for world harmonization.

Political pressure will undoubtedly serve to maintain some forms of taxation that should logically have been abolished. The main example is the tax on corporations. Although it is a discriminatory tax against a particular type of organizational form, and although it is levied irrespective of the income level and taxable capacity of the final recipients of income (the shareholders), the corporation tax is too tempting a political target to forego. Political poseurs could never abjure such a tax on the "fat-cat corporations," big business, and so forth. But we have surely learned to make the tax at least moderate.

The increasing mobility of capital and the ramifications of multinationals will make the practice of setting up corporations in the most propitious tax environment more practical and attractive—the "Delawarization" of corporations. Nevertheless, politicians and their treasuries can cause enormous havoc by unilaterally abrogating tax treaties between countries. An example is the recent termination of the United States treaty with the Netherlands Antilles.

TAXATION OF INDIVIDUALS AND FAMILIES

First, regarding the income tax. In most OECD countries, income taxes, excluding social security contributions, amount to between 10 percent and 15 percent of GDP. Sweden and Denmark are the most notable exceptions, with 20 and 25 percent of GDP taken in income taxes. (If we add social security, however, the Swedes pay about one-third of their GDP in income and social security taxes.) The marginal rates of tax vary even more from country to country and with respect to income conditions than do the average rates of income tax. Note also that they cannot be sensibly calibrated against GDP but must be associated with a family income level.

There is some pressure to harmonize rates of income taxes. The alarm that has been expressed in Europe at the supposed torrential "brain drain" to the United States in response to the recent reduction in marginal tax rates is some evidence of the pressure. It is widely thought that the United States has set the standard for personal taxation in the rest of the OECD.

In my view, this pressure has been much exaggerated. Certainly the drive to equalization is much less with labor than with capital. Workers, even professional people, are much less mobile than portfolio capital and direct investment even when there are not artificial barriers to movement. In the European Economic Community (EEC), for example, although the formal barriers to movement have been lowered substantially, if not quite eliminated, there has been only modest intra-EEC mobility; indeed, it has been miniscule compared with the migratory pressure from outside the Community. And countries such as the United States and those of the EEC do have formidable barriers against the entry of would-be residents, which are unlikely to be substantially removed and more likely to be increased, during the next two decades. I therefore judge that the opportunities for considerable variations in income tax structures and levels will remain well into the 21st century.

However, I suspect that the income tax will decline in relative importance as a source of revenue. The income tax is, first of all, extraordinarily "painful" to those who pay it. The elaborate forms and complexities have elicited rage from the populace and promises of simplification from the politicians, and attempts are made to simplify, such as eliminating loopholes, widening the base, and reducing the rates. The 1986 Tax Reform Act in the United States is a shining example of such an attempt. But it is also, alas, an aberration and, in my view, is likely to be only a brief interlude in the history of increasing complexity.

Politicians, not to mention powerful lawyers, accountants, and so forth, have a vested interest in complexity. In gaining political support and campaign funds from particular groups, the main thing political candidates have to sell is tax loopholes. In the absence of any constitutional prohibition on granting loopholes and special tax privileges, these will continue to be the currency of our politicized economic life. When the incentives to complicate are great, it is doubtful that simplicity will survive.

The regression of all income tax systems is toward the "gruyere" form. Such systems are not only bureaucratic nightmares; they are demonstrably unfair and discriminatory—and so they encourage evasion and all the corrosive characteristics of a morally indefensible system. Many scholars of public finance have been looking for a system of raising revenues that is not subject to quite the political temptations of the income tax and is less painful for the taxpayer.

The most popular alternative is the value-added tax (V.A.T.). In principle, all productive activity can be characterized as business adding value to the raw materials and capital that are bought, transformed, and sold to some other business or consumer. It is the value added by the business which constitutes the base on which the V.A.T. of, say, 10 percent is levied. The deduction of the value (including V.A.T. levied) of purchases ensures that there is no double taxation (as in the simple sales tax, where taxes escalate according to the length of the chain of eligible transactions). The main attraction of the V.A.T. is that it most nearly approaches the desideratum of neutrality—at least in principle. No industry should get a discriminatory tax break.

In practice, however, different rates have often been applied to different commodities. For example, in the United Kingdom, food is rated zero compared with 15 percent on most other commodities. And as a general rule, exports are also exempt from the V.A.T., thus creating a generalized export preference.

Perhaps the big advantage, at least to governments, is that the V.A.T. is much less painful than the income tax. It is administered and collected by business and incorporated in the final price in the shops, as "V.A.T. included." It is rare that, as distinct from the sales tax, the customer sees it as a separate item. It is subsumed in the system.

The V.A.T. is a comparatively recent tax instrument, but it has become increasingly important in Europe, particularly where the income tax has demonstrated its inefficacies. The European Economic Community (EEC) requires a V.A.T. system in all its members and collects the community revenue from a V.A.T. imposed on the states. Proposals for harmonizing the V.A.T. rates in the 12-nation community by 1992 have generated much heat in Brussels. Suggestions in recent years that such taxes be imposed in the United States as a way of reducing the deficit have received some publicity and, in the Reaganomic ambience, much obloquy.

I suspect that, notwithstanding occasional setbacks, such as Nakasone's embarrassment in Japan, the V.A.T. will come more and more to replace the income tax as one of the main sources of revenue. Once the structure of the V.A.T. is in place, it is most tempting for the treasuries to increase V.A.T. rates rather than contemplate a rise in income tax rates and the flurry of loopholes they engender. It may be that the United Kingdom will be one of the leaders in such a move—but this is pure speculation.

One of the main objections to the V.A.T. is that it makes it so much easier for politicians to raise taxes. Indeed, in the United States, it is the additionality of the V.A.T. that has given rise to such opposition. Paradoxically, the fact that the V.A.T. is a tax with both low discrimination and perception is reckoned by many to be a powerful argument against it. This is odd. Good taxes are now bad. As Macbeth said, "fair is foul and foul is fair." But those who oppose the V.A.T. on these grounds—and they include Nobel laureates Milton Friedman and James Buchanan—have powerful reasons for arguing that easier taxes beget large government. They are mainly concerned with containing the expansion of the state. When it becomes less painful to collect taxes, then it is likely that expenditure will also expand to spend the proceeds.

Nevertheless, I doubt the Friedman/Buchanan argument will have much weight against the political pressures that have prevailed consistently over these many postwar years. I therefore stick to my conjecture that the V.A.T. will increasingly become the tax of the 21st century.

Its big political disadvantage is its lack of progressiveness. And there is a populist pressure to "soak the rich," or levy the burdens where they can most easily be borne. In order to assuage these demands, I suspect—and I am on much less certain ground here—that many countries will adopt some form of capital levy. Socialist governments are always tempted to take this course, and then conservative governments are unlikely to promise to dismantle such a "moral" impost. Of course, countries, even rampantly socialist ones, will learn that the tax rates have to be modest—well below those of Sweden, for example. But the need to go through some visible process to reduce the inequalities of wealth is entirely understandable.

CONJECTURES AS CONCLUSIONS

Provided there is no backsliding into protectionism and autarky, and, indeed, in the hope that markets continue to open wider, there will be continuing pressure to equalize tax treatments of capital and some more modest pressure to equalize the tax rates of income and outlay. This will have only limited success in restraining the more extreme statists (since they will erect suitably high barriers), but it will bring effective pressure to bear on the high-tax states of Western and Southern Europe. The same equalizing pressure will have the opposite effects on low-tax nations—the United States, Japan, and newly industrialized Pacific Basin countries. In the democracies, this upward tax pressure will be reinforced by the inherent process of selling loopholes and by the eventual adoption of less painful taxes, such as the V.A.T. This will be praised, in my view quite erroneously, as part of the "international coordination of economic policy," which is now so fashionable as to be regarded as the fad of the era.

Alas, the main conclusion for the United States is that taxes will increase (as a fraction of GDP). I see no Reagan redux in the 21st century; but I confess I never anticipated a Reagan in the 1980s. Perhaps, we should read the prophets rather than pretend to emulate them.

15
Faith in Market Forces

JOHN A. KAY

One of the most important characteristics of the 20th century has been the steady increase in the scale and scope of government intervention in the private sector of the economy. What of the 21st century?

Simple extrapolation would suggest that well before that century reaches its end, all economic activity would be in the hands of the state. But there is more than *reductio ad absurdum* to indicate that such an outcome is unlikely. More sophisticated extrapolation would observe that the last decade has seen a marked check in that growth. There has been a shift not only in policy but in the framework of intellectual ideas that determines policy. This shift has taken place in four broad areas: tax structures, welfare systems, privatization, and deregulation. An examination of the origins of the shift provides a basis for assessing whether the last 10 years or the first 75 years of the 20th century provide the better guide to what citizens will expect of their governments in the 21st century.

TRENDS IN PUBLIC EXPENDITURE

At the beginning of the century, public spending in major Western economies was less than 10 percent of national income, as compared with between 30 and 40 percent today. Moreover, the pattern of spending was different from today's in shape as well as size. In the United Kingdom, for example, almost half of all expenditure was on defense—actually more than half if the cost of interest payments on the national debt, which largely reflected the legacy of past wars, is included in defense spending. Education was an important component of the remaining expenditure, but the government spent very little on welfare or, directly or indirectly, on health.

The growth of public spending has been consistent through the 20th century, but the displacement effect of the two major world wars deserves to be noted. The very large increases in expenditure they entailed broke new ground in terms of the scale of government activity and in accustoming taxpayers to different levels of the tax burden. While expenditures and taxes have generally fallen when wars have ended, they have never returned to their earlier levels. For the United States, a smaller effect of this kind can be attributed to the Vietnam war. In that period, however, expenditures, as reflected in tax revenues, rose rapidly in almost all countries (see Table 1). Between the early 1960s and the mid-1970s, every major Western economy saw a substantial increase in public spending as a share of national income.

Countries differ substantially, however, both in the overall level

Table 1
Tax Revenue as Percent of National Income (GDP)

	1960	1970	1976	1985
France	35	36	39	46
Germany	31	33	37	38
United Kingdom	29	37	35	39
United States	27	30	29	29

Source: Revenue Statistics of OECD Member Countries, OECD, Paris, (1987).

of their expenditure and in the way in which it is made up. As Table 2 demonstrates, the highest spending levels are to be found in Scandinavia. Other Western European countries follow, while the United States and Japan come far behind. Although the share of spending has been increasing everywhere, the rankings have been remarkably constant over the 30 years or so for which comparable data have been collected. It is evident that trends in public spending reflect deep-seated cultural attitudes rather more than short-term political trends.

More than a quarter of British public spending is on welfare benefits. Four other program areas—education, health, defense, and debt interest—each amount to about 10 percent of the total. This composition of public expenditure is not very different from the average for Europe or for the developed world as a whole. Some of the more important deviations from the average are identified in Table 3. One important characteristic is the influence of demographic factors. Welfare spending is predominantly for the old, education for the young, and health care for both the old and young. The period of particularly rapid growth in spending was one in which the proportions of both old and young in populations increased rapidly.

Table 2
Tax Revenue as Percent of National Income (GDP), 1985

Sweden	51
Denmark	49
France	46
Italy	35
United Kingdom	39
Germany	38
Switzerland	32
United States	29
Japan	28

Source: Revenue Statistics of OECD Member Countries, OECD, Paris, (1987).

Table 3
Differences from Average
Public Spending Proportions

Defense	High	United Kingdom, United States
	Low	Japan
Education	High	Belgium, Denmark
	Low	Germany, Japan
Health	High	Germany, Ireland
	Low	United States
Social Security	High	Belgium, Denmark, Netherlands
	Low	Australia, Japan

Source: Peter Saunders and Fredrich Klau, "The Role of the Public Sector: Causes and Consequences of the Growth of Government," *OECD Economic Studies* no. 4, OECD, Paris, (1985).

The rise in expenditure is even greater, however, than can be accounted for by these demographic factors. At first glance, it might seem that increases in the numbers requiring benefits, or in expenditures, would lead to downward pressure on the levels; however, experience seems to demonstrate the reverse. The rise in the numerical importance of pensioners was matched by a rise in their political importance, and retirement provision became a political issue in many countries, often for the first time, in the 1950s and 1960s. The increase in the numbers requiring education or health spending was similarly associated with concern about the quality of provision; therefore, these expenditures also rose rapidly.

From the mid-1970s, however, the growth in public spending has been considerably slower. As Table 1 (p. 204) shows, the share of public expenditure in overall income has been broadly stable in Germany and the United States; although there were continued increases in Britain and in France, both countries have achieved some reduction since 1983. Similar trends are apparent in other countries. Why did this happen? The explanation begins roughly with the oil crisis of 1973–1974. The recession that followed tended to increase expenditure and depress tax receipts, thus throwing government budgets into severe deficits (where many of them have remained ever since). The associated inflation gave greater priority to policies of fiscal and monetary restraint. There has been downward pressure on public spending ever since.

There were also more fundamental changes. The demographic factors that had driven public spending increases in the previous two decades largely worked themselves out. Birth rates throughout the Western world have been declining since the early 1960s. The number of pensioners in European countries stabilized, and while in North America and Japan the numbers continued to increase, the rate of increase slowed. However, supporting this trend was the development of a more critical attitude toward the economic role of the state.

THE CHANGING INTELLECTUAL BACKGROUND

We talk of Reaganomics or attribute changes in Britain's economic policy and performance to Mrs. Thatcher. This personalization is superficial, however, and although political developments have played a part in recent reductions in the economic role of the state, they are more the reflection of a change in intellectual climate than the cause of it. In Australia and New Zealand, Labor governments have been setting the pace in tax reform and in deregulation, while in West Germany, Conservative governments have done much the same. The planned economies of China and Eastern Europe have recognized an increased potential for market forces. The paradigm of the deregulated industry is the Carter administration's abolition of controls on U.S. civil aviation. The trend to disengagement is not simply the result of rightward shifts in the political pendulum. It will not necessarily be reversed when that pendulum swings back.

The shift that has occurred is primarily a change in emphasis, from concern with the failure of markets to concern about the failure of regulation. In most of the Western world, it is recognized that markets are effective mechanisms for promoting efficiency, both in the static sense of allocating and distributing resources appropriately and in the dynamic sense of promoting innovation and change. But markets are also imperfect mechanisms. Public goods—justice, defense, policing—must inevitably be provided by the state. Many people feel that the ways in which the market limits access to health care or education requires modification. For some commodities, such as domestic water supply, competitive provision is simply impracticable; yet others, such as banking or military procurement, are seen as too important to be left to the market. Judgments of these kinds have motivated an increasing degree of government involvement in what have remained predominantly market economies.

Any economic views held in 1950 were inevitably influenced, on the one hand, by the obvious failures of capitalist economies in the Great Depression of 1929–1933 and, on the other, by the successes of Allied governments in mobilizing resources to fight the Second World War. It is easy to see how an exaggerated belief in the capacity of a rational government intervention to remedy market failure was formed. For those who held this belief, it was enough to specify what the criteria of intervention should be. It was taken for granted that governments and their appointees (such as the managers of publicly owned firms) would be willing and able to implement policies based of these criteria. Thus Herbert Morrison, architect of the postwar British nationalization program, stressed that:

> the public corporation must not be a capitalist business . . . it must have a different atmosphere at its board table from that of a shareholders meeting: the board and its officers must regard themselves as the high custodians of the public interest.[1]

Although Morrison's exposition is particularly clear, this view of the possibilities of rational economic management was by no means exclusively a Socialist one. Thus as Robert Skidelsky writes:

> [Keynes] meant by the state something very different from what the modern economist or political scientist means by it. For Keynes the distinguishing characteristic of the state was not mechanism or function but motive. He meant by it a nexus of institutions working for the public good. These institutions could be privately owned; they could supply goods and services through the market. But their

> tradition, prestige or situation was such that those who managed them were constrained to take the public good into account in making their decisions. Given the strong Victorian tradition of public service—which was not at all the same as working in the public service—Keynes's motivational definition of the state was well-grounded in contemporary thought and experience.[2]

The problems of this approach can now be seen. The job of the "high custodian of the public interest" is not an easy one; even Plato recognized that the philosopher-king was a very special breed. It does not require a particularly cynical view of human nature to recognize that politicians seek to appeal to public opinion, that managers may be concerned to expand or defend their organizations, and that tax administrators or legislators will respond to short-term, popular pressures. In the face of these constraints, the high custodian of the public interest is expected not only to assemble the information needed to determine what the public interest is but also to translate it into operational instructions for tax collectors and coal miners—public employees who, in turn, are confronted by their own mixture of personal interests and concern for the public good.

Regulatory failure is caused, then, by dual difficulties: of arousing appropriate incentives to pursue the public interest and securing appropriate information to determine what the public interest is. The particular merit of market organization is that it offers solutions to these problems. Markets are efficient in their use of information, and they deal with incentives by harnessing self-interest to the general good—Adam Smith's invisible hand, which led men to achieve ends that were not part of their intention. Where the market is suppressed, however, these problems of incentives and of information have to be confronted directly. The injunction to do the right thing is not enough.

I put the high point of faith in the capacity of rational intervention at around 1950. This faith was sustained, however, by the economic success of the two decades that followed, and its rapid erosion coincides with the relatively disappointing economic performance of the 1970s. We see a similar phenomenon in macroeconomic policy as well, where belief in the ability of governments to sustain full employment evaporates in the face of accelerating inflation.

THE EFFECT ON TAX STRUCTURES

In few other areas is the shift of concern from the failure of market to the failure of regulation as clear as it is in tax policy. Traditionally, the concern of tax legislators was to stimulate the good and discourage the bad. Views of what was good or bad changed from time to time, but differences of opinion predominantly reflected alternative views of what should and what should not receive political favor. Revenue authorities saw themselves as fighting a difficult battle for integrity of the fiscal system against the depredations of a collection of vested interests.

The influence of such lobbies has not disappeared, and, within an open political system, it cannot disappear. But there is a new concern today with fiscal neutrality. The idea behind fiscal neutrality is that tax structures should raise revenue with a minimum distortion of private sector economic decisions. The issue is no longer simply what the tax system should favor or disfavor, but whether the tax system should favor or disfavor anything at all. Throughout the world, there is a pressure for structures that involve lower rates of return but a broader tax base.

Tax systems of a scale or scope likely to have a major effect on economic decisions or activities were the product of the Second World War. Before 1939, for example, a British worker on average earnings paid no income tax. There was no sales tax or payroll tax and no corporation tax. (Curiously, companies were taxed as if they were individuals. The introduction of the British income tax had preceded the invention of the corporation by about 50 years.)

As the burden of taxation increased, so did the perception that tax policy would be used as an instrument of economic management. The size and structure of investment was a subject of particular concern. Any tax on corporate profits discriminates against investment, but the degree of discrimination can be varied by altering either the basis on which depreciation allowances are provided or through extended deduction of capital costs (through investment tax credits, initial allowances, or other devices).

Both devices have been widely used—and to discriminate between different kinds of investment. Plant and machinery have almost always been favored; commercial buildings and investment in inventories have not. Political attitudes towards investment in energy and energy conservation have fluctuated with the price of oil. Within the last two years, however, both Britain and the United States have largely eliminated investment allowances in favor of rates of corporation tax reduced from 52 percent to 35 percent and from 46 percent to 34 percent.

A classical system of corporation tax, such as that of the United States, discourages dividends and stimulates retention of profits. Until recently, this was thought to be desirable, and the introduction of a similar system in the United Kingdom in 1965 was promoted by a conscious desire to increase investment by increasing retained profits. The European Commission's first draft directive required all member states of the European Community (EC) to adopt such a system. But by the 1970s, discouraging the distribution of profits was thought to be a disadvantage rather than a bonus. It was felt that companies ought to be required to subject their investment plans to the scrutiny of the capital market. Britain and France adopted imputation systems. Germany eliminated the double taxation of dividends through a two-rate system. The U.S. structure, far from being the model for the rest of the world, became the target of increasing domestic criticism.

In personal tax systems, too, the postwar pattern has been one of initial extension of tax preferences, followed more recently by attacks on them and retreat from them. Of equal or greater significance, however, has been the movement of maximum rates of tax. These generally raise little revenue: They are more a symbol of political attitudes toward taxation than a means of financing public services. For most of the 20th century, they have steadily increased, but recent falls have been almost as dramatic as earlier rises. The top rate in the United States is down from 70 percent to 28 percent; the fall in the United Kingdom is from 98 percent to 60 percent (with more to come).

Although the general trend is clear, there are alternative routes to fiscal neutrality. The two main options are the comprehensive taxation of income and comprehensive taxation of expenditure. Much current discussion stresses the former, but this reflects what I think is a chimerical belief that if only reliefs and allowances were swept away from the present personal and corporate income tax structure, the resulting outcome could be substantially simpler. The more significant long-term trend is to derive a major part of government revenue from a broad-based consumption tax. Within the last two decades, more than 60 countries, including all the states of the EC, have adopted a value-added tax (V.A.T.).

PRIVATIZATION

Perhaps the most remarkable retreat from state economic intervention has been privatization—the sale of state industrial assets to the private sector. This has gone furthest and fastest in the United Kingdom. In the early years of the Thatcher government, a number of smaller public industries were sold, such as state road haulage operations and hotel businesses of the nationalized railways. The program developed with the sale of major public utilities such as British Telecom and British Gas. In France, the sale of nationalized industries is proceeding even more rapidly, and privatization is an issue in many developing countries.

Privatization is partly motivated by budgeting pressures. The proceeds of sales provide an immediate boost to public revenues. Total receipts so far in the United Kingdom amount to about 10 percent of annual government spending, and the program is currently targeted to raise about 3 percent of expenditure each year. In addition, future capital requirements of the industries concerned are taken out of the public accounts. The confusion of current expenditure and capital receipts has led to criticism—"selling the family silver," in the words of Lord Stockton, an aristocratic former prime minister. The activity is, moreover, ultimately self-exhausting, since the supply of saleable public assets is limited.

The ideological rationale, at least in the United Kingdom, has been just as important as the fiscal justification. The early hopes of the Socialist nationalizers, epitomized in Herbert Morrison's concern that the industries "must not be a capitalist business," were dashed by the disappointing performances of the firms concerned. In retrospect, it is hardly surprising that organizations with such an ill-defined sense of corporate purpose were not successful. In particular, the years immediately following nationalization were characterized by a poor productivity record, as well as an emphasis on technical and engineering standards at the expense of marketing, responsiveness to consumer needs, and effective financial control. The resulting dissatisfaction led to increasing direct government intervention in the industries concerned, which undermined managerial morale and authority and created tension and frustration in relations between government and industry.

When the industries concerned are small firms operating in competitive markets, privatization appears to be an effective solution to these problems. Following on some of the earlier privatizations, those of Cable and Wireless (an operator of foreign telecommunications systems), Associated British Ports, or Amersham International (a medical isotopes company), the improvements in performance have been striking. However, the issues are considerably less clear cut when major utilities, such as British Telecom, are examined. If the organizational structure and the composition of management remains unchanged after privatization, it is not clear that merely reconstituting the nationalized industry as a corporation with many shareholders changes things in any fundamental way. Moreover, if a public utility becomes a private monopoly, public regulation is inevitable, along with its own detrimental effects on performance. Also, there is an opportunity to rerun, in a somewhat different institutional framework, the tensions associated with the relations of government and industry under nationalization.

Much of the difficulty arises because privatization has, to date, retained the centralized structure that was imposed on the industry under nationalization. This has happened for two principal reasons. One is that more revenue is obtained by selling a monopoly than a competitive industry (an observation as familiar to present governments as to the medieval kings who balanced their budgets from the proceeds of selling trading monopolies). The second, and more important, is that it is difficult to privatize an industry without the support of the incumbent management, and such support is almost invariably contingent on retention of the existing organizational structure and a restrictive attitude toward the introduction of new competition. So privatization and deregulation are not only not identical but directly inimical.

Thus the privatization of major public industries is a less fundamental change than it appears at first sight. Continued government involvement in the privatized industries is inevitable, but through direct regulation, and as a result of the problems privatization has created. Privatization of government activities that remain publicly financed may in time prove more significant than the large-scale flotations, with their attendant publicity.

DEREGULATION

If privatization spread to the rest of the world from the United Kingdom, the move to deregulation began in the United States. Criticism of government regulation of industry was directed both from the right, which saw it as an inappropriate interference with the operation of markets, and from the left, which observed the capacity of regulated industries to manipulate the systems of regulation for their own benefit and to the possible detriment of consumers. This critique developed the concept of "regulatory capture"—the notion that regulators, initially charged with obligations of consumer protection, may be won over by the better organized, better informed, and better financed resources of the regulated firms.

Much of the early discussion of deregulation in the United States was focused on the airline industry, and ultimately price controls and entry restrictions were dismantled. The example has been followed, rather feebly, in the rest of the world. Many of the restrictions on North Atlantic aviation have been removed, but in most of Europe and on many other intercontinental routes, tight controls on fares and frequencies of flights remain. Other transport industries, which have a long history of regulation, have seen a degree of liberalization in the United States and other countries.

Statutory and government-supported barriers to new competition have lowered in many other areas of economic activity. As financial markets have become more international, governments have found it impossible (even if they thought it desirable) to maintain restrictions on who may do business or to police demarcations between areas of the financial sector. Thus the Eurodollar market developed in London primarily to escape regulation of similar activities in the United States, while lines between brokering and market-making or between investment and commercial banking have become increasingly difficult to maintain. Paradoxically, these developments have often involved the simultaneous removal of old rules and the implementation of new ones. The old restrictions become unsustainable, and new competitors on the scene cannot necessarily be expected to understand the traditional tacit understandings under which financial markets are organized, so they must be restrained by new regulation.

When industries were nationalized, it was usual to restrict private operation in the activities concerned. The post and telephone authorities in most countries have enjoyed a statutory monopoly of these functions. This monopoly has normally extended, for example, to the supply of subscriber apparatus. The rules governing energy production are typically somewhat more liberal, but not much. For example, the British nationalization statutes basically limited the private generation of electricity to production for the producer's own use and prohibited private coal mining without a license from the nationalized coal industry. These restrictions followed from the underlying logic of the approach to nationalization. The executives of the industries concerned were seen not just as the managers of a commercial concern that happened to be owned by the state but, as the regulators of a whole industry, charged with overseeing the supply of communication services or energy on behalf of the public. With such a view of the objectives of nationalization, it could not make sense to permit production outside the supervision or control of the nationalized firm.

As this vision of high altruistic purpose became eroded, so did the rationale of these restrictions on competition. Part of this change was evident long before privatization became an issue. When British Labor governments extended nationalization in the 1960s and 1970s, they did not, as they had in the 1940s, legislate to bring all of the activity concerned under public ownership. They purchased control of a number of specifically-named undertakings. Although the major steel and shipbuilding firms were nationalized, anyone was free to continue private steelmaking or shipbuilding operations and to establish new ones—and this in fact happened. In the last phase of French nationalization at the beginning of the 1980s, the government simply bought some large firms in certain sectors of the economy: Paribas, a bank; Thomson-Brandt, the largest electrical producer; St. Gobain, the glass manufacturer. The intended impact of nationalization was now to be on major decisions of corporate strategy rather than on the day-to-day operations of the corporation. Although nationalization continued, the scope and intensity of the government intervention implied by it diminished.

At the same time, then, governments began to reduce barriers to competition with the nationalized industries. But progress was usually slowed by the political influence of nationalized industry managers themselves. What happened in telecommunications has been the focus of most discussion. Technological changes have vastly extended the range of facilities available and allowed competition in areas where it had previously been technically infeasible, while state monopolies have generally been slow in responding to these new developments. Most European countries have now liberalized the provision of subscriber apparatus. Britain and the United States have permitted competitive supply of long-distance facilities. Many value-added network services, such as cellular radio or packet switching, have been developed outside the scope of the National Posts and Telecommunications Authority (now called OFTEL).

If the British experience is to be a guide, however, merely allowing competition in areas where it was previously prohibited may not have much practical effect. The endowment of financial resources, technical dominance, and political skills established by a firm that has enjoyed a long period of legal protection from competition may be considerable. It is now five years since Britain liberalized energy supply to allow the private generation of electricity and to enable industrial customers to contract directly with gas producers, using the British Gas network as the common carrier. In fact, there are still no private generators of significance and no substantial contracts for gas supply to which British Gas is not a party. More surprising still is the evolution of competition in the express coach industry, where the nationalized operator has used its financial muscle and exclusive access to city-center terminals to establish what is probably a larger market share than it enjoyed before deregulation. One of British Airways' first exercises of its now commercial freedom as a private company was to announce a takeover bid for its principal domestic rival, British Caledonian.

WELFARE SYSTEMS

Welfare spending has been the largest single factor governing the growth of public expenditure through the 20th century. It has grown to somewhere between one-quarter and one-third of total public spending in most countries. Beneficiaries fall in four main categories: the old, the sick, children, and the unemployed (see Table 4). Provision for the elderly dominates everywhere.

There are as many different schemes of provision for the elderly as there are countries in the world. Some countries, such as Italy,

Table 4
Government Welfare Spending as a Share of National Income (GDP), 1981

	France	Germany	Japan	1979 United Kingdom	1978 United States
Pensions	11.9	12.9	4.7	6.5	6.7
Sickness	1.2	0.6	0.1	0.4	0.1
Child Benefits	2.2	1.2	1.6	1.4	0.5
Unemployment	1.9	1.4	0.4	0.7	0.4

Source: Peter Saunders and Fredrich Klau, "The Role of the Public Sector: Causes and Consequences of the Growth of Government," *OECD Economic Studies* no. 4, OECD, Paris, (1985).

have an extensive state system of pensions related to earnings, and there is little private provision for retirement either by employees or by individuals themselves. In France, the state supports industry-wide pension schemes funded by employers, while in Japan, responsibility for pensions rests primarily with individual employers. In Germany and the United States, there are public schemes of different degrees of generosity, supplemented by employer and private pensions. In the United Kingdom, there is both a state and an occupational sector, with an opportunity for employers to contract out their workforce who then receive reduced state benefits and an assurance that their private pension will at least make up the difference.

After several decades of rapidly increasing expenditures, the future financing of pension benefits has become an issue everywhere although the precise form of response has generally been the same—trimming of state benefits and stimulus to private provision of savings and retirement benefits. The United States has reduced government benefit promises and increased tax subsidies to private retirement plans, most substantially through Individual Retirement Accounts (IRAs), although these subsidies were limited somewhat by the 1986 Tax Reform Act. The United Kingdom attempted to abolish the portion of state pensions related to earnings, and when that was defeated by political opposition, reduced the projected benefit levels and allowed more attractive terms for the private elements of the public-private pension partnership.

In Europe, the growth of state provision of sickness and unemployment benefits largely destroyed the markets for insurance against these contingencies, which had been provided at an earlier stage of development through trade unions and private insurers. There is little sign of any redress of this position although the issue is now on the political agenda to an extent that would have been difficult to envisage two decades ago. But the general European structure of welfare benefits, based on a concept of social insurance, is now increasingly vulnerable.

The concept behind social insurance is that benefits are provided for the contingencies that might give rise to need rather than as a result of need itself. The analogy is with private insurance where contributions generate benefit entitlements—although the analogy is a weak one if, as is inevitably the case, the contributions are compulsory and the scheme as a whole is heavily redistributive. The price to be paid, however, is either that benefits are set at a level too low for the needs of those who have no other resources, or the costs of providing benefits are increased by the extent of provision to those who have no specific need. As costs have grown, there has been increasing pressure to relate benefits to specific needs rather than general contingencies.

CONCLUSION

The fiscal pressures created by the growth of public expenditure until 1975, combined with increasing disenchantment with the performance of government as regulator or industrial manager, have provoked in the following decade a clear reaction against the trend to increased government intervention in the economy. The benefits of extended involvement are no longer taken for granted. The motives and incentives of public officials are viewed with skepticism. Public expenditure is no longer growing as rapidly as it did. For the first time in industrial history, public ownership of businesses is diminishing, rather than increasing, and at a rapid rate. Deregulation is becoming more common, and taxes are being imposed at lower rates and in less distortionary ways.

Are these permanent changes or just temporary reactions to earlier excess? Certainly the exaggerated claims made for current reforming trends will generate an inevitable reaction. The hope that tax systems shorn of special-interest group pressures will be substantially simpler is already appearing illusory. Privatization that fails to solve the problems of market failure, which provoked nationalization, or the issues of regulatory failure, which led to denationalization, will breed discontent. There are inevitably losers as well as gainers from more competitive market structures, and not everyone will applaud the results of deregulation.

The change in intellectual climate, and the reasserted faith in market forces that goes with it, however, is a much more enduring phenomenon. If the trends I have described continue for 50 years rather than for 10, the results may be dramatic indeed. The coverage of welfare programs may diminish rather than increase. Overall expenditures on health and education will certainly go on rising, because both are goods that take an increasing share of higher incomes. However, the public sector's share of these expenditures is likely to fall as competitive private provision is encouraged and recognition grows that even if activities are publicly financed they do not need to be publicly managed. As a result, the number of public employees may fall faster than the level of public spending.

Partnerships between the public and private sectors are likely to grow. The development of private insurance systems integrated with the public welfare system is one important means of reducing welfare costs. Within the public sector itself, an increasing variety of activities may be contracted out to private management, and there will be increasing pressure to introduce the reward and incentive structures of the private sector.

In the United States, where suspicion of the economic role of government has been vigorous since the days of the founding fathers, these changes may seem neither surprising nor dramatic. In Europe, where both the citizen and the firm have routinely looked to government for protection from a hostile economic environment, they seem far more radical. And in countries of the Third World, where development and state involvement have often been seen as synonymous, their impact may be greater still.

16

The U.S. Supply-Side Revolution

PAUL CRAIG ROBERTS

There has been a fiscal revolution in the United States. This revolution has taken place in both theory and practice. The supply-side emphasis on incentive effects of fiscal policy has supplanted the Keynesian emphasis on demand effects. One consequence of this revolution has been the destruction in the 1980s of the consensus in both political parties that supported high tax rates.

Prior to the supply-side revolution, the economy's performance was believed to depend on the total amount of spending or demand in the economy. In this view, taxes affected only disposable income and the ability of private individuals to spend. As long as government spent the tax revenues, taxation was not considered costly to the economy. It simply shifted spending from the greedy private sector to the benevolent government sector; total spending remained the same. Indeed, many macroeconomists argued that higher taxes would actually help the economy by raising total demand. Their reasoning was that people would partly pay a tax increase by reducing their saving, so the increase in government spending would not be completely offset by a drop in private spending. Thus economists concluded that higher taxes were a stimulus to the economy because they increased total spending.

Supply-side economics showed that taxation (and government spending) affect incentives and relative prices and that these supply-side effects are not washed out when spending is transferred from the private to the government sector. The disincentive effect of the higher tax rate remains. Therefore, as government grows, the incentives to produce decline. This accumulation of disincentives leads to stagflation and worsening trade-offs between inflation and unemployment as successive increases in government spending call forth weaker increases in real output and stronger increases in prices or inflation.

No American policymaker any longer believes that taxes do not matter. In 1981, legislation was passed that cut marginal tax rates for all brackets and reduced the top tax rate from 70 percent to 50 percent. In 1986, both the U.S. House of Representatives and the U.S. Senate passed legislation that slashed the top tax rate further and collapsed the progressive step system into two or three brackets. The House bill reduced the top statutory tax rate to 38 percent, and the Senate bill cut the rate to 27 percent. The compromise between the two legislative committees settled on 28 percent. (The Administration's bill proposed a 35 percent top rate.) The corporate income tax rate was cut from 46 percent to 34 percent. American taxpayers have not seen tax rates this low since 1925, when tax-cutter Andrew Mellon was Secretary of the Treasury.

ORIGINS OF THE REVOLUTION

Many factors contributed to the fiscal revolution that began in 1975: a moribund Republican party hoping to make a comeback; a dynamic and articulate political spokesman (Jack Kemp); a small group of economists on the Congressional staff who were willing to challenge the establishment; stagflation and the inability of the Keynesians to explain it or to offer a hopeful way out.[1]

These factors alone might not have prevailed against the ideology of redistribution, which had seized upon the Keynesian macroanalysis of taxation. Redistributive politicians were brought into the supply-side camp by two additional factors. They realized that high tax rates do not necessarily mean high tax revenues. They were given a practical demonstration of this when the maximum tax rate on capital gains was cut in 1978 from 49 percent to 28 percent, and the revenues rose.

Redistributionists also discovered that in a welfare state redistribution takes place as a result of income transfers through the expenditure side of the budget. A proportional tax levied on all but redistributed only to lower income groups can accommodate massive income redistribution. The idea that redistribution requires progressive taxation dates from an earlier time when the only "public goods" were highways and national defense. Prior to the income-support programs of the welfare state, the only way to redistribute income was to require the rich to bear a disproportionate burden of the budget of the minimalist state. Once redistributionists caught up with their times they were no longer willing to pay the deadweight loss of punishing the successful with high tax rates.

BUDGET DEFICITS AND INFLATION

Many people think that the large budget deficits discredit the supply-side idea and make the fiscal change ephemeral. They mistakenly equate the "Laffer curve" with supply-side economics and believe that the large budget deficits prove the Laffer curve did not work. However, the 1981 tax rate reduction was not predicated on the premise that it would pay for itself through increased revenues. The Reagan Administration planned to "pay for" the tax rate reduction through a combination of revenue reflows from better economic performance, an increase in the private sector saving rate, and a reduction in the growth rate of government spending.

The budget deficit is not an indication that this plan failed. The budget deficit was caused by unexpected disinflation. In 1981, the Administration's five-year forecast projected declining inflation. At that time, few critics could reconcile this projection with the proposed tax cuts. However, actual inflation came in far under the projections. In his book, *The Triumph of Politics,* former budget director David A. Stockman shows that the unexpected disinflation and 1981–1982 recession reduced nominal gross national product (GNP) for the 1982–1986 period by $2.145 trillion. My own estimate is $2.5 trillion.[2] In 1986, the revenues lost to this unexpected disinflation accounted for about 75 percent of the budget deficit.

The sudden collapse in inflation also wiped out the spending cuts the Administration thought it had achieved in 1981. The cuts were in nominal terms, and when inflation fell below the forecast, the cuts were transformed into increases in real spending. In other words, the Reagan fiscal plan failed because it overbudgeted for inflation. It is obvious that tax rate reduction cannot cause government spending to rise as a percent of GNP, and it is the relative rise in spending that accounts for the deficit.

The inflation rate fell more than expected because the Federal Reserve Board implemented a much tighter monetary policy than the Administration had requested. The central bank misinterpreted the supply-side policy as an excessive fiscal stimulus that would greatly expand consumer demand at a time of double-digit inflation. Concerned that it would be blamed for a new burst in inflation, the Federal Reserve took defensive action and unexpectedly collapsed the growth of the money supply. Believing in the primacy of fiscal policy, as many economists did, it did not expect the consequences of its action.

In thoughtful policy-making circles in the United States, the facts about the deficit are understood,[3] even if not admitted for reasons of political jockeying. However, the rhetorical war against the supply-side camp has made it difficult for other people to get good information. The more the results are studied, the more it seems that the Administration underestimated the incentive effects of its tax policy. Professor Lawrence Lindsey of Harvard University, in a study for the National Bureau of Economic Research, found that the behavioral response to the tax rate reduction resulted in 47 percent of the revenues being recovered.[4] Treasury policymakers had not expected a revenue feedback of this magnitude. Similarly, Allen Sinai and his associates at Data Resources, Inc., in a paper published in the *National Tax Journal,* reported a private-sector saving response that exceeded the Treasury's expectations.[5] Politicians who have no time for economic research have been guided by the fact that the United States experienced falling inflation despite a long expansion that has created 13 million new jobs. Since the results of economic policy during the 1970s had convinced them that no such result was possible, they think there must be something to the supply-side approach.

A PERMANENT CHANGE

Absent an economic catastrophe that could make it politically profitable to repudiate "Reaganomics," an appreciation of the incentive effects of taxation is likely to remain a permanent part of the world's policy knowledge—although it is always possible for envy to cause democratic electorates to cut off their noses to spite their faces. If the U.S. government cannot control its penchant to buy votes with taxpayer dollars or if a legitimate need for revenues arises, the increase in taxation is likely to take the form of consumption taxes.

The extraordinary rise in federal government spending from 3 percent of GNP in 1929 to 24 percent in 1986 is unlikely to continue in the easy way characterizing growth of government in the 20th century. One reason is that economists no longer believe taxation is a burden only to the taxpayer. It is generally recognized today that disincentive effects of taxation impose a deadweight loss to the economy. Only an ignorant ideologue would deny that the true measure of the tax burden must include all the production that is lost to disincentives.

Another reason is that the ideology that led to welfare economies in the West, and to irrational and bureaucratized economies in the

East, has left governments with responsibilities they cannot meet and do not want. The extensive privatization in the United Kingdom and the repudiation of central planning in China and the Soviet Union are indications that the growth of government in the 20th century has exceeded its natural boundaries. With governments today saddled with massive responsibilities, there is no rational reason for them to continue to grow relative to the economies that support them. If economies continue to grow, government should shrink as a share of GNP.

THE TAX BIAS AGAINST SAVING

The next logical step to follow from the new view of tax policy is to reduce and eliminate the bias resulting from the multiple taxation of saving. U.S. tax law is biased in its treatment of saving in two ways. The most important is the multiple taxes it imposes on income from saving. The choice people make between current consumption and saving determines the level of investment. The multiple taxation of saving biases the choice toward consumption and away from investment. This bias retards the growth of the capital/labor ratio and productivity. As a result, the United States experiences a lower real economic growth rate than a neutral tax system would provide.

The second source of bias affects the choice among different investments. For tax reasons, some are better than others. This bias is secondary since it affects the mix of investments, whereas the first bias affects the overall level of investment.

As a result of the multiple taxation of saving, the rate of return an individual realizes from his investments is substantially smaller than the economic return of the investment to society. The amount of money an individual has for investment is first reduced by personal income tax. If he invests after-tax savings in a corporation which uses the investment to purchase capital equipment, the earnings from the capital investment are taxed at the corporate level. Furthermore, if the remainder is passed on in the form of a dividend, it is taxed as regular income at the personal level. If the remainder is reinvested instead, the return will be capitalized in the worth of the stock, adjusted for future corporate taxation. If the individual were to sell the stock and realize a capital gain, then this amount would be subject to further taxation. These multiple layers of taxation are further compounded by other taxes, such as the property tax, with the end result being less investment and lower growth in labor productivity.

Specific investment incentives can distort the choice of investments, and gains in economic efficiency can be obtained from abolishing differential "tax preferences," or loopholes, which distort the choice of investments. However, such specific investment incentives also reduce the tax bite on saving and, thereby, the tax bias that reduces the level of investment.

The Tax Reform Act of 1986 was a confused affair because it set out to reduce the distortions that affect the mix of investments in a way that did not take into account the contribution tax preferences make to reducing the bias against the level of investment.[6] Old-fashioned economists occupied solely with efficiency gains could not come to grips with the more important issue. Consequently, whereas the 1986 reform may have achieved some efficiency gains, it gave up larger economic gains that would accrue from a more neutral tax treatment of saving.[7] Continuing concern with the U.S. saving rate is likely to lead the makers of tax policy to redress the bias against saving.

Another Side to the Supply Side

DONALD F. KETTL

Supply-side economics has certainly revolutionized tax policy in one respect: Never again will analysts contend that the level of tax rates does not matter. Even skeptics now concede that the rate at which individuals and corporations are taxed critically affects their behavior. However, the supply-side revolution of the 1980s has not ended the war. If it closed, perhaps only temporarily, the front on tax rates, it also created powerful incentives for combatants to shift the battle to other fronts.

The debate over supply-side economics is based on this much broader question: Which problems are society's, and in dealing with the societal problems, what should be the role of government?

Taxes are not the only governmental tool for dealing with problems. If political or economic circumstances restrict revenue increases, pressures inevitably grow for using other governmental tools, such as tax expenditures (deductions, credits, or exclusions that reduce taxes due) or regulations or loan programs to achieve the same results. Just as squashing one side of a pillow pushes up the other side, limiting one form of governmental action increases pressure for other forms.

Two points must be emphasized. First, regardless of the level of services a society decides its government should produce, there are many different ways of producing those services. Second, different governmental strategies have different implications for equity among citizens, for efficiency in using society's resources, and for accountability in government programs.

Despite the supply-side revolution, demands for governmental services continue. For example, the aging of the population is likely to dramatically increase service demands. These needs can be met in four different ways, some governmental and some not:

1. *Economic growth.* We can hope that the rising tide of economic growth will lift all boats, including those of the elderly. But will all boats be raised to the same level? Inequity seems inevitable, and the needs of the less privileged will still call for societal intervention.

2. *Private assumption of the burden.* Private sector organizations can create benefit programs to care for their former employees' special needs. Increasingly, however, families are likely to include second wage earners who will not have become fully vested in retirement programs; service workers who will not be covered by any plan at all; and divorced women, who will find themselves bereft of coverage when they need it most. Private pension plans are likely to fall short of carrying the burden.

Nothing guarantees that corporations will willingly shoulder such a burden. Government could mandate coverage, but this would simply be a tax covered by the veil of regulation. Even such a mandated program would probably leave many citizens uncovered and create further demands for governmental services. Thus pressures might shift to creating incentives for individuals to save.

3. *Incentives for saving.* Government could create incentives for taxpayers to save privately for their retirement. As the Individual Retirement Accounts demonstrated before the 1986 Tax Reform Act changed their structure, such incentives are most attractive to upper-income taxpayers. A program to convince middle-income taxpayers to save large sums of money would have to offer huge incentives, for these families seem to value current consumption far more than future security. If the incentives are large enough to encourage a high level of savings to deal with the future costs of security in old age, the government subsidy, even if hidden, would be huge. And finally, there is the problem of the poor, who have no money to save.

Such tax expenditures are just as real as direct spending programs. However, they have different economic costs and distributional effects. And they do not reach everyone, which inevitably leaves some share of the needs of the elderly to be covered by the government—or not at all.

4. *Government programs.* Even the most "privatized" strategy—short of one that abjures any societal responsibility—contemplates some governmental role. The crucial questions are what that role ought to be and how it can best be structured to achieve society's broader values. Taxes are a part—an important part—of this debate, but taxation is only one of many possible governmental strategies. In the case of caring for the 21st century's elderly population, the government can use regulation and tax incentives as well as direct spending funded by taxation.

Each of these tools has its own politics, its distinctive distributional effects, its different effects on efficiency, and its unique effects on society. Regulation shifts the cost burden from government to the private sector and intrudes on private decisions. Tax incentives represent large, sometimes inefficient, and often uncontrollable losses of government revenue. Direct spending programs funded by taxes can be more narrowly targeted, but they most sharply raise the problems of "big government."

The lesson here is an important one. The supply-side revolution, in broadening the battle to many more fronts, increased the incentives of claimants to look for new forms of governmental action. Many of these forms are more complex, are harder to manage and hold accountable, and have more varied effects of equity and efficiency than more traditional taxing and spending decisions. The supply-side revolution has not solidified the wall between the public and the private sectors. It has made those relationships far more porous and intricate, and this trend, we can confidently predict, will continue into the 21st century.

17

Richer Means Harder to Tax

HENRY J. AARON

INTRODUCTION

Unless a striking reversal of fortunes occurs, in the 21st century the United States and most other countries will be richer than they are today in at least two ways: Annual incomes will have grown, and the ratio of wealth to annual income is likely to have increased. With greater incomes and wealth will come increased international trade and capital movements. If the projections of the Social Security Administration (SSA) are even close to accurate, men will devote a smaller part and women a larger part of their adult lives to work outside the home.

The likely consequences of such trends for tax policy are my subject. First, I shall indicate the direction and general magnitude of the trends in income and wealth that we can anticipate. Then I shall suggest that these trends are likely to make it even harder than it now is to tax income fairly and without distortion. Problems will grow because the relative importance of capital income and capital transactions will increase. In the past, tax authorities have had far greater success in designing rules for taxing labor income than they have had in fashioning fair and efficient rules for the taxation of capital income. It will become increasingly important either to solve the many remaining problems in taxing capital income or to shift reliance from taxes that purport to measure capital income annually to taxes that measure capital income less frequently, if at all. Finally, I shall explore alternative possible responses to the problems generated by the economic trends.

PROJECTIONS OF INCOME, WAGES, WEALTH, AND CAPITAL INCOME

The following projections come from a project now under way at The Brookings Institution, under a contract from the SSA, to explore the economic implications of alternative budget and Social Security financing policies.[1] For this purpose my colleagues and I have developed a simulation model based on SSA projections of the labor force. We project the growth of the capital stock owned by Americans and of the capital stock located in the United States. These projections are based on alternative assumptions regarding private saving, the surplus or deficit of the federal government, and decisions to invest U.S. saving at home or abroad.

Baseline Assumptions

In our baseline projections, we assume that private saving, the federal budget deficit, and domestic investment will remain at their historic average levels of 18 percent, 1.5 percent, and 16.5 percent of gross national product (GNP), respectively. We have assumed that U.S. net foreign investment will become zero in the mid-1990s and remain at that level thereafter. We have explored the implications of modifying each of these assumptions, and I report some of these results next. Using as our basis the supply of labor as projected by the SSA and the capital stock as projected by our model, we assume a rate of growth of productivity that reproduces the growth of GNP implicit in the SSA's intermediate projections.

WAGES AND COMPENSATION

These assumptions lead to the following general conclusions. Real hourly compensation will grow by 33 percent between 1986 and 2000 and by 84 percent in each of the succeeding 30-year periods (see Table 1). This growth of compensation reflects a combination of technical change and increases in the capital stock.

Money wages will become a progressively poorer index of total compensation as the ratio of fringe benefits to total compensation continues to grow. Between 1986 and 2000, total money wages will grow 34 percent, and total employee compensation will grow 45 percent. From 2000 to 2030, wages and compensation will grow by 61 and 76 percent, respectively, and from 2030 to 2060, they will grow by 58 and 73 percent, respectively.[2] These discrepancies would not matter if all workers received the same ratio of fringe benefits to money wages. Since they do not, however, the importance of including fringe benefits in the tax base for reasons of fairness is heightened. Of course, the argument that taxing fringes increases economic efficiency depends on marginal tax rates as well.

Capital Income and the Capital Stock

Although wages rise rapidly, the growth of capital income and of the capital stock is even more striking (see Table 2, p. 236). The capital stock grows faster than capital income because, according to our projections, the ratio of capital to output rises, signaling a drop in the rate of return.[3]

ALTERNATIVE PROJECTIONS

These projections are based on many debatable assumptions. One is the rather extreme assumption that after the mid-1990s, net foreign

Table 1

Indices of Actual and Projected Growth of Wages, Earnings, and Compensation in Constant Dollars Based on The Brookings Macroeconomic Simulation Model, 1960–2060

	Hourly Compensation				Total Wages				Total Compensation			
	Baseline Saving[a]		Increased Saving[b]		Baseline Saving[a]		Increased Saving[b]		Baseline Saving[a]		Increased Saving[b]	
Year	Domestic Investment Only[c]	International Capital Mobility[d]	Domestic Investment Only[c]	International Capital Mobility[d]	Domestic Investment Only[c]	International Capital Mobility[d]	Domestic Investment Only[c]	International Capital Mobility[d]	Domestic Investment Only[c]	International Capital Mobility[d]	Domestic Investment Only[c]	International Capital Mobility[d]
1960	73	—	—	—	47	—	—	—	44	—	—	—
1970	91	—	—	—	73	—	—	—	70	—	—	—
1980	97	—	—	—	85	—	—	—	87	—	—	—
1986	100	—	—	—	100	—	—	—	100	—	—	—
1990	111	111	111	111	108	108	108	108	114	114	114	114
2000	133	128	136	128	134	129	137	129	145	140	148	140
2010	162	151	168	151	162	151	167	151	180	168	186	168
2020	199	179	208	179	187	168	195	168	215	193	224	193
2030	245	217	256	217	216	190	225	190	255	225	266	225
2040	300	265	314	265	252	222	263	222	307	271	321	271
2050	368	324	385	324	293	257	306	257	368	323	385	323
2060	452	397	473	397	342	301	358	301	443	389	464	389

[a]National saving is 16.5 percent of gross national product (GNP). Private saving equals 18 percent of GNP. Government saving is − 1.5 percent of GNP.

[b]National saving equals 18 percent of GNP.

[c]The current foreign trade deficit is assumed to be eliminated by 1991 and the current account is assumed to remain in balance thereafter.

[d]Domestic investment is just sufficient to maintain the domestic real rate of return. If national saving exceeds this amount, it is invested abroad.

Table 2
Indices of Actual and Projected Growth of Capital and of Capital Income in Constant Dollars Based on The Brookings Macroeconomic Simulation Model, 1960–2060

Year	Capital Stock				Capital Income			
	Baseline Saving[a]		Increased Saving[b]		Baseline Saving[a]		Increased Saving[b]	
	Domestic Investment Only[c]	International Capital Mobility[d]	Domestic Investment Only[c]	International Capital Mobility[d]	Domestic Investment Only[c]	International Capital Mobility[d]	Domestic Investment Only[c]	International Capital Mobility[d]
1960	39	—	—	—	41	—	—	—
1970	59	—	—	—	50	—	—	—
1980	83	—	—	—	75	—	—	—
1986	100	—	—	—	100	—	—	—
1990	114	114	114	114	115	116	115	116
2000	158	143	169	143	152	155	157	162
2010	211	173	235	173	193	203	202	220
2020	272	199	308	199	232	257	246	285
2030	336	232	385	232	279	321	296	362
2040	410	281	472	281	340	398	361	453
2050	501	338	577	338	411	489	437	560
2060	608	410	701	410	499	600	531	689

[a]National saving is 16.5 percent of gross national product (GNP). Private saving equals 18 percent of GNP. Government saving is −1.5 percent of GNP.
[b]National saving equals 18 percent of GNP.
[c]The current foreign trade deficit is assumed to be eliminated by 1991 and the current account is assumed to remain in balance thereafter.
[d]Domestic investment is just sufficient to maintain the domestic real rate of return. If national saving exceeds this amount, it is invested abroad.

investment of the United States will be zero every year. Another is that national saving will remain at historic averages. We have examined the sensitivity of our projections to variations in these and other assumptions.

INTERNATIONALLY MOBILE CAPITAL

While the large and recalcitrant contemporary deficits on current account may make the achievement of a foreign-trade balance by the mid-1990s seem unreasonably optimistic, the more questionable aspect of our baseline projections concerns our assumption that the United States will export no capital to the rest of the world in succeeding years. This assumption is debatable because our simulations indicate a sharp drop in the rate of return to capital in the United States if national saving remains at historic levels and if all savings are invested domestically. Only a major change in the nature of technical growth—causing productivity of capital to rise sharply despite an increase in the ratio of capital to output—could prevent such an occurrence.

Faced with a drop in domestic rates of return, investors would be likely to look abroad to maintain rates of return. If net foreign investment were positive, the domestic capital stock would be smaller and U.S. capital income would be larger than they would be if net foreign investment were zero. To explore the effect of shifting investment abroad, we introduced the alternative assumption that the net flow of capital from the United States will be just large enough to maintain the domestic rate of return to capital at the average rate prevailing from 1986 to 1990. We assumed that net foreign investment earns a rate of return halfway between the domestic rate of return gross and net of corporation income tax.[4]

Under this assumption, our simulations indicate that the growth of the domestic capital stock will be significantly reduced. By 2000, the capital stock will be 9.5 percent smaller than it would be if all national savings were invested domestically; by 2030, it will be 31 percent smaller; and by 2060, it will be 33 percent smaller.

Because the movement of capital overseas slows the growth of the domestic capital stock, it also retards increases in money wages and total compensation. If capital moves overseas when the domestic rate of return tends to fall, hourly wages will be 4 percent lower by the year 2000, and 12 percent lower in 2030 and 2060 than it would be if all capital were invested domestically. Capital income, however, rises more rapidly—2 percent higher by 2000, 15 percent higher by 2030, and 20 percent higher by 2060—if capital is invested overseas, because savers are not forced, as they are in the baseline case, to accept progressively lower rates of return.

GOVERNMENT SAVING

The fact that the federal government deficit has averaged roughly 1.5 percent of GNP is no guarantee that it will not be higher or lower in the future. Since 1981, the deficit has considerably exceeded that level. Current law calls for the elimination of these deficits, however. It also calls for the Social Security system to move into surplus by as much as 2 percent of GNP. To indicate the sensitivity of our projections to variations in national saving, we explored the effects of variations in both government and private saving. Tables 1 and 2 present results of simulations in which the federal deficit is assumed to be balanced in every year. Such balance could result if the general fund deficit just offset the projected Social Security surpluses, which are projected to persist until about 2030. In succeeding years, a general fund surplus would just offset projected Social Security deficits.

If all capital is invested domestically, the additional national saving results in faster domestic capital accumulation and wage growth. The effect is significant. If the federal government runs a perennially balanced budget, rather than operating with an annual deficit that equals 1.5 percent of GNP, the capital stock is 7 percent larger in 2000 and 15 percent larger in 2030 and 2060. Hourly wages are 2 percent higher in 2000, 4 percent higher in 2030, and 5 percent higher in 2060.

If capital flows abroad whenever the domestic rate of return tends to fall, the level of national saving has no effect on the domestic capital stock or wage growth, but it has a profound effect on capital income. When national saving rises, additional capital flows abroad, and capital income increases 7 percent by 2000, 30 percent by 2030, and 38 percent by 2060.

Even if the government deficit remains at historic averages, private saving might increase, because of demographic factors, for example. The effects would be qualitatively similar to those resulting from a reduced government deficit. If the saving rates of various age groups were to remain at levels indicated by the 1983 Survey of Consumer Expenditures, saving would rise by about two-thirds as the population ages. It would do so because the proportion of young adults, who dissave, will drop sharply, while the proportion of mature, preretirement adults, who save a large proportion of their income, will rise. The proportion of retirees will also increase, but the survey indicates that they will remain net savers. Even if one assumes that the elderly save nothing on balance and that the young dissave negligibly, demographic factors will increase saving by about one-third. (Another researcher, Michael Boskin of Stanford University, assumes that young workers save half as much as older workers and that retirees dissave. He concludes that demographic factors will cause a slight drop in private saving.)

WHERE THE PROJECTIONS LEAD

I infer from these projections that the taxation of capital income will become ever more important to the achievement of a fair and nondistorting income. I also infer that international capital flows are likely to increase if United States national saving responds to the demographic reality of an aging baby-boom generation or if the large projected Social Security reserves materialize. An increase in the national saving rate brought about by a rise in either government or private saving will contribute to growth of the capital stock and capital income. If some or all of that increased saving is invested domestically, it will also accelerate growth of earnings. It is likely to increase the importance of international capital flows and the relative importance of foreign-source capital income.

IMPLICATIONS FOR TAX POLICY

How will these trends affect the U.S. federal tax system? The United States currently derives most of its revenues from the personal income tax (46 percent of all revenues), the payroll tax (36 percent), and the corporation income tax (11 percent). The relative importance of the payroll tax has risen sharply with the cost of the Social Security system, and it is projected to rise somewhat more in the next few years as payroll tax increases scheduled under current law go into effect. The proportion of federal revenues derived from the corporation income tax fell from 32 percent of total federal revenues in 1952 to 8.4 percent in 1985, before the Tax Reform Act of 1986 boosted it slightly.[5]

The rising importance of capital income and wealth poses a challenge to tax authorities. They must either improve the quality of taxation of capital income or choose one of the two following courses: (1) reconcile themselves to a deterioration of the fairness of the income tax and an increase in the economic distortions it causes or (2) reduce the degree to which the tax system relies on taxes that purport to reach capital income.

WHY CAPITAL INCOME IS ESPECIALLY HARD TO TAX

It is far easier to measure labor income than it is to measure capital income. Both kinds of income consist of gross receipts less costs incurred in earning that type of income. The measurement of capital income poses a large number of problems which either do not occur in the taxation of labor income or are far less serious:

- *Inflation.* Many problems arise from the fact that the generation of capital income often takes far longer than does the generation of labor income. This fact means that changes in prices during the life of an investment can distort income measurement. The current tax system makes no adjustments for the effects of inflation on the measurement of income. (Inflation adjustments for tax brackets, personal exemptions, and standard deductions concern the rate structure, not the tax base.) Although the U.S. Treasury in 1984 recommended such adjustments, the White House elected not to include many of them in its final recommendations to Congress in 1985. The Committee on Ways and Means of the U.S. House of Representatives rejected the rest.

- *Accrued Income.* The fact that capital transactions often take considerable time creates a dilemma for an income tax that purports to measure income relatively frequently. Unless accrued as well as realized income is taxed, the tax system will create a bias toward investments that generate realized income infrequently.[6] This distortion makes the annual taxation of capital income, both realized and accrued, attractive. To tax both accrued and realized capital income, authorities would have to measure the income generated during the taxable period even if the transaction were incomplete. They would have to value assets and liabilities that had not been traded during the taxable period. Estimates of asset values are essential for the measurement of accrued gains and losses and for the accurate measurement of income.[7] Such a system would be nondistorting but administratively cumbersome.

With some exceptions, Congress has chosen to tax only realizations and not accruals. (The exceptions include bonds purchased at discount and various futures contracts. A large legal literature has developed on this issue, which is sometimes referred to as the "time-value of money.") This policy is certainly defensible on administrative grounds. But it has resulted in a host of measures to minimize opportunities for tax avoidance, such as limitations on capital losses, at-risk rules, marking certain assets to market, limits on interest deduction, passive-loss rules, statutes and regulations concerning the timing of capital income and of deductions, and other provisions to which tax lawyers owe much of their ample incomes.

Similar but far less serious problems arise in the taxation of labor incomes. Wages and salaries are typically paid many times during the annual taxable period and usually shortly after the employee undertakes expenses associated with earning income.[8]

INTERNATIONAL TRADE AND CAPITAL MOVEMENTS

The growth of international trade and capital movements and the increasing importance of income generated through such transactions means that a growing share of personal and business income is associated with such transactions. The taxation of international transactions is among the most complicated and least satisfactory aspects of income taxation. The problems include, but are not limited to, the following:

- *Transfer Pricing.* When subsidiaries of a single parent company carry out transactions with each other, how should tax authorities determine at which price such transactions occur? This problem is critical because without restrictions (and, perhaps, even with them!) companies might manipulate intracompany transactions to shift income to jurisdictions with low tax rates or unused deductions, or they might try to take advantage of differences in tax years in different jurisdictions.

- *Multiple Currencies.* When branches of a company are subject to taxation in several countries, what exchange rates should be used to measure income?

- *Foreign Tax Credit.* Most developed nations allow a credit for taxes paid to foreign jurisdictions. Such credits would be straightforward if all countries taxed all types of capital income at the same rate. Because rates differ among countries, capital-exporting countries place limits on the amount of credit that will be permitted because of taxes paid in other countries, thus preventing capital-importing countries from setting rates arbitrarily high and tapping into the treasuries of capital-exporting countries. Because rates differ on various types of capital income, capital-exporting countries must also decide whether or not they wish to allow concessionary rates on types of income from abroad that would be favored if earned domestically.

Each of these problems is heightened by the probable growth in international trade and capital movements as economies become increasingly open and wealth increases. These trends raise questions regarding the capacity of sovereign states to carry out independent policies for taxing capital income. The questions are similar to those with which the members of the European Economic Community (EEC) have grappled. The EEC has moved gradually to coordinate tax structures.

Among the approaches tax authorities have developed for dealing with the growing importance of capital income are the following:

- reformed and improved income tax systems
- alternative approaches to taxing capital income
- abandonment of the taxation of capital income

Reformed and Improved Income Taxation

The movement to reform the income tax rather than abandon it, which reached a high water mark in 1986, has shown that rates could be greatly reduced without loss of revenues if the tax base is broadened. The major elements for broadening the tax base in the U.S. Tax Reform Act of 1986 extend taxation to previously untaxed capital income. These elements include the repeal of the investment tax credit, repeal of the 60 percent exclusion of long-term capital gains, and extension of depreciable lives on structures. Also included are limits on deductions of interest expense and passive losses, strengthening of at-risk rules, the personal and corporate minimum taxes, and other provisions. While additional elements of capital income remain untaxed, currently excluded labor income—notably, fringe benefits—is the major area for future broadening of the tax base.

The measurement of capital income remains quite inaccurate, however. The distortions from inflation remain. Each new bout of inflation, like the last one in the early 1980s, will cause taxes on different types of capital income to change by widely differing amounts. As always, inflation will reduce the value of depreciation; result in fictitious deductions for interest paid and fictitious income from interest received; distort inventory accounting; and generate tax on nominal, but unreal, capital gains. When inflation accelerates—as at some future time it surely will—Congress is likely to succumb to the legitimate complaints of recipients of capital income that inflation is, if not the cruelest tax, then surely the most capricious.

Unless the tax system is insulated from inflation-induced distortions, the inevitable result will be the reintroduction of the familiar ad hoc concessions whose repeal represented the most important accomplishments of the 1986 tax reform. The threat posed by an unindexed tax system does not depend on any increase in capital income or wealth but would be greatly magnified by such trends.

Inaccuracies in the measurement of capital income are not limited to the absence of adjustments for inflation, however. The retention and expansion of personal and corporate minimum taxes proclaim eloquently the continuing opportunities for tax avoidance that the post-1986 reform system retains.

A central and inescapable problem of the measurement of capital income revolves around the "realization" principle. The current system is a mix of alternative treatments. Tax falls on interest and dividends that flow to ordinary accounts of individuals but not on interest and dividends that flow to individual retirement accounts, other tax-exempt savings vehicles available to individuals pension funds, or insurance companies on policyholder reserves. Unrealized capital gains usually escape tax, but they are taxed if they have been earned on certain futures contracts. Realized capital losses may be offset against gains or deducted up to a modest limit, even if unrealized capital gains are far greater. The current rules governing deductibility of interest payments are so complicated and confusing that I can only describe them as a last-ditch attempt by a desperate Congress to curb serious abuse.

All of these problems of the current system are serious. Will they remain tolerable as the number of people with substantial assets and the average amount of such assets increases? The answer to this question will determine the future place of the personal income tax in 21st-century America.

Other Approaches to the Taxation of Capital Income

Most of the problems with the taxation of capital income previously described arise from congressional efforts and frequent failures to tax capital income annually. However, the taxation of capital income at less frequent intervals would have major advantages. First, it would reduce the distortions in the timing of consumption associated with annual taxation of capital income, as noted earlier. Second, it would reduce the considerable administrative burden in calculating and verifying capital income both for taxpayer and tax collector. Third, it would reduce the distortions of investment decisions that arise from different effective rates of tax on various types of capital income:

- *Constructive Realization.* Capital income could be taxed less than annually in a number of ways. The first is to tax previously unrealized capital gains at the time the taxpayer dies or transfers assets to others. Such "constructive realization" would reduce the lock-in effect of the current capital gains tax, the disincentive to sell appreciated assets that grows progressively more powerful as the taxpayer ages. This modification in the current tax structure would not entail any additional valuations for taxpayers subject to estate or gift tax. It could be part of an effort either to strengthen the current annual income tax or to tax capital income at less frequent intervals.

- *Annual versus Lifetime Income.* Second, it is well established that under certain rather restrictive conditions, income is defined as the discounted present value of either earnings plus inheritances or consumptions plus bequests. This definition implies that if the objective is to tax lifetime resources of the taxpaying unit, an income tax properly should not fall on annual capital income. Instead, tax should be imposed annually on consumption and gifts given in that year, with bequests treated as terminal consumption (subject to averaging).[9] Alternatively and equivalently for the individual, taxes could be imposed on all earnings and inheritances.[10] Whether such taxes would be more or less progressive than ones imposed by the current system would depend on the rate structure that was chosen.
- *Taxing Only Earnings.* David Bradford has suggested a third approach. Individuals would be taxed only on their earnings. Businesses would be taxed on gross receipts less wage payments (fringe benefits would not be deductible if they are not taxed at the individual level), payments to other businesses, and depreciation. Because investments would not be deductible when purchased, capital income would be taxable at the business level. The tax schedule for individuals could be proportional or progressive. The rate imposed on businesses would be at the maximum rate imposed on individuals.

Each of these approaches to taxation of capital income avoids many or all of the pitfalls encountered under the current system. The taxation of constructive realization of capital gains (which would increase revenue) could be combined with adjustment of some elements of capital income for the effects of inflation (which would reduce revenue) into a revenue-neutral package, both elements of which would improve the fairness and reduce the distortions of the income tax and buffer taxpayers from inflation-induced distortions.

- *Estate and Gift Taxation.* The estate and gift tax, the one tax that falls on wealth only once per generation, has become less important than it once was. It accounted for 2.3 percent of federal revenues in 1965, but today it represents only 0.7 percent, and it is projected to fall to 0.5 percent in 1991. Revenue from the tax is small and getting smaller for two reasons. First, Congress has so liberalized exemptions that few decedents have sufficient wealth to be taxable. Second, the avenues of avoidance are so numerous and well-traveled that George Cooper subtitled his careful review of this source of revenue *The Voluntary Tax.* Reversal of this trend would be essential to continued taxation of income should Congress conclude that annual taxation of capital income is infeasible. In that event, a tax on correctly measured lifetime income would have to fall on the sum of consumption plus gifts and bequests.[11]

Abandoning the Taxation of Capital Income

A strong minority of philosophers and political analysts and, perhaps, a majority of young economists have argued that consumption is a fairer and less distorting base for an economy's major tax than is income. The arguments run the gamut: Some economists take the philosophical position that people should be taxed for what they withdraw from the common pool of resources rather than for what they contribute to it; others claim the economic argument that capital income taxes inevitably distort individual decisions about when to consume; still others point to the administrative argument that abandonment of capital taxation would greatly simplify assessment and collection.

Two major ways of reaching this goal are available. The most commonly applied in many countries of the world, and widely discussed in the United States, is the tax on value added. Although the value-added tax (V.A.T.) comes in variants that fall on national income or GNP, the only versions in wide use fall solely on consumption.[12] The V.A.T. could be used either to supplement revenues or to reduce the absolute importance of some other tax. Various proponents have suggested that the V.A.T. replace all or part of the corporation income tax, the payroll tax, or the personal income tax. Alternatively, some experts have proposed a personal consumption tax, either as a supplement to or as a replacement for the personal income tax.

CONCLUSION

Most of the complexity and the provisions that create opportunities for planned tax avoidance under the personal income tax arise from the difficulty of taxing capital income. Although the Tax Reform Act of 1986 represents a landmark effort to limit such opportunities for avoidance, it did far less than the Treasury staff had suggested in 1984 that it would; and even the Treasury's recommendations would not have reached some of the fundamental problems with the taxation of capital income. Nevertheless, it remains to be seen whether the taxation of capital income has been improved sufficiently to remain an acceptable component of the income tax.

I argue that the stakes in this effort will rise continually because the relative importance of capital and capital income are likely to increase steadily and dramatically. In particular, international movements of capital and capital income are likely to grow in time. In short, economic trends are raising the importance of the segment of income that the personal income tax is least effective in reaching. This shortcoming must be overcome if the personal income tax is to remain the dominant source of revenue that it is today.

A Second Word about Taxing Affluence

YOLANDA KODRZYCKI HENDERSON

Across the 23 OECD countries, there is no general relationship between a country's GDP per capita and its overall level of taxation. In Europe, affluence and taxes are positively related; in particular, the Scandinavian countries have high incomes and a high profile for government. But the opposite is true in the United States, Canada, Japan, and Australia; all have relatively low taxes and government expenditures, even though incomes are high. Thus I do not expect that increased affluence will necessarily bring about more government.

What does stand out vividly in the OECD is that the more affluent countries rely more heavily for their revenues on income and profits taxes. (Relative to the overall pattern, the U.S. reliance on income and profits taxes is a bit low.) This positive association between affluence and income taxation is not guaranteed to hold true in the future. But given that income taxes are the most progressive form of taxation, they naturally tend to account for a larger share of revenues as national incomes rise. To reverse this trend takes a specific breakdown in acceptance of this form of taxation.

Because income taxes are such a large share of revenues in many countries, we are continually reforming their structure in order to make them acceptable. The recent tax reform effort in the United States reacted to abuses and excesses in order to make the tax structure more durable. Exemptions, deductions, and credits had not only become more targeted to taxpayers engaging in certain activities rather than being available generally but also appeared to be less equitable than they had been in the past. Incentives to promote capital formation were sometimes used for unproductive projects. Tax reform responded by limiting tax avoidance through tax-shelter partnerships, by promoting general tax preferences such as an increased personal exemption at the expense of specialized tax preferences, and by equalizing the tax treatment of different investment projects. Tax reformers did not deal with all the traditional objections to our income tax structure, but they did reverse some disturbing trends.

The United States should continue to evaluate its income tax structure to make it acceptable in the 21st century, but I am unconvinced as to whether or not the stakes will be significantly higher. It appears that capital transactions will increase, but the share of capital income may not be much greater. A key determinant is whether the United States will find investment opportunities overseas so that capital deepening in the United States does not lower the rate of return to savings.

In the case of domestic capital markets, the ratio of capital income to labor income is projected to be about 10 percent higher in 50 years than it is today; this is well within the range of historical fluctuations. In the case of open capital markets, the ratio is 50 percent higher. This view assumes that foreign countries will not also be increasing their saving. I think we need to take a closer look and include this factor in an expanded model. A worldwide increase in saving could serve to depress worldwide returns, leaving capital incomes in the United States at about the same level relative to labor incomes.

We should not underestimate the potential role of fringe benefits in preserving a strong income tax structure. Exclusions of employer pension plans and medical insurance premiums are the two largest tax expenditures under the personal income tax. Together, they account for about $70 billion in foregone revenues in fiscal year 1988, and Henry Aaron's projections indicate continued growth in these items. The increasingly widespread nature of these benefits makes them popular tax preference items, but coverage differs significantly, and thus this tax preference reduces the equity of the income tax.

Turning to capital taxation, I would agree that the recent U.S. tax reform left major imperfections that threaten to undermine our support for capital taxation. Corrections for some of these problems are feasible; in particular, the Treasury I proposals for indexing depreciation allowances and capital gains for inflation. On the other hand, indexing interest payments and receipts is a tougher problem, and one for which we do not have workable blueprints. The Treasury proposal would not have produced correct results for financial intermediaries, and it was flawed in excluding home mortgage interest. Until a comprehensive plan for indexing can be devised, I doubt we will adopt partial solutions.

To tax capital income at less frequent intervals, as Aaron mentions, would open the door to abuses of the system, I fear. One of the important innovations of 20th-century taxation has been withholding taxes on wage income at the source, which essentially is a way of tallying up tax liability more frequently. Several years ago, withholding was proposed also for interest income, but it was not enacted. This was unfortunate for tax compliance. I also think that stiffer estate taxes, while a good idea, are unlikely to be enacted until we can convince people that their neighbors are complying with the tax. Any tax that is levied infrequently is more easily avoided, and any tax that is easily avoided is perceived to be unfair.

Another solution would be to move to a tax on consumed income, since its zero tax on capital income averts many of the problems of income taxation. But whatever the merits of a consumption tax, it introduces all sorts of new challenges, including intergenerational equity and international coordination. I am convinced that some of the benefits of consumption taxation can be achieved via a broad-based income tax with a low rate.

For example, take the failure to index the tax code. If we mismeasure income during inflationary times by understating depreciation allowances or overstating capital gains and interest, then the distortion is much worse if we take this mismeasured income and apply a high tax rate. If the rate of taxation is low, then errors in measuring income lead to relatively low costs in terms of errors in computing tax liability. Just by lowering tax rates, the Tax Reform Act achieved some lessening of the sensitivity of taxes to inflation.

Significant potential for lowering rates still exists even in the wake of tax reform: the individual income tax base remains less than 50 percent of total personal income. Although we should try to develop workable rules for indexing incomes for inflation, we should not ignore the simpler approach of broadening the tax base and lowering rates.

18

A Pollution Tax Makes Sense

WALLACE E. OATES

Most people would say that the central role of the tax system is to produce the revenues needed to finance the activities of government. While this may be true, it is also true that taxes impinge in important ways on the functioning of the economy. For example, a system of taxation typically embodies a myriad of incentives for individuals and firms.

The trouble is that the vast majority of these incentives are harmful. They introduce distortions into the functioning of the economy, with resulting losses in social welfare. A tax on wage or salary income, for example, alters work incentives for individuals. If 50 or 60 cents of an extra $1 earned is drained off in additional taxes, people have a compelling incentive to cut back on work effort and substitute untaxed leisure pursuits. The welfare loss to society from such distortions is not trivial. In a recent survey, the economist Edgar Browning reports that although the magnitude of the distortion associated with taxes on labor earnings is still uncertain, it is potentially very large. Estimates range from a low of about 8 cents lost per $1 of tax revenues to a figure in excess of $1. The true cost to society of the taxes we pay is larger—probably much larger—than the amount of revenues actually collected.

As economists have long noted, however, certain kinds of taxes can correct existing misallocations of resources rather than distort the economy. Such taxes effectively cost society less than the revenues that they generate.

Taxes on polluting activities are a major case of such "corrective taxes," and in economic terms they present a very attractive source of revenues. The primary function of such taxes is to make the economy function more efficiently. Through their use, we have an opportunity to employ the tax system not only to raise revenues but also to enhance the operations of the economy. In thinking about the future evolution of tax systems throughout the world, it is important to give careful consideration to such corrective taxes.

Taxes on pollution deserve special consideration. During the coming decades, growing populations and economies will place increasing pressure on the world's limited environmental resources. A judicious use of taxes on polluting activities can help to achieve two objectives: the establishment of a powerful set of incentives for the protection of the environment and the raising of needed revenues to finance the public sector, including expenditures on important public environmental programs. The first tasks are to develop the economic rationale for this form of taxation and to explore its potential in a policy setting. We then examine some alternative policy instruments for protection of the environment.

THE ECONOMIC CASE FOR THE TAXATION OF POLLUTION

Economists have devoted much of their effort to understanding the properties of a free market system, and in the process they have developed important insights into the efficiency-enhancing potential of a competitive system. They have established, in principle at least, that a competitive market system, characterized by decentralized choices by individual consumers and producers, can provide an efficient allocation of resources. This is really a formalization of Adam Smith's famous "invisible hand." In a sense, the competitive system provides the right set of incentives to producers and consumers, so that the goods and services people want get produced, and in the least costly way.

Essential to this result, however, is the requirement that an appropriate price be attached to each of society's scarce resources. In other words, any activity that imposes a cost on society must be accompanied by a price, and that price must equal the social cost. For most goods and services, the market takes care of this matter. The forces of supply and demand lead to a market price that accurately reflects the cost of such items as bread and refrigerators.

There are, however, certain circumstances under which such a price may not emerge—and pollution is a classic case. Early in the 20th century, at Cambridge University, A. C. Pigou set forth the basic economic perspective on pollution and developed its policy implications in *The Economics of Welfare.* Later economists have developed Pigou's analysis with greater care and in more formal terms. The basic idea is straightforward: The lack of an appropriate price for certain scarce environmental resources, such as clean air and water, has led to their excessive use and resulted in what the textbooks call "market failure."

The source of this failure is what economists term an "externality." For example, a producer whose factory spews smoke on a neighboring residential area is imposing a real cost on those who must live with the dirty air, but this cost is "external" to the firm. The firm need not bear this cost as it does for the labor and raw materials it employs. While the price of such labor and materials leads the firm to economize on their use, it has no such incentive to control its smoke emissions. The point is simply that whenever a scarce resource is made available free of charge (as is the case with our limited stocks of clean air and water), it is bound to be used to excess.

From this perspective, the source of excessive environmental degradation is the absence of the appropriate price for an important class of society's scarce resources. The policy implication of this perspective is also straightforward; as Pigou pointed out, in the absence of the interplay of supply and demand, the government must intervene and impose an artificial price—a tax, or effluent fee, as it is sometimes called, on damaging waste emissions. As microeconomic analysis easily shows, if this tax or fee is equal to the value of the damages from an additional unit of emissions, then sources will have the proper incentive for controlling their discharges of pollutants.

Economic analysis thus suggests the need for taxation of pollution to correct for a serious "failure" in a competitive market system. Apart from any revenues that such taxes would produce, they would have a beneficial effect on society's use of its scarce resources. Rather than distorting economic decisions as most taxes do, a system of effluent fees would establish the correct incentives for the use of our environmental resources.

Economists are virtually unanimous in their support of these kinds of pricing incentives for protection of the environment, but to their dismay, they have not had much influence on the design of measures for pollution control. Instead, regulators across the world have opted for the more traditional "command-and-control" (CAC) techniques, under which the environmental agency specifies the levels and kinds of treatment technologies to be adopted by the industrial sources of emissions. A substantial body of empirical studies now documents the enormous wastes associated with such programs.

Unfortunately, the CAC approach is a relatively clumsy and costly way to achieve our environmental objectives. It is impossible for an environmental agency to know what is the least costly control technique for each source of waste discharges.

Pricing incentives are well suited to the task, however. In principle at least, a pollution tax set at the appropriate level can attain our standards for environmental quality in the least expensive fashion. In responding to the taxation of their discharges while seeking to minimize costs, firms will adopt and use the least expensive control technologies, and this will lead to the least-cost pattern of discharges among sources. Each source will adjust its emissions so that the marginal cost of additional control equals the tax.

For example, if the tax were 10 cents per pound of sulfur emitted, it would pay each source to continue to reduce its discharges to the point where the cost of cutting emissions by one more pound is 10 cents. So long as the source can reduce its discharges further, at a cost of less than 10 cents per pound, it pays to do so. After all sources have established their cost-minimizing levels of control, the cost at the margin of reducing emissions for every source will thus be 10 cents, and this is just what is required for the least-cost solution for society. Note that there is no way discharges could be shifted from a source with higher control costs at the margin to one with lower costs. Since all sources have the same marginal control costs, it follows that aggregate emissions will have been reduced in the least expensive way to society.

Pollution taxes can thus make use of the decentralized, efficiency-enhancing forces of a market economy to achieve our environmental goals at relatively low cost. Compared to existing CAC programs, the potential savings are very large. Studies of U.S. programs for the management of air and water quality indicate that the costs (the control costs to sources, not the administrative costs of environmental agencies) run from about twice to more than ten times what the least-cost outcome would be! These studies also reveal that marginal control costs for some sources are many times higher than those of others, so a straightforward rearrangement of control efforts among sources could effect large savings in pollution control expenditures. We are effectively paying far more than necessary to clean up the environment.

Under the CAC approach to environmental policy, there is also a longer-run source of wastes that is more difficult to quantify, but that source may be even more important than the short-run waste. The long-term success of our environmental programs will depend on our capacity to discover more effective and less costly ways to control pollution. It is thus very important to have in place incentives that promote research and development activities in abatement technology. The CAC approach not only fails to provide such incentives but may actually discourage such pursuits. A source that finds a new and better way to control its waste discharges may be "rewarded" by the environmental agency with a tougher set of abatement directives. Under a CAC system, it is not clear that it is in the interest of sources to seek out new control techniques.

On the other hand, under a system of pollution taxes, such innovations in control technology are directly profitable. A firm that discovers a new, less expensive way of controlling its waste discharges can employ this new technique to reduce its discharges even further. It will realize savings both on its control activities and on the reduced tax bill associated with a lower level of waste emissions. Note also that society benefits further from the cleaner environment that results. In short, pollution taxes provide an effective set of incentives for the development over the long run of new and better ways to reduce pollution—incentives which are either absent or seriously muted under existing CAC programs.

THE REVENUE POTENTIAL OF POLLUTION TAXES

The basic economic rationale for the taxation of polluting activities is thus to correct a malfunctioning in the market system—namely the absence of an appropriate price on our scarce environmental resources, including clean air and water. This implies that the level of tax rates should be determined by our environmental objectives, not by revenue considerations. Tax rates should be set so that waste discharges are cut back to levels consistent with our targets for air and water quality. As a kind of beneficial side effect, such taxes will produce revenues for the public sector.

How much in revenues would such taxes be likely to generate? This is not an easy question to answer. One careful study of this question was made by David Terkla of Boston University. Terkla examined a hypothetical national effluent tax on emissions of particulate matter and sulfur oxides by stationary sources. Considering a range of tax rates sufficiently high to attain U.S. environmental targets for air quality, he estimated that the annual revenues in 1982 dollars would range from a low of $1.8 billion to a high of $8.7 billion. The great bulk of these revenues, incidentally, would come from the tax on sulfur oxides, with the revenue estimates for this tax alone ranging from a low of $1.7 billion to an upper limit of $8.5 billion.

Another recent estimate comes from the Joint Committee on Taxation of the U.S. Congress. Taking as a potential proposal a tax of 45 cents per pound on sulfur dioxide and nitrogen dioxide emissions from boilers and furnaces, the committee's staff estimated annual revenues for 1988–1990 of about $6.3 billion. In addition, they considered a tax on the emission of chlorofluorocarbons—chemicals thought to deplete the planet's ozone layer. The potential revenues associated with this particular tax were estimated at about $500 million per annum.

These revenue estimates are not large when compared to the overall needs of the public sector. Pollution taxes could not replace in their entirety the major taxes, such as income and sales taxes, in our revenue systems. Nevertheless, they could play a significant role in the evolution of national tax structures. The estimates previously mentioned are for revenues from taxes on only a few air pollutants. A broader set of pollution taxes encompassing most of the major air and water pollutants (and, perhaps, other wastes as well, such as those that find their way into landfills) would obviously produce greater amounts of tax monies.

In certain instances, it may make sense to earmark some of these revenues for pressing environmental programs. This has been done to some extent in Western Europe. Several countries, including Belgium, France, and West Germany, have made a limited use of effluent charges for water-quality management. These charges are not "pure" effluent fees: They have not been designed with the primary objective of regulating levels of waste emissions. In fact, the levels of the taxes are low and sometimes do not apply directly to marginal emissions, so they do not provide a direct incentive to cut back on waste discharges. The taxes have typically been used to produce revenues needed to underwrite the operations of the water management authority. Nevertheless, these programs do represent a beginning in the taxation of pollution. Moreover, the Organization for Economic Cooperation and Development (OECD) countries have adopted the so-called "Polluter-Pays-Principle." This at least represents a general commitment to exploring the role for pollution taxes.

From the perspective of revenues, the potential role for taxes on pollution involves the substitution of these revenues for revenues from "harmful" taxes. For example, effluent fee receipts could reduce the extent of reliance on income taxes and excise levies on particular products. Terkla, in his study, goes beyond the basic revenue estimates to examine the potential "efficiency gains" from employing effluent charges. These gains result from reducing the distortions to the economy caused by other forms of taxation. And these gains turn out to be of measurable significance.

Terkla calculates, for example, that if his estimated revenues from the taxes on particulate matter and sulfur emissions were substituted for tax receipts on labor income, there would be a saving to society ranging from $.6 billion to $3.1 billion. If these revenues were substituted for corporate income taxes, the efficiency gains would be even larger—ranging from $1 billion to $4.9 billion. These results suggest that the gains from an improved functioning of the economy might offset as much as half of the revenues themselves. Pollution taxes thus offer an appealing opportunity to adjust the tax system in a way that reduces reliance on the more harmful forms of taxation.

THE TAXATION OF POLLUTION IN A POLICY SETTING

If the taxation of pollution has such compelling economic attractions, why have public officials been so reluctant to introduce these measures? This is an intriguing and important question, one that must be addressed if we are to pursue proposals for such taxes seriously.

Some critics have objected to the proposal on practical, administrative grounds. Pollution taxes, since they are levied on levels of emissions, would seem to require continuous monitoring of waste discharges. It is true, of course, that any system of pollution control must have a monitoring system, but the CAC approach typically requires only that checks be made to ensure that the requisite equipment or treatment procedures are in place and are being properly employed. Pollution taxes, in contrast, require the actual measurement of the quantities of wastes discharged, since the source's tax bill is based on its level of emissions.

This is admittedly a matter needing some attention, but it does not seem to constitute an insurmountable obstacle to a system of effluent fees. In some instances, such monitoring is a fairly straightforward and economical matter. In other cases, there may be acceptable proxy measures for emissions; for example, it should be possible to obtain reasonably reliable estimates of sulfur emissions from knowledge of the sulfur content of the fuel that is burned and the efficiency of the treatment procedures used. The monitoring issue, at least for many major pollutants, is not likely to be a decisive objection.

Pollution taxes are a source of concern also because they result in higher costs for polluters, who, therefore, will find it harder to compete both in domestic and world markets. But it is important to remember that the fundamental principle at issue here is attaching an appropriate "price" to society's scarce resources. We could obviously reduce the costs to firms if we made labor and raw materials available without charge (as in a sense we have done with certain of our most basic environmental resources), leaving no incentive to economize on their use, but economic chaos would result from such an absence of prices. A price should be attached to the environmental resources, too, so the users pay the full cost of all the inputs they employ in the production of products.

Taxes on pollution will raise the cost of goods that make

comparatively heavy use of the taxed environmental resources. This is as it should be, since the new pattern of relative costs and prices will more accurately reflect the true costs to society of the goods and services it produces.

Some interesting longer-run consequences for the world economy are also involved, particularly a shift in patterns of comparative advantage. Countries that pursue active pollution control programs and employ taxes to curtail waste emissions will in the long run find that their international cost advantage is in those goods for which production involves few polluting side effects. In contrast, countries that ignore their environmental problems and do not make polluting industries bear the costs of their damaging waste discharges will come to specialize in and export goods with a relatively heavy "pollution content." They will become the home for the world's "dirty" industries. Thus pollution taxes can play a role in the evolution of a national economy specializing in the production of relatively "clean" goods for purposes of world trade.

It may be, however, that the most serious obstacle to the introduction of effluent taxes is a matter of misunderstanding, for economists seemingly have not made the case for such taxes in a clear and compelling way. In a fascinating study, Steven Kelman, a political scientist at Harvard, explored with great care the politics of environmental policy in interviews with policymakers and lobbyists. Kelman's findings are quite striking. Of the 61 individuals he interviewed (including staff members of U.S. congressional committees dealing with environmental matters and the professional staff members of Washington environmental and trade organizations), not a single person was able to explain the basic economic efficiency argument for effluent charges! Instead, each expressed support or opposition to pollution taxes in basically ideological terms. Opponents of such taxes often referred to them as "licenses to pollute," while supporters typically cited ideological arguments about replacing bureaucratic administration with the market. What is clear from Kelman's study is that the basic economic case for a system of pollution taxes is not well understood in the policy arena. This is why it is especially important to bring the proposal for effluent taxes out into the open—to encourage discussion in order to improve the level of understanding.

In considering the various policy options for pollution control, an intriguing alternative to taxes has received some response at the policy level: a system of transferable discharge permits. The basic idea is that the environmental agency issues discharge permits for particular pollutants to industry and limits the total number of permits in order to ensure the achievement of environmental targets for concentrations of each pollutant in the environment. These permits can either be auctioned off to polluters or simply distributed according to some sensible formula. The key feature of the permits is that they are transferable: They can be bought and sold among sources. The appeal of this system is that, as markets for these permits develop, they will be purchased by those to whom they have the greatest value, that is, by those for whom abatement efforts are the most expensive.

As with pollution taxes, such a permit system can, in principle, achieve any specified level of environmental quality at the minimum cost. In fact, there is a kind of symmetry in the two systems. Using the pollution tax approach, the environmental agency sets the tax at the appropriate level, and sources respond by cutting back their waste discharges to the target amount. Using the permit system, the agency issues the requisite quantity of permits, and sources respond by bidding up the price of these permits to the market-clearing level. In principle, the price that emerges from the operations of the permit market should be precisely the same as the charge that the agency would have set under the tax regime.

There are, of course, some important administrative differences between the two systems. The marketable permit approach has the advantage of giving the environmental agency direct control over the level of discharges. The tax system allows the agency only indirect control in that it sets the level of the tax but depends on sources to cut back discharges in response to the tax. If the tax is not set at the right level initially, further adjustments will be needed to attain the target level of environmental quality. For this and other reasons, there has been a tendency in recent years for policymakers to lean in the direction of transferable permits.

The Environmental Protection Agency has introduced a program of "emissions trading" for the management of air quality. Under this rubric, states may design air-pollution control programs that allow sources, subject to various rules, to trade entitlements for waste discharges for certain pollutants. In a similar vein, the state of Wisconsin has proposed a program of transferable discharge permits for the management of water quality on some of its rivers.

The choice between a system of pollution taxes and one of transferable permits is far from resolved. It depends in large part on how well the markets for transferable permits can be expected to function, but experience with such markets is still limited and inconclusive. From the perspective of revenues, fees are attractive; they generate tax monies. Of course, permits can also be a source of revenues if the environmental authority auctions them off. Under existing systems, however, these permits have effectively been distributed without charges to sources, so they have not produced any revenues for the public sector.

Various countries have shown an interest in the U.S. experience with emissions trading; the West Germans, in particular, have been studying the program carefully but have not yet come to a conclusion. Systems of pollution taxes and transferable discharge permits both have compelling attractions as policy instruments for environmental management. I think both should play a role in the development of our overall programs of environmental policy.

CONCLUSION

During the coming decades we should concern ourselves not only with developing a tax system that can produce revenues sufficient to eliminate currently existing deficits but also with one that promotes our other social and economic objectives. One of these objectives is to facilitate, rather than impede, the functioning of the private market sector of the economy. Most of our major forms of taxation, such as income and sales taxes, have harmful side effects on the market economy. But other taxes, such as taxes on pollution, have beneficial side effects—they correct rather than distort incentives for market behavior.

Taxes on pollution can contribute in two important ways to our well-being: They can generate revenues to finance needed public programs, and they can provide powerful, direct incentives for protection of the environment. The potential revenues from such taxes are not so large as to supplant entirely the major, more traditional forms of taxation, but they can serve to reduce reliance on these more damaging types of taxes. For these reasons, the taxation of pollution merits serious consideration in any long-term investigation of the reform of our revenue system.

19
Forces That Shape Tax Policy

VITO TANZI

In recent years, economists have had little interest in the question of whether or not a relationship exists between structural changes in a country's economy and changes in the structure and, perhaps, the level of taxation. This question did attract some attention about 20 years ago, especially in connection with the tax systems of developing countries. At that time, a small group of fiscal economists, including Professor Richard Musgrave, attempted to determine the extent to which various structural characteristics of national economies influence both the level and the structure of tax systems. The results of these attempts were used by tax experts to advise policy makers on changes that they could bring to the tax systems of their countries.

However, the relationship between economic structures and taxation is an important element of any forecast about the future of taxation. The main question is: How might future structural changes influence tax systems? This chapter begins with a brief review of the history of changes in tax structure in the course of economic development.[1] I then consider economic changes likely to occur in industrial countries, especially the United States, during the next several decades. The last consideration, looking into the future, is a task that would greatly benefit from the wisdom of a crystal ball, but I must rely on the power of informed speculation.

A LOOK AT THE PAST

The levels and structures of tax systems have changed dramatically during the 20th century. Table 1 shows the remarkable increase in tax levels that have occurred in four major industrial countries since the beginning of the 1900s. Similar changes have occurred in other industrial countries. A cross section of present taxation levels of countries would show an average tax level of about 13 percent of gross domestic product (GDP) for the poorest 20 developing countries and more than 37 percent for the industrial countries. The level of taxation, as revealed through the study of "time series" information, rose fairly regularly over the years along with per capita incomes. Cross-sectional studies confirm that the level of taxation is influenced by the level of income at any given time.[2]

Changes in the structure of taxation are particularly apparent in many industrial countries where large increases in revenues have been realized through increases in income taxes (especially personal income taxes) and social security taxes. These two taxes now

Table 1
Tax Levels in Major Western Countries, 1900–84

	1900–01	1913–14	1924–25	1965	1975	1984
France	15.0	14.1	20.0	35.0	37.4	45.5
United Kingdom	10.0	11.3	24.8	30.6	35.5	38.5
Germany	8.0	10.5	29.2	31.6	35.7	37.7
United States	7.8	6.7	11.1	26.3	29.6	29.0

Sources: Edwin R. A. Seligman, *Studies in Public Finance* (New York: Macmillan, 1925), Ch. 1; and *Revenue Statistics of OECD Countries,* 1965–85 OECD, Paris, (1986).

Note: For 1900–01, 1913–14, and 1924–25, the figures are percentages of national income. For later years they are percentages of gross domestic product.

account for about 63 percent of the total tax revenues of the countries in the Organization for Economic Cooperation and Development (OECD) and for 24 percent of GDP.

Customs duties, once an important source of revenue, have become insignificant in industrial countries, but they continue to generate about a third of total tax revenues in developing countries. For the U.S. government, the share of customs duties in total receipts fell from 56 percent in 1880, to 41 percent in 1900, and to 14 percent in 1925. By 1955, customs duties were contributing less than 1 percent of total federal government receipts. Similar trends have occurred in other industrial countries. In developing countries, however, as the level of per capita income rises, the share of foreign trade taxes in total tax revenue also falls; but even so, these taxes remain important at all levels.

Some economists have theorized on these changes in tax structures in order to predict the future. Harley Hinrichs, in his 1966 book, *A General Theory of Tax Structure Change During Economic Development,* argues that the early phase of economic development was accompanied by a shift from traditional "direct taxes" (on land, livestock, water rights, etc.) to "indirect" taxes, especially those connected with the foreign sector. Eventually, he points out, modern, direct taxes will replace indirect taxes.

In *Fiscal Systems,* Richard Musgrave emphasizes that economic, political, and social factors all affect a country's tax structure and that it may be difficult, therefore, to distinguish the economic effects from the others. Musgrave points out that economic factors influence tax structure through the creation of new tax bases and "tax handles." By tax handles he means the ability of tax administrations to collect taxes imposed on particular tax bases. However, changes in tax handles are inevitably accompanied by changes in the economic objective of tax policy.[3]

Musgrave argues that, with the development of the economy, more tax bases and more tax handles become available, giving policymakers more freedom in determining the tax structure of the country. He theorizes that as a consequence, the tax structure comes to depend more on social and political objectives, such as the redistribution of income, and less on purely economic factors, so the structure of the economy becomes progressively less important in determining tax structure. In Musgrave's words, the tax structure becomes a "free policy choice." He attributes the increasing importance of income taxes less to the changes in the structure of the economy, which facilitated the imposition of these taxes, than to the spreading of "social and political trends toward redistribution that have characterized the last half century or more."

When the income tax was permanently introduced in the United States in 1913, it was generally considered the "fairest tax"—a reputation it probably lost in the 1970s.[4] By 1965, in the OECD countries income taxes had reached 9.6 percent of GDP and 35.2 percent of total tax revenue. By 1982, these percentages had risen to 14.5 percent of GDP and 40 percent of total tax revenue. Furthermore, these figures do not include social security contributions, which are also taxes on income. These represented another 5 percent of GDP and 18.19 percent of total taxation in 1965 and 9 percent of GDP and 24 percent of total taxation in 1982.

The growing importance of income taxes in industrial countries was a result not only of changes in social and political trends but also of structural changes in the economy. Two merit mention: first, the increased proportion of total personal income that individuals derived from the sale of their labor services or the lending of their wealth (tangible or financial) to others; and second, the gradual concentration of income in fewer, larger economic units (governments, large corporations, etc.).

It has always been difficult to tax the self-employed, so in an economy characterized by much self-employment, it would be very difficult to have a tax system that relies on income. The Internal Revenue Service has collected considerable evidence indicating that tax compliance is highest when taxes can be withheld at the source by those who pay the incomes. Similar evidence is available from other countries. There is also evidence from many countries that tax compliance is a function of the size of an establishment: the larger the enterprise, the higher its tax compliance. This conclusion is of particular importance for income taxes.

THE EFFECTS OF INNOVATION AND EXPENDITURE

Two other factors have influenced the structure of taxation in past years and are likely to continue to do so in the future: tax innovation and the structure of public expenditure.

By tax innovation, I mean the "discovery" of new taxes. For instance, when the income tax was introduced in the United States in 1913, it was still a relatively new tax even though it had been levied for some time in Europe and even in the United States for a few years during and after the Civil War. (The income tax was probably invented in Europe, perhaps in Florence, during the 16th century.) Another example is the value-added tax (V.A.T.). Although the concept had been known at least since 1918, when a German industrial executive first proposed it, the V.A.T. was first introduced in 1954 in France. (The Shoup Mission had proposed it to Japan in 1949, and the state of Michigan used a version as early as 1953.) Within three decades the V.A.T. has become a very popular tax that is now levied in at least 40 countries.

Today, there is much interest in a tax on "cash flow," just as there was around 1960 in an "expenditure tax." The point is that the future structure of taxation is likely to depend to some extent on the inventiveness of tax experts in devising new tax forms. What these will be depends, in part, on the availability of new tax handles.

As Musgrave emphasizes, policy objectives influence tax structures and tax levels. However, policy objectives are achieved by instruments other than taxes, such as public expenditure and regulation. In the future, the same is likely to hold. That is, changes in social objectives are likely to affect the structure and the level of taxation but so are any changes in attitude toward the use of instruments, while policy objectives remain the same. For example, in recent years deregulation and privatization have been popular in many countries. Even in the absence of changes in policy objectives, deregulation and privatization may make necessary the introduction of assistance to some groups (who were being protected by the regulations or the public activities) in the form of subsidies or tax expenditures.

There has also been an increasing awareness of and concern about the efficiency effects of high marginal tax rates. To reduce these rates, tax bases have been broadened, often through the elimination of tax preferences (tax expenditures). Again, in the absence of changes in policy objectives, the elimination or reduction in tax expenditures may eventually require increases in public spending and thus increases in tax levels.

FUTURE SHOCKS

Over the next several decades, many changes—political, social, and economic—are likely to take place throughout the world. Already in the past 20 years we have witnessed a reversal from the attitude that justified and demanded a large role for the government to one that considerably restricts that role. One future possibility is that the present conservative trend will continue for years to come. Another is that the political cycle will repeat itself so that, in future decades, the electorate will once again demand a larger role for government.

While the present conservative trend has slowed down the growth in the level of taxation of many countries, it has not yet reduced that level by any significant amount. The latest OECD statistics indicate that the share of total taxes in GDP is still growing in most industrial countries, though at a slow pace. So far, the conservative climate has had a greater impact on the structure of tax systems than on levels of taxation.[5]

Changes in political attitudes may require a rearrangement of policy objectives. For example, the electorate may come to consider the pursuit of growth to be more important than that of a fair distribution of income as an objective of economic policy. Alternatively, changes in political attitudes may be related less to the ultimate objectives of economic policy than to the means of achieving them—such as doubts about the ability of governments to achieve those objectives or achieve them at acceptable costs. For example, taxpayers decide that in the presence of large underground economic activities and growing tax evasion and avoidance no real social objective can be achieved by highly progressive statutory rates.

What we have observed in many countries over the past two decades may not be so much a demand for changes in the ranking of economic objectives as a change in the popular perception of what government can do. In the 1960s, many people thought, unrealistically, that government could do everything. In the early 1980s, many thought, equally unrealistically, that government could not do anything right. Perhaps between these two periods, people's objectives—such as fair distribution of income—did not change, but they became skeptical about the government's ability to bring them about. This led to demands for lowering marginal tax rates and for flat-rate taxes. If the government cannot implement a tax system that is effectively fair and progressive, why keep an instrument that is likely to create problems of horizontal equity while generating economic distortions that may have a high cost in terms of growth? However, if in the future the perception about the ability of the government to efficiently control its policy instrument changes, people's attitudes toward the government may change once again. Increased information and changes in the structure of the economy may increase or decrease the effectiveness of policy instruments.

Social attitudes toward government programs—toward the level of taxation, the relative importance of taxes on consumption as compared to taxes on incomes, and so forth—change over time. Some of these changes are brought about by changes in the structure of the population. The old are likely to prefer taxes on income rather than on consumption since they spend a greater portion of their incomes on consumer goods than the young do. Young workers are likely to favor taxes on capital income rather than on labor income since they do not have much capital income. Older workers and retirees are likely to favor taxes on labor income compared to capital income, and so forth. Thus the demographic structure of the population inevitably influences the structure (and the level) of taxation.

Future years will bring about major demographic changes. In the next 40 years, the populations of the United States and other industrial countries will age considerably. As the share of the population made up by the elderly increases, changes will occur in patterns of consumption (perhaps reducing the level of saving), the attitude toward the tax structure, and the demand for some government services. The burden on social security systems will become heavy.[6] Projections for the year 2000 recently released by the U.S. Bureau of Labor Statistics indicate that future growth of the labor force will come mainly from blacks, Hispanics, and Orientals. The proportion of women in the labor force will also increase.[7] All of these trends are likely to affect both the need for tax revenue and the structure of the tax system.

The growing interdependence of the world economy is also bound to have a great influence on the tax system. This interdependence has several dimensions. Financial markets are being integrated to such an extent that some observers already talk about a world financial market with major centers in New York, Tokyo, London, and Frankfurt. Goods markets are becoming progressively more integrated because of the high growth of world trade as compared to the growth of the world economy and also because of the growing role of multinational corporations. (Intracompany trade now accounts for half of all exports.) The basket of goods one finds today in different countries is bigger, more varied, and more similar to that of other countries. World trade is growing faster than world income (despite the ominous threat of protectionism). It seems realistic to assume that this trend will continue and the goods markets will become progressively more integrated.

Movements of workers from country to country are likely to continue to be restrained except, perhaps, within particular markets, such as the European Community (EC). At the same time, movements of people—tourists, pensioners who retire to foreign countries—will continue to grow, thus increasing the lack of correlation between the places where individuals earn their incomes and the places where they spend them.

Finally, countries will become progressively more aware of the fact that there are "public goods" and "public bads" (such as pollution, overfishing, destruction of the forests) that are international in character and that require more policy coordination. This must extend to systems of taxation, for all of these changes have strong implications for tax systems. There may come a time when the

Internal Revenue Service may have to be supplemented by an "International Revenue Service." Supranational tax systems already exist in the EC and other common markets.

LINES OF GROWTH

Short of a major catastrophe, per capita income should continue to rise during the coming decades. An annual real rate of growth of about 2 percent seems to be a realistic possibility. If this growth is not accompanied by wide fluctuations in economic activity and by increasing poverty for some groups, the combination of increased affluence and a continuation of a conservative political environment should lead to reductions in transfer payments, which, in turn, would result in lower tax levels.

However, the aging of the population would require more transfers to older people. Furthermore, it should be recalled that over the past decades, increased affluence was associated with more rather than fewer transfers. But the instability (the cyclical character) of past economic performance may have been partly responsible for these trends. The instability of economic performance in the past may have also been partly responsible for the popularity of the income tax since this form of revenue is characterized by considerable built-in flexibility. In a period of stable growth, however, the built-in flexibility of the income tax, which implies that revenue grows faster than income, would become an obstacle to growth.

Technology has also been changing rapidly in recent decades, and many people suspect we are at the threshold of a new technological revolution, especially with the widespread use of computers. Technological changes are likely to continue to influence the structure of the economy and, through it, the tax systems.

The technological developments of the recent past were associated largely with processes that required increasingly large plants. Economies of scale brought about a concentration of production in relatively few large units. This process facilitated the use of income taxes. Current trends indicate that future technology is for the most part less likely to require these large establishments except in a few sectors (the production of airplanes?), and economies of scale will become less important. Probably much future output will take place in very small units producing customized products for particular consumers. (Much of the employment recently created in the United States takes place in small production units.) In addition, affluence is likely to reduce the demand for standardized products and to increase the demand for products made to specific orders.

For some lines of production, workers may not have to leave home at all. They may be able to get most of the information they need by computer. This process is already happening. For example, shoe factories have almost disappeared in Italy, which is still the world's leading exporter of shoes. Instead, shoe production has gone "underground," moving from large factories into very small production units. Many workers with small machines fill orders directly from home. A manager with a good secretary can coordinate the production. The same process is apparently going on in the manufacture of fashionable clothes, which can be produced efficiently in very small units. In many sectors, highly decentralized, small units are likely to become as efficient as larger units or perhaps more efficient, especially for high-quality or customized products.

This decentralization, or even the atomization, of production activities will have important implications for tax systems because it will become increasingly more difficult to tax wages and profits. As already mentioned, it has always been difficult to tax the self-employed, and larger establishments have had a higher degree of tax compliance than smaller ones.

By the same token, technological changes in communications are generating enormous amounts of information on individuals, including data on their credit worthiness, bank accounts, purchases, travel, meals, accommodations, and so forth. Such information is now routinely stored in the memories of hundreds of computers owned by private companies. If somehow it could be collated and made accessible to the tax authorities, it could be used for tax purposes, for example, to develop estimates of "presumed incomes" or "presumed total expenditures" for individuals. Major legislative changes would be required to accomplish this objective, and it is likely that taxpayers would resist such legislation as a massive invasion of their privacy. (The Japanese tax authorities have not yet succeeded in assigning an identification number to taxpayers.)

Another major structural change now taking place, and likely to continue, is the growth of services. Modern economies seem to have relatively fewer needs for products as compared to services. This explains, in part, the sharp decline in the prices of commodities in spite of several years of uninterrupted growth in the economies of the industrial countries. Services for health and education, for the maintenance of durables, personal services, and so forth now account for a very large and growing proportion of total employment. Much of the recent growth in employment in the United States has, in fact, taken place in the service sector.

Current forecasts about the growth of employment over the next 10 years indicate that the trend toward a service economy will continue. What has been happening is that the share of national output accounted for by manufacturing has remained relatively constant, but that share is being produced by a progressively smaller share of the labor force.[8] However, many service activities are difficult to tax, and tax evasion is often much higher than in the manufacturing sector. We must thus contemplate a considerably changed and more difficult future for taxes.

WHERE IT ALL MAY LEAD

We can now attempt to speculate about the kind of tax systems that we are likely to have, say, 30 or 40 years from now, and to draw some general conclusions. Let us assume a scenario whereby (a) the present relatively conservative environment continues; (b) the aging of the population takes place as predicted; (c) the growth of the labor force is made up predominantly of minorities (including women); (d) the process of integration of the world economy continues; (e) per capita income continues to grow at the present average rate; (f) large establishments are progressively replaced by smaller productive units; and (g) the trend toward a service economy continues. What effect will these trends have on the tax system?

It is conceivable that they will make it difficult for countries to maintain their present levels and structures of taxation. For example, in a highly integrated world, where capital will be able to move freely across countries, it will become increasingly difficult to maintain high tax rates on capital incomes. Such rates would simply stimulate capital to emigrate from the high-tax to the low-tax countries. The trend toward atomization of the productive unit may make it more difficult to tax profits and labor income. It may also become more difficult to tax consumption because a larger share of it will be made up of services rather than commodities and, especially, durables. A further complicating trend is that, to an increasing degree, individuals would earn their incomes in one country and spend them in another, as tourists or pensioners. Of course, how much the tax system will be affected will depend on how far these trends progress.

Not all the trends, however, point toward increasing difficulties. The "information revolution," now well under way, and the large amounts of information on individuals that it has caused to be stored away in computers, may give governments new tax handles, if they succeed in getting access to it. The governments of various countries will increasingly need to share some of this information. It is conceivable that the day may come when the countries create an "International Revenue Service" to collect taxes that could not be collected by separate governments and to allocate them either to the provision of international public goods or back to the countries. Such an international institution might also collect information on taxpayers for the benefit of the member tax administrations.

Whether the political process would allow such an enormous invasion of privacy, with all its inherent political dangers, would depend in part on the political environment. The more conservative that environment, the less likely any such change is. However, without access to better information, countries will find it progressively more difficult to levy taxes and to do so equitably. The structure of the tax system may not be a "free policy choice;" it may be determined partly by the structure of the economy. Thus government would have lost part of its control over certain tax instruments.

20

Computerized Tax Collecting

JOSEPH E. STIGLITZ

The focus of this chapter is the relationship between technical change and taxation. I want to explore both sides of this relationship: how technical change affects our tax system and how our tax system affects the rate of technical change.

The perspective of the 21st century is somewhat longer than what we normally take. The vagaries of the tax laws in the past decade should make us wary about making any predictions concerning what the tax law is likely to be in five or ten years, let alone the next century.

There are two predictions, however, in which we can have some confidence. First, changes in technology will have potentially important effects on our tax system—if not on tax legislation, at least on its administration. Second, the tax law itself will affect the pace and direction of technological change in the United States. At the same time, I do not see that any likely changes in technology in the near future will have a revolutionary effect on the design of our tax system.

Although I focus on taxation in the United States, the issues I raise have implications for the tax systems of other countries as well. We have much to learn from the Tax Reform Act of 1986, one of the most sweeping attempts at reform since the enactment of the income tax some 70 years ago. Although it seems unlikely that there will be another major reform in the near future, the limitations and failures of the act provide useful hints about the likely course of the evolution of the tax system in the coming decades.

HOW TECHNICAL CHANGE AFFECTS OUR TAX SYSTEM

Changes in technology have already affected our tax system, and the future holds out the possibility of even more profound changes. While for the most part the technological changes so far have reduced the administrative costs of collecting taxes and increased compliance with the tax laws, some innovations in technology have made the problem of revenue collection more difficult for government. I argue that government has not fully taken into account some of the advances in technology, and if it were to do so, we could have a better tax system, with a higher degree of compliance at lower administrative costs.

Computerization and Reporting

In the past, certain types of income were consistently underreported. As recently as 1981, the government claimed that one out of six dollars of dividends that should have been reported was not; one-fourth of estate and trust income, almost two-fifths of royalties, and more than two-fifths of capital gains went unreported. This should be contrasted with only 6 percent of wages and salaries that went unreported and the more than one-half of the income of partnerships and small business corporations (and almost one-half of nonfarm proprietor income) that went unreported.[1]

Computerization has made it easy for corporations to report on dividend payments, banks to report on interest payments, and stockbrokers to report on sales of securities. The matching of these reports with income reported by individuals allows a check on the accuracy with which individuals report income, and the very fact that the government has this capability will increase the extent of compliance.

This increased compliance is important. If there is to be a general acceptance of our income tax system, there must be a belief that taxes are not only levied in a fair manner but are also collected fairly.

There is, however, one potential problem. As the degree of compliance in these categories increases, the gap may grow between the effective tax rate imposed on these forms of income and the rates on income for which compliance remains low (such as small businesses and farming). This may not only have allocative effects but also may erode confidence in the equity of our tax system.

Computerization may eventually be able to alleviate some of these problems. Farmers, for instance, have extensive dealings with the U.S. Department of Agriculture. They may report the amount of acreage they have in a given crop and receive support payments from the government. In principle, this information could be used to ascertain the extent of compliance with the tax law. Using this information raises some thorny philosophical problems: Should information that the government obtains for one purpose (running the agricultural program) be used for another? To what extent does this violate "rights to privacy"?

On the one hand, one may argue that since only those who lie would be concerned with this use of information, there is nothing wrong in the Department of Agriculture making this data available to the IRS. On the other hand, there is a question of the long-run consequences of an excessive concentration of information about individuals in the hands of the government. Although the particular use of this information—enforcing the tax laws—might be unobjectionable, it might be put to other uses that are more objectionable.

DESIGNING TAX POLICIES WITH THE NEW TECHNOLOGIES IN MIND

The existence of these new technologies raises a fundamental question: How can we design our system of taxes to minimize the burden of compliance and maximize the extent of compliance? This question, which should have been near the top of the agenda in the discussions leading up to the U.S. Tax Reform Act of 1986, was, to my knowledge, hardly mentioned. It has been increasingly evident that at least one of the three main objectives of the tax reform—simplification—has not been achieved; numerous new forms have been created, and it is estimated that there will be a substantial increase in the number of hours that many taxpayers will have to spend to complete the required forms.

As an example, the change in the rules for individual retirement accounts (IRAs) shows how compliance costs were ignored not only in the design of the new law but also in its implementation. The government still allows upper- and upper-middle income individuals to contribute to IRAs, but these IRA contributions will no longer be deductible, although interest earned on these accounts will be tax-deferred. This poses a horrendous recordkeeping problem for any purchaser. When individuals start to draw funds out of their IRAs, on some of these funds they will already have paid a tax on their original contributions, while taxes on others will not have been paid. Since the tax-deferral advantages of tax-exempt state and local bonds will probably exceed those of IRAs and thus attract the upper-income buyer, it is likely to be middle-income individuals who will take advantage of the tax deferrals offered by the IRAs. The record-keeping and computational requirements imposed by these regulations are accordingly likely to be particularly burdensome.

A slightly different administrative arrangement could have achieved most of the objectives at a much lower cost of compliance. Assume the government had declared that there were to be two types of IRA accounts: type I, on which individuals had not paid taxes on their contributions, and type II, on which they had. In the latter case, the financial institution managing the account would be required to keep records of the individual's original contribution. Then the government could have offered the following option: When the individual began to withdraw funds, all of type I and type II accounts could be consolidated with a "qualified" financial intermediary (a bank, a securities firm, etc.).[2] Any distributions from the IRA accounts would then be taken from both accounts, in proportion to the value of the assets in them. Since the financial intermediary would have the full data on the individual's original contribution to the two types of accounts, the amount of the withdrawal on which a tax was due could easily be calculated. The whole burden of the calculations would be borne by the financial intermediary.

The point is that for the financial intermediary, the calculation is virtually costless, given that the records are already computerized. For the individual recipient, the costs of calculations would be enormous. I suggest this proposal as an option. Individuals who prefer not to consolidate their accounts with a single financial institution could, of course, make the calculation themselves.

More generally, I would increasingly place the burden of performing calculations and keeping records on financial institutions, for whom the incremental costs of such calculations would be slight. For instance, it would be easy for these institutions to report not only the price at which a security was sold but also the price at which it was purchased.

Similarly, current regulations concerning the capital gain due on mutual funds, in which individuals reinvest their income, are, to say the least, cumbersome. Many individuals purchase shares, often fractional shares, each month by reinvesting their dividends. In a ten-year period there will be 120 monthly purchases. If in some months the individual purchases additional shares and in other months sells some of the shares, the calculations required to ascertain the realized capital gain at each sale are indeed awesome. However, a computer program to perform the calculation can be easily written. Why burden the taxpayer when the mutual fund could easily assume the task?

I would also place more of the burden of tax compliance on the IRS. Take, for instance, our present regulations regarding capital gains from the sale of an owner-occupied house. In principle, an individual selling a house at the age of 70 would need to have kept detailed records of the prices at which that person purchased and sold houses over a lifetime, as well as capital expenditures for home improvement. Most householders are not equipped to be accountants; and even if a person had hired an accountant some 35 or 40 years ago, the likelihood is small that the accountant survived, let alone that accurate records survived, over that length of time.

The point is that if we pass tax laws that require this type of onerous recordkeeping, the government should assume the burden. With computerization, it would be possible for the government to keep records on the purchase and sale prices of each house; indeed, it would be easy for the individual to submit large capital expenditures to be added to the file. When the individual finally sells the house, the government could easily calculate the individual's capital gain. If the government feels that it is not cost-effective to keep such records and make the requisite calculations, that it cannot do this kind of job effectively, we should change the tax law. It is surely no less burdensome for the individual than it is for the IRS.

CHANGES THAT MAKE TAX COLLECTION MORE DIFFICULT

To an extent that we are only fully coming to appreciate, the effectiveness of our system relies on market imperfections. The tax law imposes provisions that—if capital markets worked perfectly, as they typically do in economists' models—would enable individuals to avoid much or all of their taxes on capital income.[3] For instance, individuals can postpone realizing a capital gains tax by not selling their securities that have appreciated in value, but they can accomplish nearly the same portfolio objectives by buying securities that are very negatively correlated with the security they would like to sell or by selling short securities that are highly positively correlated. Similarly, before 1986 (and to some extent even today), the favorable treatment of capital gains provided an incentive for firms to distribute funds from the corporate sector to the household sector through share repurchases and cash mergers and acquisitions. Firms are belatedly recognizing these tax advantages, so today nearly two-thirds of distributions take this form.[4]

The problem is that firms are becoming increasingly sophisticated and markets increasingly efficient. The opportunities available for tax arbitrage are increasingly seized upon. Only a few months after the passage of the 1986 tax reform it became apparent that the corporation was tax disadvantaged. Most, if not all, of the advantages of the corporate form can be retained with the master limited partnership (MLP), while the MLPs have distinct tax advantages. The government can obviously respond by declaring that MLPs are to be treated as corporations. However, this simply forces another line to be drawn—some partnerships will be tax advantaged relative to others. Innovations, new forms of organization that satisfy the requirements to obtain partnership tax treatment but have much of the advantages of the corporate form, will be developed.

When types or sources of income that are really not much different are taxed differently, opportunities for recharacterizing the income and for tax arbitrage are opened up. Capital gains are not really different from other forms of capital income. The distinction between partnerships and corporations is not a clean one. The increasing efficiency of the economy in recognizing these opportunities for reducing taxes puts a heavier burden on the tax authorities in designing tax laws. The Tax Reform Act of 1986 provides little evidence that we are up to the task.

THE EFFECT OF TAXATION ON INNOVATION

There has been increasing concern in this country about our lack of competitiveness. Are we losing the competitive edge to the

Japanese? Given the intrusive role that taxes play in all aspects of modern economic life, it is no surprise that taxes get blamed here, too. No doubt, there are many explanations for our problems; taxes can be only a part of the story. Our tax rates are far lower than those in most Western European countries, yet our savings rate is far lower than theirs. Taxes may discourage savings, but they simply cannot account for our current consumption spree.

Accordingly, I focus on a more narrow set of issues: To what extent did the 1986 Tax Reform Act serve to encourage or discourage innovation? It will be recalled that the tax reform had three major objectives: to simplify the tax code, to stimulate growth, and to increase equity. We have seen how it is already apparent that it failed in the first. I want to suggest that it may have failed in the second objective as well; by and large, its provisions will serve to discourage rather than encourage innovation.

The most important effect on innovation is probably the treatment of capital gains. Capital gains tax rates actually increased rather than decreased, from a maximum rate of 20 percent to a maximum of 28 percent. Since entrepreneurs and investors in high-technology companies typically received a large fraction of their returns subject to capital gains taxation, this change meant that high-technology industries effectively experienced a tax increase, not a tax decrease.

Other provisions adversely affect high-technology firms. The alternative minimum tax may limit their ability to take advantage of preferences they previously enjoyed. Certain restrictions against loss carry-forwards (i.e., when there is more than a 50-percent change among certain shareholders in a three-year period) may affect how funds are raised. These and other provisions of the tax code may affect the ability of firms to realize losses for tax purposes.

Although these provisions have an impact on all industries, their effect on high-technology industries may be particularly acute. There is an old argument, put forward some 40 years ago by Richard Musgrave, then at Harvard, and Evsey Domar of MIT, that taxation may actually encourage risk taking.[5] The government acts as a silent partner, sharing in the gains, but if expenses are deductible, also sharing in the costs. This risk-sharing role of the government is particularly important in those instances where equity markets do not work well. However, this argument requires that the government share in the costs. Investments in research and development are particularly risky; in many years and on many projects, losses are recorded. When these losses are not fully tax deductible (even when they get carried forward, their present discounted value is reduced), then the government is taking a share of the profits but paying a much smaller share of the costs. It is this asymmetry which gives rise to the problem—which results in investment in research and development being discouraged.

The problem is exacerbated by inherent difficulties in raising funds for start-up companies.[6] Informational problems often make it difficult for such companies to raise funds on equity markets or to borrow extensively from banks. The original entrepreneurs in these firms typically have to surrender a large fraction of their stake in the company in order to raise the requisite funds. While the original entrepreneurs may be driven by other than financial concerns, those who supply the firms with capital look at these investment opportunities dispassionately; and if the tax law reduces their net return from investing in these ventures, they will allocate their funds elsewhere.

Even in the next stage of the life cycle of a high-technology firm, the tax laws may have a deleterious effect. Now firms typically reinvest a large fraction of their after-tax cash flow. They are reluctant to attempt to raise additional equity because of the typically high cost of doing so. They may be reluctant to borrow too extensively because of the high risks that borrowing (as opposed to equity) imposes; and their bankers may feel the same way, so their access to borrowing may be restricted as well. Thus when the average tax rate is increased, their after-tax cash flow is reduced as is their investment in research and development. (More generally, there is considerable evidence for the importance of this effect in smaller companies.) The current tax law not only has raised the effective marginal tax rate on high-technology companies, but also it has probably raised the average tax rate. The companies suffered on both accounts.

Not all the changes in the Tax Reform Act were negative. The research-and-development (R & D) tax credit was extended, but it is a credit only on incremental expenditures. It can be shown that this form of the credit encourages instability in the pattern of expenditures; that is, a firm with a steady stream of R & D expenditures would be disadvantaged relative to a firm that had varying expenditures but the same present discounted value. The tax is of limited value to new firms with no income against which to offset the R & D expenditures.

In general I am sympathetic with the original spirit of the Tax Reform Act and the elimination of special preferential treatment for different categories of investments and expenditures. On the other hand, corrective taxes also have their place. Beginning at least with the great Cambridge scholar, A. C. Pigou, economists have contended that taxes can be used to improve the efficiency with which resources are allocated—for instance, when externalities are involved.

Suppose the actions of one individual or one firm have positive consequences for other individuals or firms, but no compensation is made for those actions. One can argue, I think, that research and development results in such externalities; that is, not all of the benefits accruing from expenditures on R & D are captured by the firm engaging in the research. Indeed, even with an effective patent system, firms seldom capture more than a fraction of the returns from their successful innovations. As a result, a strong case can be made that in market economies there will be insufficient expenditures on R & D. A correspondingly strong case can be made for government subsidies to R & D, and tax credits provide an effective way of providing these subsidies.

However, in the Tax Reform Act, Congress again demonstrated its inability to distinguish between industries for which there is some good economic justification for special treatment (based, say, on externalities) and those for which no good justification exists.

It is the inability of Congress to make these distinctions that has persuaded most economists not to use tax policy to correct market failures. The Tax Reform Act confirmed those views, and as it passed through Congress, it did not even stay true to its original spirit. Preferences for the oil and gas industries were retained.[7]

Where does this leave us today? Had the Tax Reform Act been true to its original intentions, I would be arguing that we should not have a special R & D tax credit. I would be in favor of limiting capital gains to real capital gains, but perhaps more importantly for R & D, I would argue for provisions allowing the full realization of losses. This could be done in a number of different ways. If losses are carried forward, they should be interest-bearing. Losses could be made cashable or more easily transferable. In short, the first order of business would be to eliminate those provisions which discriminate against risky R & D investments.

Given that the 1986 law retained the principle that certain industries should receive favorable treatment, then at least a reasonable case can be made that the R & D sector is as deserving of such favorable treatment as other sectors. The benefits that accrue from technological leadership are not limited to the economic returns; they extend in a wider sense to the American spirit. We are apparently confident enough that R & D confers these benefits to adopt a tax credit on incremental expenditures. Does it not make sense then to extend the credit to all expenditures, thus avoiding the special problems associated with the incremental R & D credit, such as the incentives for varying expenditures?

Time—along with econometric studies—may eventually reveal exactly how negative an impact the 1986 law will have on the R & D sector. The question is: Do we wish to wait, or can we afford to wait, to find out the answer?

Summary: The Value of Warning

HERBERT STEIN

Nobody is looking forward with great eagerness to being taxed in the 21st century. But as the need for revenues increases—and it will increase—obtaining them will be increasingly difficult, and that leaves the question of what's going to give. The common, if not quite universal, conclusion is that we are going to be living with increasingly unsatisfactory taxes.

I must explain what I mean by the increasing "need" for revenues. I think there is a general presumption that without radical changes of policy and attitudes, which most economists do not foresee, expenditures will rise relative to our national incomes. Three sources of this rise are foreseen.

First, there are the costs of the aging of the population—the pension costs and the health costs. Second, there are the growing interest burdens that we foresee, as the ratios of debts to national income and gross national product rise. Third, there is something commonly labeled egalitarianism, which more broadly means, I suppose, the general political pressures.

Almost no one, so far as I can see, wants this increase in spending. We speak of it with despair and disdain, as very nearly inevitable and totally unfortunate. Hardly any case is made for more spending on education and health and infrastructure in order to increase productivity. Almost no one speaks about the need to spend money to defend Western civilization, which is certainly an important consideration.

Some people foresee some change in attitudes towards government which would slow down this trend of expenditures. But the expectation of a change in attitudes seems to be a minority view. So is a position that foresees a rise in affluence by itself tending to reduce the demand for government services relative to our incomes.

The need for more revenues will result not only from the trend of rising expenditures but also from the need to reduce deficits. In many countries, deficits are big enough to raise the ratio of debt to GNP. As economists are fond of saying, this cannot go on forever. And as I have said—this is Stein's first law—if something cannot go on forever, it will stop. This does not mean that it cannot go on throughout the 21st century. But presumably at some point in the 21st century, there will be a desire or a need to reduce deficits, and that will require revenues to rise more than expenditures.

This brings me to the other side of the equation: the difficulty of raising revenues. Most people assume that raising revenue relative to the national income will require raising taxes. That is, we cannot raise revenues by cutting taxes. If this assumption were incorrect, if we could raise revenue by cutting taxes, the future would look much brighter and easier. But few believe this is so.

To say that raising taxes is difficult can mean any of three things. First, that it is administratively difficult; second, that it has adverse economic consequences; and third, that it is politically unattractive.

Several reasons are adduced for thinking that further tax increases will become increasingly difficult in all of these senses. First, there must be some law of increasing marginal costs. It hurts more to raise a 50 percent rate to 51 than to raise a 25 percent rate to 26, because the percent change in after-tax incomes is greater in the first case.

Second, international integration of business and international resource mobility increase the difficulty of raising taxes. From the standpoint of business, higher rates increase the damage from the double taxation and the inconsistencies that exist in a system in which businesses operate in more than one jurisdiction. From the standpoint of government, international competition limits the rates that can be charged.

Third, various structural changes domestically will make taxation more difficult. As our economies advance, an increased share of total income will come from capital, which is more difficult to tax than labor income, mainly because of measurement and timing problems. The increased flexibility of the financial organization of businesses enhances the ability to escape some kinds of taxes. Since we can expect the relative size of business units to become smaller, at least relative to the size of the economy, the difficulty of collection will further increase. And a larger share of the workforce will be self-employed, a development that also increases the difficulty of collecting taxes. A larger share of the national output will take the form of services, which are traditionally difficult to tax. And we will probably see, if tax rates continue to rise, a growth of the underground, or informal, economy.

On the other side, only one factor seems to make the increase of revenue easier: the improvement of the management of information and recordkeeping. Some have suggested that this could be a very important factor in view of the large amount of revenue that now escapes collection.

But there does seem to be, as some have pointed out, a kind of Parkinson's Law at work here, in that the complexity of the tax system rises to meet the capability of handling information.

So the question arises, what are we to do about this unfortunate trend toward higher expenditures and higher needs for taxes, combined with greater difficulty in raising them? Is it feasible to reduce the difficulties and costs of raising taxes, and if so, is it desirable to do so?

Some have suggested that we can reduce the costs of raising taxes, or reduce the adverse consequences, by several kinds of tax changes. The income taxes could be reformed by broadening their base. Reliance on income taxes, especially on the taxation of income from capital, could be reduced by more reliance on a broad-base consumption tax, or expenditure tax. A value-added tax has numerous proponents in the countries that do not already have it—the United States and Japan. International agreements could harmonize accounting standards and reduce the likelihood of double taxation and the influence of tax differences on the location of business. International coordination could reach agreement on tax levels and limit the erosion of revenue by international competition. And there could be more reliance on user charges and effluent fees.

A minority view presents some doubts about whether such reforms of the tax system would have any significant economic effect. What really counts, it is claimed, is the average rate of taxation, or even more, the level of total spending, which will not be reduced by tax reform.

There is even more doubt about the political feasibility of these reforms. This seems to be especially acute with respect to matters that require international agreement. Many people find it difficult to envision any substantial submergence of national sovereignty about taxes. Also, public opinion in Japan and the United States does not seem to be receptive to broader-based consumption taxes, such as the value-added tax, although the tax's proponents hope that opinion about them will change in time.

A provocative question that is occasionally raised is whether tax reform would be desirable if it could be achieved. The argument is that the "badness" of taxation and international competition both serve to limit the amount of taxation and, therefore, the growth of government, which is the real evil to be feared. But I suppose most economists have too much of a stake in preaching tax reform to be willing to entertain the notion that tax reform might be a bad thing.

But what is to be said about the gloomy predictions that we are going to live for a long time with more expenditures than we would like, financed by more and worse taxes than we would like?

I would make two observations. First, there has been little attempt to estimate how much difference this all makes. It would be important to know whether we are expressing an aesthetic preference for small budgets and neat tax systems, or whether the differences we are talking about matter seriously. In another connection, I have made a simple comparison of the performance of the United States economy in the 40 years since the end of World War II, which was a period of high budgets and high taxes, to the 40 years before 1929, which was a period of much lower taxes and budgets, relative to national incomes. I found, to my surprise, that in this period of high budgets and high taxes the economy has grown as rapidly in total GNP, per capita GNP, and productivity—in the usual measures of economic performance—as it did in the period of much smaller budgets and lower taxes. This suggests to me a certain warning against drawing weighty conclusions about the performance of the economy as government grows.

I would also refer to a recent study by Angus Maddison of Groningen University in The Netherlands, covering the growth experience of the United States, the Western European countries, and Japan over a fairly long period.[1] Professor Maddison shows that in the 25 years or so after World War II growth was much higher in all of these areas than in the preceding 50 years or so, when governments had been smaller and taxes lower.

Of course, since 1973 rates of growth have declined, and there has been a general deterioration of economic performance as it would ordinarily be measured. But in most cases—the United States is an exception—performance has been superior to what it was in the earlier days, when budgets were smaller and taxes lower.

A good deal of attention has been paid to the very weak performances of European economies in the last 10 or 15 years, difficulties that are commonly associated with tax systems, budgets, and related variables. We should be aware, however, that this attribution is disputed, and we still know very little about what moves the big aggregates of our economies.

Growth washes out a lot of other problems, as a little experiment will show. Let us assume that per capita income before tax will rise by 1 1/2 percent per annum for 50 years, which would approximately double before-tax income. And let us suppose that during this period, taxes rise from 25 percent of before-tax income to 35 percent of before-tax income. We find that per capita income after tax still rises by 70 percent in that period. Apparently, we can survive the next 50 years despite the drag of these rising budgets and these terrible taxes. Except for the youngest among us that must be some comfort.

A second, more serious point is that even if these predicted trends have serious consequences, we should not feel hopeless about the possibility of changing the trend. Economists and a lot of other people these days seem to be in the grip of a very pessimistic view of public policy. This has something to do with public-choice theory. We are a bit obsessed with the notion that public policy is determined by pressure groups, politicians, and bureaucrats who, unlike us economists, are all very selfish, short-sighted, and unresponsive to considerations of the long-run national interest.

While this notion may often be accurate, there are critical points at which it seems not to have been correct. There are some cases in which talking, writing, thinking, and ideas have made some difference. It seems to me unquestionable that the Keynesian revolution in economic thinking made a difference. (Now many people are unhappy about the difference it made, but the important point is that it made a difference.) More recently, the revival of thinking and writing about the virtues of the free-market system has had an influence on policy in the United States and elsewhere.

In both of these cases, the influence of thinking on policy was certainly accentuated or facilitated by a present crisis. There was the crisis of the Great Depression. In the 1970s, there was a much smaller crisis, but nevertheless an acute concern, about inflation. The question is really whether we are capable of exercising any forethought about policy as applied to some date out there 50 years from now when we are not face to face with a crisis. Can we adapt our policies to concerns whose consequences will not be felt for quite a long time? That, of course, is a more difficult question, but I do not think you can be entirely negative about it, either.

We do see, at least in the United States and in many other countries, that we go on spending large amounts for national defense as security against some danger that is certainly not imminent and whose timing we cannot see but that we know we have to do something about now. The United States and many other countries have invested fairly large amounts in aid to foreign countries, where the benefits to us were remote in both time and proximity for a considerable period. In most countries, the increase of the ratio of debt to GNP (aside from war) is a fairly recent phenomenon. We do see in the political process a good deal of what we would call responsibility about that. So I do not think it would be appropriate or even permissible for us to accept as inevitable too many gloomy predictions.

Our need is to try to make these predictions as vivid and believable as possible, so that they will have some affect on policy. And I think we should regard the more worrisome thoughts as warnings, rather than predictions, of what is going happen.

Biographical Notes

The Editor

Herbert Stein, Ph.D., Senior Fellow, American Enterprise Institute for Public Policy Research. Dr. Stein is a member of President Reagan's Economic Policy Advisory Board and has served as Co-Chairman of the Committee to Fight Inflation. During the Nixon Administration he was a member and then Chairman of the President's Council of Economic Advisers.

Dr. Stein was the A. Willis Robertson Professor of Economics at the University of Virginia from 1974 to 1984. For 22 years (1945–1967), he was an economist with the Committee for Economic Development and its director of research for most of that time.

For the past decade he has been on the board of contributors of the *Wall Street Journal*. He is the editor of the *AEI Economist*.

Dr. Stein served as chief consultant and chairman of the Advisory Board for the "Tax Policy in the Twenty-First Century" conference.

The Authors

Henry J. Aaron, Ph.D., Senior Fellow, The Brookings Institution. A professor of economics at the University of Maryland and a former staff member of the President's Council of Economic Advisers, Dr. Aaron has also served as Assistant Secretary for Planning and Evaluation in the U.S. Department of Health, Education and Welfare. He is a senior associate of the Policy Economics Group of Peat Marwick Main & Co. and a trustee of the Teachers Insurance and Annuity Association. Among his recent publications is *Economic Choices of 1987*.

James A. Baker, III, U.S. Secretary of the Treasury. Secretary Baker also serves as Chairman of the President's Economic Council and is a member of the National Security Council. From 1981 to 1985 he was President Reagan's Chief of Staff. A lawyer from Houston, Texas, Mr. Baker was appointed Under Secretary of Commerce by President Gerald Ford in 1975. In 1980, he became senior adviser to the Reagan/Bush campaign. Secretary Baker is on the board of trustees of the Woodrow Wilson International Center for Scholars at the Smithsonian Institution. He has received the Jefferson Award for distinguished public service from the American Institute for Public Service, a John F. Kennedy School of Government Award for Distinguished Public Service, and the Woodrow Wilson Award from Princeton University, his alma mater.

JACK F. BENNETT, Ph.D., Senior Vice President and Director, Exxon Corporation. Dr. Bennett's current responsibilities include Exxon's accounting, finance, and tax functions. He held various posts in government before he went to work for Exxon, where he served in the United States and Europe. In 1971, he joined the U.S. Department of the Treasury and later became Under Secretary for Monetary Affairs, then rejoined Exxon the next year. He is on the Advisory Committee on International Capital Markets of the New York Stock Exchange.

RICHARD M. BIRD, Ph.D., Professor of Economics, University of Toronto. A former director of the Institute for Policy Analysis at the University of Toronto, Dr. Bird has lectured around the world and researched the economies of more than a dozen countries. He is a member of the editorial boards of various journals, including *Public Finance Quarterly* and *Government and Policy.*

MARIO S. BRODERSOHN, Ph.D., Minister of Finance, Republic of Argentina. Dr. Brodersohn is a former president of the National Bank of Development and a former vice president of Arla Bank International. A one-time consultant to the United Nations, the Organization of American States, the Inter-American Development Bank, and the International Organization of Labor, he has taught at various Argentine universities and been a visiting researcher at The Brookings Institution and the University of California.

SIJBREN CNOSSEN, Ph.D., Professor of the Economics Faculty, Erasmus University Rotterdam. Dr. Cnossen served for 12 years as a staff member in the Fiscal Affairs Department of the International Monetary Fund, where he researched the tax systems of several countries. He started his career as a tax inspector with the Dutch Ministry of Finance. His most recent publication is *Tax Coordination in the European Community,* which he edited for the International Seminar in Public Economics.

YUJI GOMI, M.A., Chairman, Chuo Coopers & Lybrand Consulting Co., Ltd. Mr. Gomi was a longtime staff member of the Japanese Ministry of Finance in the National Tax Administration Agency. He is a past president of the National Tax College and has served as director of a number of taxation bureaus in Japan. He is the author of *Guide to Japanese Taxes,* among other titles.

BILL GRADISON (R.-Ohio) represents the second district of his state in the U.S. House of Representatives. A member of Congress since 1974, he is on two committees of the House, Ways and Means and Budget, and he is the ranking Republican member of the Health Subcommittee of the Ways and Means Committee. He is also Chairman of the Biomedical Ethics Board, created by Congress to examine the ethical implications of current medical practice and research. A former investment broker, Mr. Gradison has served in both the U.S. Department of the Treasury and the U.S. Department of Health, Education and Welfare. For 13 years he was on the Cincinnati, Ohio, City Council. He has been both Vice Mayor and, briefly, Mayor of that city, his place of birth.

YOLANDA KODRZYCKI HENDERSON, Ph.D., Economist, Federal Reserve Bank of Boston. Dr. Henderson has served as a research assistant at the National Bureau of Economic Research and with the Fiscal Affairs Division of the U.S. Congressional Budget Office. She has been a consultant to the President's Council of Economic Advisers. Presently, she is a consultant to the Massachusetts Special Commission on Tax Reform and a member of the advisory council of the American Enterprise Institute Project on the Economics and Politics of Fiscal Policy.

HIROSHI KANEKO, L.L.B., Professor of Law, University of Tokyo. A graduate of the law faculty of the University of Tokyo, Professor Kaneko has been associated with it for more than three decades. He is president of the Japanese Society for Tax Law and a member of the Tax Policy Committee of the Japanese Government. He also sits on the Tax Policy Committee and the Foreign Trade and Exchange Committee of the Japanese Ministry of Finance. He is chairman of the Japanese branch of the International Fiscal Association.

JOHN A. KAY, M.A., Director, Centre for Business Strategy and Professor of Industrial Policy, London Business School. A former editor of the *Economic Journal,* Professor Kay is a noted broadcaster and a columnist for the *Daily Telegraph.* He has served as director of the Institute for Fiscal Studies in London and is the author (with M.A. King) of *The British Tax System.* He is also the founder and chairman of London Economics, a consulting group.

DONALD F. KETTL, Ph.D., Associate Professor of Government and Foreign Affairs, University of Virginia. Dr. Kettl has been the director of the Graduate Program in Public Administration and Public Affairs in the Department of Government and Foreign Affairs at the university. He is on the executive committee of the American Political Science Association's section on public administration and is a member of the editorial board of *State and Local Government Review.*

CHARLES E. MCLURE, Jr., Ph.D., Senior Fellow, Hoover Institution, Stanford University. Dr. McLure is a former Deputy Assistant U.S. Secretary of the Treasury for Tax Analysis and a former vice president of the National Tax Bureau of Economic Research. Formerly the Cline Professor of Economics and Finance at Rice University, he has served as a senior economist on the staff of the President's Council of Economic Advisers and as a consultant to the World Bank.

FERENC E. MOLNAR, J.D., Associate (International Group), Arent, Fox, Kintner, Plotkin & Kahn. Mr. Molnar provides counsel to Latin American clients (particularly those in the Mexican public sector) on international trade, litigation, and general matters. He is a graduate of Harvard College and Harvard Law School.

WALLACE E. OATES, Ph.D., Professor of Economics, University of Maryland. Professor Oates has taught at Princeton University, San Jose State College, and San Diego State College. He has been a consultant to the National Science Foundation (economics subpanel) and the National Oceanic and Atmospheric Administration. He is a member of the Association of Environmental and Resource Economists.

PAUL CRAIG ROBERTS, Ph.D., The William E. Simon Chair in Political Economy, Center for Strategic and International Studies. A former Assistant Secretary for Economic Policy of the U.S. Department of the Treasury, Dr. Roberts has served with the Hoover Institution and as economic counsel to Representative Jack Kemp (R.-New York). Formerly a professor of business administration and a professor of economics at George Mason University, he is a columnist for *Business Week.*

STANFORD G. ROSS, J.D., Senior Partner, Arnold & Porter. A specialist in federal tax law and administrative law, Mr. Ross is an adjunct professor of law, Georgetown University Law Center, and an ex-Commissioner of Social Security. He has served in the U.S. Department of the Treasury and on the White House staff. He has taught at the law schools of New York and Harvard Universities, and he is a member of the council and a former vice president of the International Fiscal Association.

DALLAS L. SALISBURY, M.P.A., President, Employee Benefit Research Institute. Mr. Salisbury served as Executive Assistant to the Administrator of Pension and Welfare Benefit Programs in the U.S. Department of Labor and as assistant executive director of the U.S. Pension Benefit Guaranty Corporation. He is a consultant to the U.S. Administration on Aging and the American Association of Retired Persons.

JOSEPH E. STIGLITZ, Ph.D., Professor of Economics, Princeton University. Dr. Stiglitz, who is a research associate of the National Bureau of Economic Research, has been on the faculties of Oxford, Stanford, and Yale Universities, the Massachusetts Institute of Technology, and other institutions in the United States and abroad. He has been a consultant to the Office of Technology Assessment and the U.S. Department of the Interior (offshore oil leasing programs).

LAWRENCE H. SUMMERS, Ph.D., Professor of Economics, Harvard University. Dr. Summers was a Domestic Policy Economist for the President's Council of Economic Advisers in 1982–83. He has been a consultant to the U.S. Departments of the Treasury and Labor and to the governments of Jamaica, Indonesia, Canada, Mexico, and Japan. Currently, he is a member of the Panel of Economic Activity of The Brookings Institution, a research associate at the National Bureau of Economic Research, and editor of the *Quarterly Journal of Economics.*

VITO TANZI, Ph.D., Director, Fiscal Affairs Department, International Monetary Fund. Dr. Tanzi is a former consultant to and a senior economist with the Organization of American States. His work with the IMF and the OAS has included missions of economic and technical assistance to many countries in Central and South America, as well as locations in Asia and Africa. He was chairman of the Department of Economics at American University and also taught at George Washington University.

KLAUS VOGEL, Dr. iur., Professor of Public Law and Director of Research for Foreign and Tax Law, University of Munich. Dr. Vogel has taught at the Universities of Erlangen-Nuernberg and Heidelberg. A member of the Permanent Scientific Committee of the International Fiscal Association, he has been a visiting scholar at Harvard Law School and a visiting professor at the University of California Law School, Berkeley.

SIR ALAN A. WALTERS, M.A., Senior Fellow, American Enterprise Institute for Public Policy Research, and Professor of Economics, Johns Hopkins University. Former personal economics adviser to Prime Minister Margaret Thatcher, Sir Alan (who was knighted in 1983) has taught at the University of Birmingham and the London School of Economics. Currently an adviser to the World Bank, he has written extensively on economic theory and development.

ARNOLD H. WEISS, J.D., Senior Partner, Arent, Fox, Kintner, Plotkin & Kahn. Mr. Weiss serves as counsel for banking institutions in Mexico, Argentina, Brazil, and Germany in their relationship with U.S. public and private institutions. He is trade counsel for Petroleos Mexicanos and special counsel to the African Development Bank. Formerly general counsel of the Inter-American Development Bank, he was also counsel to the U.S. Office of International Finance.

Notes and References

Chapter 3 Experience from a Century of Change

Richard M. Bird

1. The figures are interpolated from R. A. Musgrave, P. B. Musgrave, and R. M. Bird, *Public Finance in Theory and Practice* (Toronto: McGraw Hill-Ryerson Limited, 1987), 128. Other sources may show different figures for some of these countries in the years mentioned because of the degree of estimation inevitable in such historical data, but the basic picture of huge governmental growth remains unchanged.
2. All figures for recent years quoted throughout are based on various documents published by the Organization for Economic Cooperation and Development (OECD), notably *National Accounts of OECD Countries* (Paris, 1985) and *Revenue Statistics of OECD Member Countries* (Paris, 1985).
3. Carolyn Webber and Aaron Wildavsky, *A History of Taxation and Expenditure in the Western World* (New York: Simon & Schuster, 1986), 214.
4. See OECD, *Personal Income Tax Systems Under Changing Economic Conditions* (Paris, 1986) and *An Empirical Analysis of Changes in Personal Income Taxes* (Paris, 1986).
5. Richard A. Musgrave, *Fiscal Systems* (New Haven: Yale University Press, 1969). Harley H. Hinrichs makes a similar, though more complex, argument in *A General Theory of Tax Structure Change During Economic Development,* Harvard Law School International Tax Program, Cambridge, MA, 1966. Hinrichs also stresses the importance of different cultural patterns in determining tax structure, a theme recently elaborated by Webber and Wildavsky, in *Public Finance in Theory and Practice,* Chapter 10. Dozens, if not

hundreds, of variations of "tax handles" and related models have been econometrically estimated over the past three decades, although with little more light being cast on the subject than by the similar deluge of papers on Adolph Wagner's "law" of expanding state activity.

6. The clearest exposition of the state as revenue maximizer is in Geoffrey Brennan and James M. Buchanan, *The Power to Tax* (Cambridge, MA: Cambridge University Press, 1980). Political-economic modeling has been most developed by Bruno Frey and his colleagues in such papers as B. S. Frey and F. Schneider, "A Political-Economic Model of the United Kingdom," *Economic Journal* 88 (1978): 243–53, although perhaps the most promising application to tax structure development is in Stanley Winer and Walter Hettich, "The Evolution of Revenue Systems: A Theoretical and Empirical Investigation," Unpublished paper, Carleton University, Ottawa, January 1987. As yet, however, there have been relatively few empirical studies along the lines suggested in these models.
7. Carolyn Webber and Aaron Wildavsky, *A History of Taxation and Expenditure in the Western World* (see note 3), 526.
8. Henry Simons, *Personal Income Taxation* (Chicago: University of Chicago Press, 1938).

CHAPTER 4 DEMOGRAPHIC SHARK IN THE FISCAL WATER

Charles E. McLure, Jr.

1. Charles E. McLure, Jr., *The Value-Added Tax: Key to Deficit Reduction* (Washington, DC: American Enterprise Institute, 1987).
2. M. J. Boskin, "Future Social Security Financing Alternatives and National Saving," *Working Paper No. 2256,* National Bureau of Economic Research, Cambridge, MA, May 1987.
3. Suppose that an individual lends \$100 at an interest rate of 10 percent for one year, receiving \$110 at the end of the year. If the same interest rate is used to determine the present value of the two flows of cash involved, it is apparent that the deduction for the \$100 of lending at the beginning of the year is exactly offset in present value terms by the taxation of \$110 of interest and principal at the end of the year. Thus in present value terms, the income from lending is, in effect, exempt from tax.

CHAPTER 6 TAXATION IN A SMALL WORLD

Lawrence H. Summers

1. Joel Slemrod, "International Capital Mobility and the Theory of Capital Income Taxation," in *Assessing Tax Reform,* edited by Henry Aaron and Harvey Galper (Washington, DC: The Brookings Institution, 1985).
2. Jerome Hellerstein, *Corporate Income and Franchise Taxes* (Boston: Warren, Gorham, and Lamont, 1983).

CHAPTER 7 THE SEARCH FOR COMPATIBLE TAX SYSTEMS

Klaus Vogel

1. The distinction between "tax neutrality" and "equity aspects" seems to have been pointed out first by Richard A. Musgrave in "Criteria for Foreign Tax Credit," a contribution to the 1960 symposium, "*Taxation and Operations Abroad.*" It was taken up and broadened by Peggy B. Richman (now Musgrave) in *Taxation of Foreign Investment Income: An Economic Analysis* (Baltimore: Johns Hopkins Press, 1963).

2. R. Musgrave and P. Musgrave, *Public Finance in Theory and Practice,* 4th ed. (New York: McGraw Hill, 1984), 766.

3. For details see K. Vogel, "Fiscal Obstacles to the International Flow of Capital Between a Parent and Its Subsidiary," *Cahiers de Droit Fiscal International (Studies in International Fiscal Law),* General Report, LXIXA (Deventer, The Netherlands: Kluwer Law and Taxation Publishers, 1984), 97, 108, and the national reports reproduced in that volume.

4. On tax credits in double taxation treaties see P. Gann, "The Concept of an Independent Treaty Foreign Tax Credit," *Tax Law Review* 38 (1982): 1. On tax treaties in general, including their history and usual structure, see K. Vogel, "Double Tax Treaties and Their Interpretation," *Int'l Tax and Business Lawyer* 4 (1986): 1.

5. Terms were originally used in R. Musgrave, "Criteria" (see note 1), 84.

6. P. Musgrave, *Taxation of Foreign Investment Income* (see note 1), 8. See also P. Musgrave, *United States Taxation of Foreign Investment Income: Issues and Arguments,* Harvard Law School International Program in Taxation, 1969, 83–84; R. Musgrave, *Fiscal Systems* (New Haven: Yale University Press, 1969), 249; R. Musgrave and P. Musgrave, "Inter-Nation Equity," in *Modern Fiscal Issues: Essays in Honor of Carl S. Shoup* (Cheektowaga, NY: University of Toronto Press, 1975), 69; B. Snoy, *Taxes on Direct Investment Income in the EEC* (New York: Praeger, 1975), 37; Mitsuo Sato and Richard M. Bird, "International Aspects of the Taxation of Corporations and Shareholders," *IMF Staff Papers* 22 (1975): 384, 408; H. W. Sinn, *Kapitaleinkommensbesteuerung: Eine Analyse der intertemporalen, internationalen und intersektoralen Allokationswirkungen,* 1985, 178, 179.

7. K. Vogel, "Fiscal Obstacles" (see note 3), 102.

8. N. Ture, "Taxing Foreign Source Income," in *U.S. Taxation of Foreign Business Abroad* (Washington, DC: American Enterprise Institute, 1975), 37.

9. K. Vogel, "Fiscal Obstacles" (see note 3), 122, and the national reports contained in that volume.

10. See *Bulletin for International Fiscal Documentation* 38, International Bureau of Fiscal Documentation, Amsterdam, 1984, 545.

11. See International Chamber of Commerce, "Avoidance of Double Taxation: Exemption versus Tax Credit Method," Resolution of ICC Council and Report of Commission Taxation, February, 1955.
12. O. Gandenberger, "Kapitalexportneutralitt versus Kapitalimportneutralitt," 7 *Aufsaetze zur Wirtschaftspolitik,* Forschungsinstitut fr Wirtschaftspolitik an der Universitt Mainz, 1983.
13. N. Ture, "Taxing Foreign Source Income" (see note 8), 38, 39.
14. For more details see K. Vogel, *World-wide vs. Source Taxation of Income: A Review and Reevaluation of Arguments* (manuscript ready for publication).
15. See H. Kuhn, *The Structure of Scientific Revolutions.*
16. Regarding equity in international taxation, see P. Musgrave, *Taxation of Foreign Investment Income* (see note 1), 7, 5, 11; P. Musgrave, *Issues and Arguments* (see note 6), 122; R. Musgrave and P. Musgrave, "Inter-nation Equity" (see note 6), 68.
17. See R. M. Dworkin, *Law's Empire* (Cambridge, MA: Belknap Press of Harvard University Press, 1986).
18. The subsequent discussion can only be very brief. See also K. Vogel, "Taxation of Foreign Income, Principles and Practice," *Bulletin for International Fiscal Documentation* 39, International Bureau of Fiscal Documentation, Amsterdam (1985): 4, 10. For more details see K. Vogel, *World-wide vs. Source Taxation* (see note 14).
19. Professor Peggy Musgrave was the first to make this distinction (see note 1).
20. James M. Buchanan, *Fiscal Theory and Political Economy: Selected Essays* (Chapel Hill, NC: University of North Carolina Press, 1960), 12.
21. Nearly 100 years ago, Georg von Schanz suggested assigning three-quarters of the tax base to the state of source and one-quarter to the state of residence. This suggestion still deserves consideration. See G. von Schanz, "Zur Frage der Steuerpflicht," *9 II Finanzarchiv,* (1892): 1, 4.
22. R. Dworkin, *Law's Empire* (see note 17), 219.

CHAPTER 8 INTERNATIONAL TAX LAW: THE NEED FOR CONSTRUCTIVE CHANGE

Stanford G. Ross

1. See S. G. Ross, "A Perspective on International Tax Policy," *Tax Notes* (Arlington, VA: Tax Analysts, 1985), 701.
2. The classic studies of the foreign tax-credit mechanism are E. A. Owens, *The Foreign Tax Credit,* Harvard Law School International Program in Taxation, 1961, and E. A. Owens and G. T. Ball, *The Indirect Credit,* Volumes I and II, Harvard Law School International Tax Program, 1975 and 1979.

3. See B. J. Arnold, *The Taxation of Controlled Foreign Corporations: An International Comparison,* Canadian Tax Foundation, 1986.

4. See S. I. Langbein, "The Unitary Method and the Myth of Arm's Length," *Tax Notes* (Arlington, VA: Tax Analysts, 1986), 625.

5. See *Competent Authorities from Six Countries,* International Tax Institute, Inc., 1986. For a proposal to use arbitration, see J. H. Guttentag and A. E. Misback, "Resolving Tax Treaty Issues: A Novel Solution," *Bulletin for International Fiscal Documentation* 140 (1986): 350.

6. For a general introduction to this subject and others, see R. Hellawell and R. C. Pugh, *Taxation of Transnational Transactions* (New York: Commerce Clearing House, 1987).

7. See J. H. Guttentag, "Tax Treaty Shopping," *Bulletin for International Fiscal Documentation* 38 (1984): 3.

8. For an exploration of these basic tax reform issues, see David F. Bradford, *Untangling the Income Tax* (Cambridge, MA: Harvard University Press, 1986).

9. See H. J. Ault, S. G. Ross, and G. M. Brannon, "Foreign Tax Provisions of H.R. 3838," *Tax Notes* (Arlington, VA: Tax Analysts, 1986), 775.

10. For an analysis of the political aspects of the U.S. tax system, see J. F. Witte, *The Politics and Development of the Federal Income Tax* (Madison, WI: University of Wisconsin Press, 1985).

CHAPTER 11 DAY OF RECKONING APPROACHES FOR THE EUROPEAN COMMUNITY

Sijbren Cnossen

1. Richard Rose, "Public Employment and Public Expenditure," in *Public Expenditure—The Key Issues,* edited by John Bristow and Declan McDonagh (Dublin: Institute of Public Administration, 1986). Rose points out that as a percentage of the workforce, public employment in the big member states grew on average by 11 percent in the period 1951–1981. More tellingly, while employment in social programs, as a percentage of public employment, increased by 18 percent, employment in economic programs dropped 13 percent (pp. 76–77).

2. I. Hansson, "Marginal Cost of Public Funds for Different Tax Instruments and Government Expenditures," *Scandinavian Journal of Economics* 86, No. 2 (1984). Hansson has estimated that the marginal cost of collecting $1 extra of income tax in Sweden (which has a revenue ratio of 59 percent of GDP) ranges from $3 to $7. This means that the benefits of related government spending would have to be three to seven times greater than the income that is taxed away to justify the tax increase. In a similar exercise with respect to the U.S. tax system, Ballard, Shoven, and Whalley compute

marginal welfare costs in the range of 17 to 56 cents. See Charles L. Ballard, John B. Shoven, and John Whalley, "General Equilibrium Computations of the Marginal Welfare Costs of Taxes in the United States," *American Economic Review* 75, No. 1 (1986).

3. For a comprehensive review, see "Tax Structure Developments," in *Tax Coordination in the European Community,* edited by Sijbren Cnossen (Deventer, The Netherlands: Kluwer Law and Taxation Publishers, 1987).
4. Such a system, however, would not be feasible for the excises levied at manufacturing and importing stages. In their case, the Commission proposes near-complete harmonization, that is, uniform rates of tax in conjunction with a community-wide system of excise suspension, so that excisable products are taxed as close to the consumer as possible.
5. See also the excellent report, "Efficiency, Stability, and Equity," by a study group appointed by the Commission of the European Communities and presided over by Tomasso Padoa-Schioppa, Brussels, 1987.
6. For a flavor of the issues, see *Personal Income Tax Systems Under Changing Economic Conditions,* OECD, Paris, 1986.
7. Munnell, Alicia H., "The Economics of Tax Simplification: An Overview," *New England Economic Review,* Jan./Feb. 1986.
8. The revenue loss of across-the-board reductions in tax rates may be partially offset by higher receipts from the increased output that results from the increased after-tax pay. Martin Feldstein ("Supply Side Economics: Old Truths and New Claims," *American Economic Review* 76, No. 2, May 1986) cites a very careful study by Lawrence Lindsey and reports that in 1982 the response of taxpayers did offset about one-third of the effect of the tax cut on federal receipts in the United States.

Additional References:

Cnossen, Sijbren. "Harmonization of Indirect Taxes in the EEC," *Tax Assignment in Federal Countries,* edited by Charles E. McLure, Jr. (Canberra: The Australian National University, 1983).

Commission of the European Communities. "Completing the Internal Market," White Paper from the Commission to the European Council, Brussels, June 1985.

——— "Report on the Scope for Convergence of Tax Systems in the Community," *Bulletin of the European Communities,* Supplement 1, 1980.

Halter, William A., and Richard Hemming, "The Impact of Demographic Change on Social Security Financing," *Staff Papers* 34, No. 3, International Monetary Fund, Washington, DC, September 1987.

Hinrichs, Harley H., *A General Theory of Tax Structure Change During Economic Development* (Cambridge, MA: Law School of Harvard University, 1966).

International Monetary Fund, *Government Finance Statistics Yearbook,* Vol. X., Washington, DC: IMF, 1986.

Lindbeck, Assar. "The Limits of the Welfare State," *Challenge,* January-February 1986.

Mueller, Dennis C., "The Growth of Government: A Public Choice Perspective," *Staff Papers* 34, No. 1, International Monetary Fund, March 1987.

Organization for Economic Cooperation and Development, *Social Expenditure 1960–1990: Problems of Growth and Control.* OECD, Paris, 1985.

——— *The OECD Observer,* No. 139, March 1986.

——— *Structural Adjustment and Economic Performance,* OECD, Paris, 1987.

——— *OECD Economic Outlook,* OECD, Paris, June 1987.

Pommerehne, Werner W., and Friedrich Schneider, "Unbalanced Growth Between Public and Private Sectors: An Empirical Examination," in *Public Finance and Public Employment,* edited by Robert H. Haveman (Detroit: Wayne State University Press, 1982).

Saunders, Peter, and Friedrich Klau, "The Role of the Public Sector: Causes and Consequences of the Growth of Government," *OECD Economic Studies* No. 4, OECD, Paris, 1985.

Stein, Herbert, *Washington Bedtime Stories: The Politics of Money and Jobs* (New York: The Free Press, 1986).

Summers, Lawrence H., "Should Tax Reform Level the Playing Field," in 1986 Proceedings of the Seventy-Ninth Annual Conference on Taxation, held under the auspices of the National Tax Association—Tax Institute of America, Columbus, OH, 1987.

Tanzi, Vito, "Public Expenditure and Public Debt," in *Public Expenditure—The Key Issues,* edited by John Bristow and Declan McDonagh (Dublin: Institute of Public Administration, 1986).

Webber, Carolyn, and Aaron Wildavsky, *A History of Taxation and Expenditure in the Western World* (New York: Simon and Schuster, 1986).

CHAPTER 15 FAITH IN MARKET FORCES

John A. Kay

1. Morrison, Herbert, *Socialization of Transport* (London: Constable, 1933).
2. Skidelsky, Robert, "Keynes and the State." In *The Economic Borders of the State,* edited by D. Helm (Oxford, England: Oxford University Press, forthcoming).

CHAPTER 16 THE U.S. SUPPLY-SIDE REVOLUTION

PAUL CRAIG ROBERTS

1. For a history see Paul Craig Roberts, *The Supply-Side Revolution* (Cambridge, MA: Harvard University Press, 1984), Chapters 1–3.

2. See Paul Craig Roberts, Testimony before the Committee on Banking, United States Senate, February 18, 1987.
3. See, for example, Michael R. Darby, "Accounting for the Deficit," *Research Paper No. 8704,* U.S. Treasury Department, October 2, 1987.
4. See Lawrence B. Lindsey, "Taxpayer Behavior and the Distribution of the 1982 Tax Cut," *Working Paper No. 1760,* National Bureau of Economic Research, Cambridge, MA, November 1985.
5. See Allen Sinai, Andrew Lin, and Russell Robins, "Taxes, Saving, and Investment: Some Empirical Evidence," *National Tax Journal,* September 1983.
6. See Paul Craig Roberts, Testimony before the Committee on Finance, United States Senate (January 30, 1986) and Roberts, et al., "The House Tax Bill: Does the U.S. Win or Lose?," The Institute for Political Economy, Washington, DC, April 1986.
7. For comprehensive proposals for neutral tax treatment of saving, see "Blueprints for Basic Tax Reform," U.S. Treasury Department, January 17, 1977.

CHAPTER 17 RICHER MEANS HARDER TO TAX

Henry J. Aaron

1. This study has been carried out by Barry Bosworth, Gary Burtless, and Henry J. Aaron. Julie Gerber-Fields gave research assistance.
2. The discrepancy between growth of money wages and of total employee compensation is based on projections of the Social Security Administration contained in "The 1986 Report of the Board of Trustees of the Old-Age and Survivors and Disability Insurance Trust Funds." In 1987, the trustees' report contained revised and reduced estimates of the growth of fringe benefits relative to money wages. These revisions would reduce the discrepancy in growth rates of money wages and total compensation reported here.
3. We assume that capital and labor combine to produce output according to a Cobb-Douglas production function. Under this production function, the rate of return on capital is equal to $(K/O)a$, where K is the capital stock, O is output, and a is the coefficient of capital in the production function.
4. What rate of return to assume on net foreign investment is something of a puzzle. The United States earns far more on assets it owns abroad than foreigners earn on investments in the United States, as indicated by the fact that U.S. net capital income continues to be positive although the United States is a net debtor. In the long run, however, there is no good reason to suppose that the United States will continue to earn more on its foreign investments than foreigners will earn on theirs. One could argue that U.S. investors must earn a higher rate when they invest abroad than they earn domestically if they are to be indifferent between foreign and domestic holdings because of greater risks or higher information costs associated with

foreign investments. On the other hand, the foreign tax credit denies the United States the portion of the gross return paid to foreign governments in creditable taxes. Our assumption regarding the relationship between the rate of return on foreign and domestic investments is clearly an uneasy compromise.

5. State and local governments continue to rely in varying degrees on real property taxes, sales taxes, and personal and corporation income taxes that in many cases are piggybacked on federal taxes. They also rely on a mix of other revenues including severance taxes, profits of state-owned enterprises, and user charges. I do not consider the implications of the trends described in the first part of this study for the tax policies of state and local governments.

6. Over n periods, an investment that generates realized income in each period at the rate of $100r$ percent per year will generate a return equal to $[1 + r(1 - t)]^n$, where t is the tax rate. An investment that yields the same before-tax rate of return in each period but that generates realized and, hence, taxable income only at the end of the period will generate a return of $(1 + r)^n(1 - t)$. The latter amount is always larger. For example, an investment that lasts 20 periods, generates a before-tax rate of return of 10 percent per period, and faces a tax rate of 33 percent on realized income will produce an after-tax return of $3.66 for each $1 invested if the returns are realized and taxed annually or $4.51 if the returns are realized and taxed only at the end of the 20 periods.

7. For a particularly careful review of the problems tax authorities must solve to impose a consistent income tax, see David F. Bradford, *Untangling the Income Tax* (Cambridge, MA: Harvard University Press, 1986). Also see Henry J. Aaron and Harvey Galper, *Assessing Tax Reform* (Washington, DC: The Brookings Institution, 1985). Aaron and Galper emphasize the distinctions in the measurement of capital income based on the frequency of measurement. Thus the conventional income tax purports to measure capital income annually. An income tax that measured lifetime income would tax consumption plus gifts and bequests. A consumption tax would, as the name suggests, tax only consumption.

8. Educational expenses might appear to be an exception, as workers normally incur them many years before they contribute to earnings. One would exclude the costs of education up to age 18 or 19, the normal age for leaving school. The largest cost of higher education is normally foregone earnings. Since these costs are, in effect, deducted when they are incurred and wages and salaries are taxed when earned, there is no problem.

9. Henry J. Aaron and Harvey Galper propose such a tax in *Assessing Tax Reform*.

10. See David F. Bradford, *Untangling the Income Tax*. The macroeconomic effects of consumption and wage taxes are quite different from one another, however, as Lawrence Summers has shown. Under the consumption tax, households must save enough not only to pay for future consumption

but also for the taxes on that consumption. Under a wage tax, savings need cover only the cost of future consumption because no additional taxes will be imposed. See "Capital Taxation and Accumulation in a Life-Cycle Growth Model," *American Economic Review* 71, No. 4, September 1981.

11. For a demonstration of this proposition, see A. B. Atkinson and J. E. Stiglitz, *Lectures in Public Economics* (New York: McGraw Hill, 1981). For a tax designed to fall on this base, see Henry J. Aaron and Harvey Galper, *Assessing Tax Reform* (Washington, DC: The Brookings Institution, 1985).
12. The standard V.A.T. falls on a company's gross receipts less its purchases from other companies, including investment. Thus investment is untaxed. The V.A.T. could be imposed on a company's gross receipts less its noninvestment purchases from other companies less depreciation. This tax would fall on net investment as well as consumption and would correspond to a tax on net national product at factor cost or national income. Alternatively, a V.A.T. could be imposed on a company's gross receipts less its noninvestment purchases from other companies. This tax would fall on gross national product at factor cost.

CHAPTER 18 A POLLUTION TAX MAKES SENSE

Wallace E. Oates

For a more extended, nontechnical discussion of the economics of environmental policy (including an exploration of the potential of a variety of policy instruments), see William J. Baumol and Wallace E. Oates, *Economics, Environmental Policy, and the Quality of Life* (Englewood Cliffs, NJ: Prentice-Hall, 1979). For a more theoretical and rigorous treatment of these issues, see William J. Baumol and Wallace E. Oates, *The Theory of Environmental Policy* (Englewood Cliffs, NJ: Prentice-Hall, 1975) (revised edition published by Cambridge University Press).

The Terkla study of revenue estimates for taxes on sulfur and particulate emissions is found in David Terkla, "The Efficiency Value of Effluent Tax Revenues," *Journal of Environmental Economics and Management* II, 1984, 107–123. The cited study reporting estimates of the welfare losses from the taxation of labor income is from Edgar K. Browning, "On the Marginal Welfare Cost of Taxation," *American Economic Review* 77 (March 1987): 11–23.

For a brief, nontechnical discussion of the case for a system of transferable discharge permits, see Wallace E. Oates, "Markets for Pollution Control," *Challenge Magazine* (May/June 1984): 11–17. T.H. Tietenberg provides a more extensive treatment including a careful assessment of the U.S. Emissions Trading program in his *Emissions Trading: An Exercise in Reforming Pollution Policy* (Washington, DC: Resources for the Future, 1985). In Chapter 3 of this book, Tietenberg provides a good summary of the findings on the potential cost savings from using economic incentives rather than existing command-and-control techniques for environmental management.

The Kelman Study of the politics of environmental policy-making appears in Steven J. Kelman, *What Price Incentives? Economists and the Environment* (Boston: Auburn House, 1981).

CHAPTER 19 FORCES THAT SHAPE TAX POLICY

Vito Tanzi

1. For a survey of this literature see Vito Tanzi, "The Theory of Tax Structure Change During Economic Development: A Critical Survey," in *Rivista di Diritto Finanziario e Scienza delle Finanze* XXXII, No. 2 (1973): 199–208.

2. Vito Tanzi, "Quantitative Characteristics of the Tax System of Developing Countries," in *The Theory of Taxation for Developing Countries,* edited by David Newbery and Nicholas Stern, (Oxford, England: Oxford University Press, 1987), 205–41.

3. Richard A. Musgrave, *Fiscal Systems* (New Haven: Yale University Press, 1969).

4. Edwin R. A. Seligman, *Studies in Public Finance* (New York: Macmillan, 1925); and U.S. Advisory Commission on Intergovernmental Relations, *Surveys of Taxpayers Preferences,* annual.

5. Vito Tanzi, "The Response of Other Industrial Countries to the U.S. Tax Reform Act," *National Tax Journal* (September 1987): 339–55.

6. Peter Heller et al., "Aging and Social Expenditure in the Major Industrial Countries, 1980–2025," *Occasional Paper* 47, IMF, 1986.

7. U.S. Department of Labor, "BLS Previews the Economy of the Year 2000," *News,* June 25, 1987.

8. Valerie A. Personick, "A Second Look at Industry Output and Employment Trends) Through 1995," *Monthly Labor Review,* November 1985.

CHAPTER 20 COMPUTERIZED TAX COLLECTING

Joseph E. Stiglitz

1. From Internal Revenue Service, Income Tax Compliance Research, *Estimates for 1973–1981,* July 1983.

2. In the absence of computerization, there would be an enforcement problem: How can one be sure that the individual has in fact consolidated all of his accounts? But computerization can solve, or at least mitigate, this enforcement problem.

   My own suspicion is that the government's concern with making sure that individuals properly allocate withdrawals between the two types of accounts is misplaced. The slight inequities and lowered present discounted value of tax collections which the government might receive if it simply allowed the individual to withdraw from whichever account he preferred (presumably first the account on which withdrawals are only partially taxed) would be more than offset by the reduced complexity.

   This is an instance of a more general problem evident in some of the recent tax reforms: There has been an excessive attempt to fine-tune the tax system, to eliminate minor inequities, without regard to the resulting administrative or more general efficiency costs. As always in economics, there are trade-offs. I am questioning whether in these instances the proper balance has been struck.

3. See J. E. Stiglitz, "Some Aspects of the Taxation of Capital Gains," *Journal of Public Economics* 21 (July 1983): 257–294. See also J. E. Stiglitz, "The General Theory of Tax Avoidance," *National Tax Journal* XXXVIII, No. 3 (September 1985): 325–338.
4. See John Shoven, "New Developments in Corporate Finance and Tax Avoidance: Some Evidence," *Tax Policy and the Economy,* ed. Lawrence Summers (Cambridge, MA: MIT Press, 1987).
5. See E. D. Domar and R. A. Musgrave, "Proportional Income Taxation and Risk-Taking," *Quarterly Journal of Economics* 58 (1944): 388–422.
6. The ideas in this and the following paragraph are developed in greater detail in Bruce Greenwald and J. E. Stiglitz, "The Incidence of the Corporation Income Tax with Equity and Credit Constrained Firms," a paper presented to a National Bureau of Economic Research conference, Cambridge, April 1987.
7. For an excellent discussion of this and other aspects of the Tax Reform Act of 1986, see the "Tax Reform Symposium," *Journal of Economic Perspectives,* Summer 1987. See also J. E. Stiglitz, *The Economics of the Public Sector,* 2d ed., (New York: W.W. Norton, forthcoming).

SUMMARY: THE VALUE OF WARNING

Herbert Stein

1. Maddison, Angus, "Growth and Slowdown in Advanced Capitalist Economies," *Journal of Economic Literature* (June 1987): 649–98.

Glossary

Alternative minimum tax is a provision of the tax code that requires tax payments to equal at least a minimum percentage of a broad measure of income when the individual's or corporation's tax preferences (e.g., accelerated depreciation allowances and itemized deductions) reduce tax liabilities substantially.

Business taxes are taxes levied on business organization income, for example, the corporate profits tax. These taxes do not include consumption taxes that are collected by businesses.

Capital income is the flow of payments to owners of financial or physical assets. Capital income includes interest payments to bond holders and dividends to equity shareholders.

Capital gains (losses) equal the change in value of an asset. Capital gains are said to be realized when an asset is actually sold.

Cash flow approach uses cash receipts and disbursements to calculate income. This method results in immediate deductibility of all business and investment expenditures rather than phased deductions of the investment expenditures over the lives of the assets.

Command economy is one in which the central government directs and organizes the economy, including determining the composition and distribution of output. The USSR is an example of a command economy.

Constrained revenue maximization is the theory by which firms try to maximize sales revenue instead of profits. A firm operating in such a manner is constrained to output levels where profits are not negative.

Consumption tax is a tax levied on purchases of goods and services. Value-added, excise, and turnover taxes as well as taxes on retail sales and manufacturer's sales are examples of the consumption tax.

Corporate tax is the tax on corporate income. Its tax base is corporate profits.

Countercyclical fiscal policy is the use of government expenditures or tax policies to minimize the fluctuation of the economy through demand management. The business cycle is dampened by reducing demand during the expansionary phase and increasing demand during the recessionary phase.

Depreciable assets are assets whose value decreases through the wear and tear of use or through obsolescence.

Depreciation allowance is the allowable portion of the cost of the depreciable assets that are used up during income-generating activity that can be included in the cost of production. The size of this allowance depends upon the cost of the asset and its expected useful life.

Direct taxes are taxes which cannot be shifted from the original payer to the ultimate consumer of the good or service. Personal and corporate income taxes, payroll taxes, and property taxes are often considered direct taxes, although the ultimate incidence of each of these taxes is subject to dispute.

Disincentive effects are the incentive-reducing effects of tax policy. For example, taxation of labor income reduces the value of labor relative to leisure and thus encourages a reduction of labor supply. Similarly, taxation of saving distorts the value of saving relative to consumption and may cause a reduction of saving. Disincentive effects vary proportionally with the marginal tax rates.

Double taxation occurs when the same activity is taxed by different governmental units or taxes. For example, corporate profits are taxed twice, first by the corporate income tax and second by the personal income tax when distributed as dividends.

European Commission is composed of technical experts and is charged with policy review and recommendation and administering of policies for the EC.

European Common Market is the economic community made up of the 12 members of the European Community.

European Community (EC), or European Economic Community (EEC), is the organization of 12 Western European states to promote free trade and a single market through coordinated economic policy. Formed in 1957, it includes the European Parliament, European Commission, and European Council. There were six original countries: Belgium, Federal Republic of Germany, France, Italy, Luxembourg, and The Netherlands. They have been joined by Denmark (1972), Ireland (1972), United Kingdom (1972), Greece (1981), Portugal (1985), and Spain (1985).

European Council is composed of representatives from the 12 nations of the European Community and has final authority to formulate and approve common policies of the EC.

Excise tax is a tax on the sale of a particular good or service. There are both fixed rate (dollars per gallon) and ad valorem (X percent per dollar) excise taxes. Cigarettes, alcohol, and gasoline are among the goods commonly subject to excise taxes.

FIFO inventory accounting is a method of valuing inventory. FIFO, first-in-first-out, accounting assumes that the first goods purchased are the first goods sold. This will lower the cost of goods sold when prices are rising and will lead to higher taxable income. (See LIFO.)

General Agreement on Tariffs and Trade (GATT) was signed in 1947 by 23 nations as a temporary means of handling tariff and other trade questions in a multilateral framework. It now includes over 100 members and is the primary vehicle for multilateral trade negotiations.

Gross domestic product (GDP) is the total output of final goods and services produced within a nation's border regardless of the ownership of the factors of production. Thus U.S. GDP will exclude all of the production of a U.S. firm in

Mexico and include all of the production of a Mexican firm in the United States. (See also GNP.)

Gross national product (GNP) is the total output of final goods and services produced by a nation's factors of production regardless of the location of the factor. Thus U.S. GNP will include the part of the production of a U.S. firm in Mexico attributable to United States-owned capital and exclude the part of the production of a Mexican firm in the United States attributable to Mexican capital while including the part attributable to U.S. labor. (See also GDP.)

Imputed income is income which is not in money form, such as the rental value of owner-occupied housing or free food and housing which is received in exchange for providing a service.

Indexation is the adjustment of future payments (or current payments previously agreed upon) through the use of a price index. Wage contracts and goods with long production times often are indexed to a price index when there is high inflation.

Indirect taxes are taxes that can be shifted from the original payer to the ultimate consumer of the good or service. Consumption taxes are generally considered to be indirect taxes.

Inflation adjustment is the method of adjusting actual prices and income to those in a base year. For example, social security benefits are adjusted annually by indexing them to changes in the cost of living.

Integration of corporate and personal income taxes refers to the process of taxing all corporate income at the individual's level using personal income tax rates.

Investment tax credit is a means by which businesses can deduct a percentage of their new investment costs from their tax liability.

LIFO inventory accounting is a method of valuing inventory. LIFO, last-in-first-out, accounting assumes that the last goods purchased are the first goods sold. This raises the costs of goods sold when prices are rising and will lead to lower taxable income. (See FIFO.)

Manufacturer's sales tax is a sales tax that is collected at the manufacturing level instead of the retail level.

Minimum alternative corporate tax—see alternative minimum tax.

Multilateral tax integration is the process of coordinating the tax policies and codes of various nations.

OASDI is the Old Age, Survivors, and Disability Insurance program in the United States, i.e., Social Security.

Organization for Economic Cooperation and Development (OECD) is an organization composed of representatives of the 18 industrialized countries in Europe, the United States, Japan, Canada, Australia, and New Zealand. Founded in 1961, it provides economic research and statistics and offers a forum for discussing and possibly coordinating policies of common interest.

Payroll tax is a tax on the payroll or labor income of a firm. In the United States, a portion is paid by employers and a portion paid by the employees. It is used to support OASDI, Medicare, and unemployment benefits.

Personal taxes include all taxes paid by individuals: income, payroll, consumption, and wealth taxes.

Progressive tax is a tax by which the ratio of tax paid to income is higher for high income individuals than for low income ones. A progressive income tax may use marginal tax rates which increase with income or use constant marginal rates and a personal deduction. The higher the progressivity the less disparity there is in after-tax incomes compared to gross incomes.

Regressive tax is a tax by which the ratio of tax paid to income is lower for high income individuals than for low income ones. Consumption taxes are often viewed as a regressive tax because consumption is a larger share of income for the poor. The degree of regressivity depends upon which goods are included or excluded in the tax.

Social Security tax is the portion of the payroll tax earmarked for the Old Age, Survivors, and Disability Insurance Trust Funds in the United States.

TEFRA is the U.S. Tax Equity and Fiscal Reform Act of 1982 which increased certain excise taxes and corporate income taxes.

Tax expenditures are the revenue losses resulting from special provisions of the tax code which grant preferential tax rates or exclude from gross income certain designated payments or receipts. Personal deductions for mortgage interest payments, property taxes, and tax credits for investment are important examples.

Tax incentive is a special provision of the tax code which promotes a particular activity such as investment, charitable giving, and home ownership.

Tax incidence is the ultimate distribution of the tax payment. The initial payer of the tax may be able to shift the burden of the tax to others. Thus an employer may be able to shift part of the payroll tax back to the employee by lowering wages or shift it forward to the consumer by raising prices.

Tax shelter is a provision of the tax code which allows individuals to reduce or eliminate tax liabilities.

Tax treaty is a treaty between nations concerning tax treatment of the income of each country's citizens and corporations which is generated in the other country.

Tax-prepayment approach uses withholding and estimated tax payments to collect taxes before the end of the tax year when final liabilities are known.

Transfer payment is a payment by governments or businesses for which no goods or services are received in return. These include unemployment benefits, welfare and social security payments, subsidies, and corporate gifts.

Treasury I is the U.S. Treasury Department's first proposal for the tax reform program which ultimately became the Tax Reform Act of 1986.

Turnover tax is a form of sales tax which is collected at all levels of business operation instead of just at the retail or manufacturer's level.

Underground economy is the economic activity which hides income—e.g., through cash transactions or exchange of in-kind services—for the purpose of tax avoidance or because the activity itself is illegal.

User charges (fees) are fees charged by the government in exchange for services. These include highway tolls, registration and license fees, and certain excise taxes. Gasoline excise taxes can be construed as user fees for highway maintenance.

Value-added tax (V.A.T.) is a tax levied on goods and services based on their increase in value as they move through the production-distribution process.

Wealth taxes are comprised of taxes on real property, estate taxes, and annual wealth taxes. The latter is a tax on the assets less liabilities of an individual or household and is levied in many European countries.

Windfall tax is a tax used to capture profits generated by dramatic price increases. In 1980, the U.S. government imposed a crude oil "windfall profits" tax based on the difference between the then current price and a base price for oil.

Index